NEW CENTURY VOICES

NEW CENTURY VOICES

Sarasota Literary Society
selected prose and poetry

NEW VOICES PUBLISHING
Sarasota, Florida

Inquiries should be addressed to:
Sarasota Literary Society
P.O. Box 4008
Sarasota, Florida 34230-4008

PUBLISHER'S CATALOGING IN PUBLICATION DATA

Rowe, Barbara
    New Century Voices: Selected Prose and Poetry Anthology 2000/Barbara Rowe.
    p.   cm.
    LCCN: 00-133413
    ISBN: 00-9712966-0-6
    1. Literature. 2. Anthology. 3. Fiction. 4. Poetry.

First Edition

10 9 8 7 6 5 4 3 2 1

Design by Carol Tornatore Creative Design
Printed in the United States of America

CONTENTS

HONORABLE MENTION
(in alphabetical order)

SELECTED FOR PUBLICATION
Fourth Grade Student Contest
(in alphabetical order)

📖 *denotes a member of the Sarasota Literary Society.*

SELECTED FOR PUBLICATION
Adult Contest
(in alphabetical order)

SARASOTA LITERARY SOCIETY

In January of 1997 a small group of writers, interested in the publication and promotion of their works, decided to form a group for that purpose. In September of 1998 they were incorporated as the Sarasota Literary Society, a 501-C3 not-for-profit organization. The stated purpose of the Society: to promote the reading, writing and publication of all forms of literature, including experimental works and new genres.

The Sarasota Literary Society has two membership classifications: Full member, $35.00 annual dues, and Friend of SLS, donations tax deductible.

Our Board of Directors has established the following as our current goals:

- To publish the Society's annual anthology, "New Century Voices"

- To continue sponsorship of our annual creative writing contest for adults (see entry form in the appendix in this book)

- To continue sponsorship of our creative writing contest among fourth graders in Sarasota County schools

- To establish a web site for the Society

- To continue participation in the Sarasota Reading Festival

- To schedule programs and speakers for our monthly meetings that are of interest to members.

ABOUT OUR CONTESTS

THIS ANTHOLOGY IS COMPOSED of entries received in the Sarasota Literary Society's two current writing contests: one for children in the fourth grade in the Sarasota County School System; and one for writers worldwide. While officers and directors of the Sarasota Literary Society, and their families, are not eligible for prizes, all other members are. All members are eligible for publication in the anthology.

In the Table of Contents, a book icon next to an author's name indicates a member of the Society. The contents are alphabetically listed within each category.

Six readers juried all submissions. Only those submissions receiving unanimous approval by this jury are eligible for publication. Three distinguished and independent judges, none of whom are members of the society, chose the finalists and prize-winners.

For those interested in submitting entries in the 2000 contest, an application form can be found in the appendix in this book with all pertinent rules and requirements.

JUDGES

SUSAN SUTLIFF BROWN

Professor of Language and Literature, Department of English, Manatee Community College, Bradenton, Florida.

Doctor of Philosophy, April, 1987
Department of English, University of South Florida, Tampa, Florida
Master of Arts, Department of English, University of South Florida, Tampa, Florida
Major Field: Anglo-Saxon and Medieval Literature

Current Professional History:
Professor of Language and Literature, Department of English, Manatee Community College, Bradenton, Florida
Special Fields: British Literature; American Literature; Creative Writing (fiction and poetry); Freshman English Honors; Magazine Production
Coordinator for PEL Creative Writing
Creative Writing Instructor
Eckerd College, St. Petersburg, Florida
Special Fields: Novel, Short Story, Poetry, Drama, Memoir, Journalism, and Feature Writing; Thesis Director
Workshop Leader: Memoir and Autobiography Workshop
Island Writing Workshops
Fire Island, Martha's Vineyard, Ventnor
Workshop Leader: Woodstock Writing Workshops
Woodstock, New York

Judge, Bayboro Fiction Contest, University of St. Petersburg, Florida

Professional Organizations:
James Joyce International Foundation
The South Atlantic Modern Language Association
Florida Association of Community Colleges

Recent Publications:
"The Joyce Brothers in Drag: Fraternal Incest in Joyce's *Ulysses*" in *Joyce and Gender.* Eds. Marlena G. Corcoran and Jolanta Wawrzycka. U of Florida P, 1997.

"Perspectives on the Fifteenth Annual James Joyce Symposium in Zurich." *James Joyce Quarterly,* October 1996: 497–501.

"Joyce at Miami." *James Joyce Broadsheet,* October, 1997: 3.

HELEN T. MEYER

Educational Administration and Adult Education
Ed.D: Rutgers University, Graduate School of Education, New Brunswick, N.J.
M.A.: Montclair State University, Upper Montclair, N.J.
B.A.: Montclair State University English and Psychology

Dr. Meyer is at present PEL Center Coordinator (Sarasota) at Eckerd College, St. Petersburg, Florida.

Recent Conference Presentations/Papers:
Options in Nontraditional Learning. Hispanic Alliance Conference, Sarasota, Florida
Adult Learners. Sarasota Thinks Festival, and Adult Learners and the Workplace, Sarasota Human Resources Association

She has been a member of the Research Committee which assisted community organizations in the development of programs for intergenerational learning in Sarasota, Florida.

CAROL H. BEHRMAN

Carol H. Behrman is the author of nineteen books for children and young adults. Her middle-grade novels include *The Lancaster Witch, Programmed for Terror,* and *Catch a Dancing Star.* Among her non-fiction books are *Fiddler to the World: The Inspiring Story of Yuzhak Perlman* and *The Remarkable Writing Machine.* Her most recent book, *The Ding Dong Clock,* a time-telling picture book in rhyme, was released in 1999 by Henry Holt Publishers.

She has also written four writing texts, published by Prentice-Hall, which are widely used in school throughout the U.S. and Canada. The latest one is *Writing Skills Problem Solver: 101 Activities for the Most Common Writing Errors.* Her books are available from book stores or online at *Amazon.com.*

Carol Behrman taught English and journalism for fifteen years at the Glen Ridge (NJ) Middle School. She has lectured at New York University and Seton Hall University and leads writing workshops regularly at Chautauqua Institution and at various writers' conferences. She conducts in-school writing workshops for teachers and students and also offers a manuscript critiquing service. For information about workshops and critiquing services, she can be reached at (941) 925-9525 or via e-mail at *cbehrman@prodigy.net.*

TWO CAR FUNERAL

by Edward Wier

IT WAS STELLA PARKER'S sixty-third birthday and the gun felt unusually comfortable in her small, strong hand. She sat calmly and noticed the stark contrast between the smooth, polished metal and the age spots on her tan but thinning skin. The difference spoke to her. Anyone walking in would have smelled a strange, hybrid odor of tobacco, coffee, garlic, beer, and bacon grease but she had lived there so long she smelled nothing. Her husband's odors dominated the house like his personality.

She had always kept the television on during the day to mask the low, steady leak of anger she felt but today she could hear the muffled sounds of birds from outside and almost forgot where she was. But then she remembered. She was waiting for her husband to come home so she could shoot him. The thought had the same impact on her as if she had just realized that she needed to get some garlic for dinner. Her list may have read:

Tomatoes
Bread
Coffee
Garlic
Beer
Bacon
Shoot husband

She felt no real misgivings about committing the crime. It was simply the next small step in a series of small steps she had been taking in her mind for quite some time. There were news reports almost every day about someone killing someone somewhere. People were starting to wise up and take action and she was going to join them. Some were dead already. She was done with the years of lies, abuses, scolding, neglect and adulteries.

Jesus, Stella, you'd screw up a two car funeral! That was his favorite thing to say to her. She must have heard it thousands of times. In fact, she anticipated hearing it whenever she tried to do anything which usually distracted her so much that she did end up hearing it. But now she was out of whatever it was that enabled her to endure for so long. She had decided he would never belittle her again. She would never again hear about how stupid she was or that she couldn't do anything right. She would never again hear, *You'd screw up a two car funeral.*

He had chipped her soul away, piece by piece, until only a small speck remained. Now she would use the last trace of her almost extinguished will in that speck to kill him. Which was worse? Killing someone all at once, or slowly, over years like he had done to her? Wasn't she being merciful? Besides, she could not torture him as he had tortured her. There was not enough life left. And, even if there was, she had no desire for justice. She was simply going to put an end to it, finally. She felt the pistol becoming part of her as it warmed in her hand.

A friend might have helped but she wasn't allowed to have any.

It wasn't some sort of official declaration by her war-hero husband, but he somehow made sure that she only had time for his desires and circumstances. He didn't want her having any frame of reference other than what he gave her. Besides, any friend who cared would have told her she was crazy to stay with a man who treated her so horribly and she could not process such an idea. She had no place to go. He was all she knew. Regardless of how unworthy he was, she had devoted her life to him. Killing him was the only solution. If he had only paced himself, she might have been able to hold out till they both died naturally but he was careless. It did not seem extreme. In fact, it seemed like the appropriate thing to do. It would be a proper killing.

So there she sat in the quietness of a bright summer afternoon with her blue eyes smoldering. She only briefly wondered what Victor was up to on *The Young and the Restless*. She had not missed an episode in years. She smiled slightly. For once there would be more drama in her afternoon than on television. Her memories confirmed her position. She thought of all the lipstick, cards, and excuses. She recalled the nights he never came home and how the lies just flowed so smoothly out of his mouth like hot, black coffee into a waiting cup. She thought about all the public humiliation. He was always proud when he had discovered a new way to ridicule her in front of the children or anyone who was handy. She could not remember an act of kindness.

But the gun was getting a bit heavy so she set it down next to the chair where he always put his beer. Besides, it would be hours before he got home and Stella Parker was not the kind of woman who wasted time, death or no death. It was twelve-thirty and he would be going to lunch. Despite how her thoughts surrounded him and their soiled past, she was nowhere in his mind. There was only room for himself there.

Even when he did think of her, it wasn't really Stella Parker he was thinking about. It was the stupid wife, the loyal but ignorant woman, the laughable creature who could not help but love him no matter how cruel he was. It was the pitiful woman he almost pitied but never did. It was the woman who needed him no matter what, the idiot who kept serving him year after year, the ace up the sleeve of his conscience. He couldn't be *that* bad. Why would a woman love him so much if he was?

Frank Parker was a department chief at a large company and everyone knew he had turned down a higher-paying position because he did not want to become a brown-noser. That one act went a long way among his peers even though he did not believe he had any. On a casual level, Frankie was charming, generous, funny, and was considered by all who knew him to be "the life of the party." He looked young for his age and never lacked female attention. He was a master at juggling situations and, more particularly, women.

Coming so close to death in the war had given him a cavalier attitude towards life which most men did not possess. His confidence came from believing that he should have been dead a long time ago. He had cheated death. What was left to fear? But it also gave him a poignant coldness. Anyone who found themselves below his carefully regulated surface would feel that stiff chill. He only made the immediate atmosphere warm and pleasant because he had to live there.

He never obeyed the dress code at work, said what he would, and was always late. But, much to the amazement of his co-workers, he was never chastised. There were many rumors. The main one being that he had Mafia ties. As Stella waited, he sat in his normal place on the corner of the bar at Rascal's substituting a vodka and orange juice for lunch. Bartik, who was his oldest friend, sat next to him. Harold, in Frank's unquestionable opinion, only had one weakness. He got emotionally attached to women. Stella liked Harold but it was embarrassing to Frank that his friend would be affected significantly by a woman. It was foolish. He pursed his lips, which looked strangely delicate approaching the glass, and took a sip of his Screwdriver while Harold talked.

"She wants me to come home after work."

"So?"

"So, I'm going to."

Frank winced as if his drink had suddenly turned sour.

"God, I can't believe you. You're whipped."

"If you're going to have a woman, then you've got to play the woman game. You should try it."

Harold said this because he knew that if he made it look like he was simply being smart that Frank could tolerate his weakness.

"What are you doing for Stella's birthday?"

"Birthday?"

"Yeah. It's the sixteenth. *Today.*"

Harold always remembered Stella's birthday because it was in the same month as his own.

"Oh shit. That's right." He said this as if he just remembered that he owed the IRS money, which he did. Then he shrugged it off.

"I've got plans. You ought to come with me. Sandy throws a *great* party man! Free booze, free food, and free..."

"Frank, you're a bastard."

"Hey, I never said I wasn't."

"And I thought you said nothing's free."

Frank picked up his drink and started singing.

I can dream about it.

"Shit! What time is it? I need to get back to work."

"Come on. At least stay here and have another drink with me. I'm buying."

"I don't have the Mafia to back me up like you do."

They both laughed.

"Take it easy, Harold."

"If you were smart, you'd go home and do some maintenance on your wife. It pays off in the long run."

"If you were smart, you'd stay here and have another drink with me and then go to that party."

"Later." Harold went for his wallet but Frank put up a hand.

"I got it." He knew better than to fight when Frank was in his generous mode.

Harold was out the door and Frank continued to sip his drink with no concern for the time. He ordered another.

Stella had done the laundry, watered the plants, cleaned the bathrooms and rearranged the freezer while humming *Happy Birthday* over and over to herself like a scratched record. Each time she drew out the last few notes longer and longer like an opera singer. Frank always told her she sang off key so she hummed instead. She even wiped the gun a few times. She had never cleaned a gun so she had a hard time knowing when to stop.

She moved Donna's old graduation picture off the wall near the door so it would not get stained or damaged during the shooting. Then she sat back down in the chair that faced the door her soon-to-be-dead husband would enter and picked up the pistol again. She took a sip of cold coffee but spilled the remainder on the recliner. She thought about cleaning it up but just let it soak into the cushion. The time for cleaning was over. Being a good Catholic, she had prayed for some other solution to her problem, but none came. She wanted to give God a chance to intervene but it looked like she would just have to kill him on faith. She stared at the weapon. *Who would make such a thing?*

Back at work, Frank found out that the party at Sandy's had been canceled. It had something to do with her children. It made sense to him. It seemed all children were good for was thwarting the plans of adults trying to enjoy themselves. That's what his kids had done. Then he thought about going home and Stella's birthday. He did not want her bad mood poisoning his atmosphere. Maybe Harold was right. Maybe it would be smart to do something for Stella. Maybe it would grease the gears a bit. But the thought of doing something for his wife on her birthday was such a strange idea that he was having a difficult time with it.

After entertaining the idea awhile, he backed off and approached it by pretending he was the kind of man who did such things. Flowers. He would get her some flowers. When he got off work, he stopped at a grocery store to commit his crime against masculinity. In the flower section, the sweet aromas reeked of male weakness. Whenever he saw a man carrying flowers he always thought sarcastically *Isn't that sweet?* Or *I wonder what he did wrong?*

He thought about the red roses but could not deal with their obviousness. He finally chose a mixed bunch with not many tiny buds. Perhaps anyone looking would think he was going to a funeral. He stood in line and held them like a tool, which was actually what they were. He was tightening up the loose bolts of his situation. The thought comforted him as he carried them out in a bag like he would a bottle of vodka.

Stella looked at the clock and took her practiced position for the last time. She aimed the pistol and then imagined the door opening. Then she lowered it again and waited. She had some stray thoughts but nothing could penetrate her resolution. Then she heard his car. He parked on the driveway and she noticed that the engine kept running longer than usual. Normally, he would have been out of the car as soon as it stopped. Soon she heard the rhythm of his swagger as he approached the steps. The door opened and she squeezed the pistol tighter. He stepped in. The flowers looked as out of place as a ring of gold in a pig's snout. The sight confounded her and, as he turned to close the door, she stuffed the pistol down between the arm and the cushion.

Frank stood there and she stared.

"Well? Happy birthday." He almost sang the words. She could tell he was uncomfortable.

"Don't you want them?"

Stella jumped out of the chair and took the flowers into the kitchen. She found a vase that had not been used in years and began arranging the flowers.

"Stella! What the hell's in this chair?"

"Oh, I spilled some coffee." But Frankie was reaching into the crack.

"Jesus, Stella, you'd screw up a ..."

The shot rang out and she heard her husband's body fall to the floor. Her mind finished the sentence... *two car funeral.* She stopped arranging and stood still. Then the smell of fresh gunpowder drifted into the kitchen. Stella's face beamed above her birthday flowers as she realized that God had answered her prayer.

Born to Polish immigrants in New Jersey, Ed lives in Atlanta as a professional musician, teacher, and a freelance writer with a BA in theology. He has written music for national television specials and film, and his articles and poetry appear in various journals and magazines such as The Formalist, Orbis, SPSM&H, Whiskey Island, The Atlanta Review, The Lyric, Troubadour, The Ledge, The Door, Windhover, Acoustic Musician *and* Guitar Review. *His first illustrated children's story is due out soon. He has won the Felix Stefanile Sonnet Award. His fiction appears in* Sideshow 1997, Fine Print, Lynx Eye, Foliage, The Bitter Oleander *and* Reader's Break, *among others.*

EDWARD WIER

❧

AFTERNOON TELEVISION

by Dan Szczesny

T HE TOAST WAS BURNT, again, for the third time in a week. Traci waved away the tiny puffs of smoke coming from the toaster so as not to set off the smoke alarm. She wasn't even sure if the smoke alarm had batteries, but she didn't want to take the chance.

She could get so distracted sometimes. There were so many things to watch on television in the morning; game shows, sunny talk shows, even cartoons sometimes. And in the afternoon, when Herb went to work and Traci had the apartment to herself, it was a whole new world. The soaps did nothing for her, but Mona and Gerry and Betty Lynn brought interesting people right into Traci's kitchen.

She absently scraped the black flakes off the toast and smeared them generously with jelly so Herb wouldn't notice. In the bathroom, the shower shut off and the kitchen pipes rattled. This was something Traci couldn't figure out. Herb had tried to explain that in an apartment as small as theirs, all the pipes were connected to one another. Every time anyone used any faucet, the whole place rattled. No matter. Plumbing was Herb's concern.

Traci set out a plate for herself, though she was on a diet. She poured two glasses of orange juice and turned up the television. The weather report was coming on and she knew Herb would want to hear it before he left for work. She was pleased at the way she had rearranged Herb's kitchen when she moved in. Herb let her, of course. He called it Traci's territory. She had found that by moving the table out in the center of the tiny kitchen, she could put the small black and white television on top of the fridge and they could watch while they ate. Breakfast was close to a ritual now and Traci was proud of that.

It wasn't like Herb was a slob or anything. Traci figured his first wife had broken him of that habit. Traci was just used to having a lot of control around the house. Before moving in with Herb she had lived as an only child, with her divorced father. This gave her lots of opportunity to be the woman of the house. That always had a nice ring to it. She was now the woman in Herb's house.

She heard a floorboard squeak behind her, but didn't have the time to get up out of her table chair before Herb's hands were on her shoulders.

"Morning, doll," he said.

He smelled fresh and soapy and his hands were still cool from the water.

"How's my cheerleader?"

She smiled. All through high school, even last year, her final year at Cleardale, she had tried out for the cheerleaders squad. She never even came close. Her weight always held her back. All those anemic mamma's girls made Traci sick. It hadn't mattered. She tried out anyway, every year, to the taunts and jeers of her classmates. Herb had been the first person to listen, really listen, to her when she told him this story. And now, she was his cheerleader and glad to be.

His fingers pressed deeply into her shoulders and neck and she felt her muscles loosening pleasantly. "I put together some breakfast, hon," she said.

"Uh-hmm."

His hands didn't let up, though, and she noticed he still had only his bath towel on. She leaned back and rested her head on his bare belly. His hands slid down, over her breasts.

They made love right there, on the table, with her fanny turning red and sticky from the toast and jelly. The orange juice spilled. Herb's grunting eventually mixed with the manic forecasting of the morning weatherman and finally all sounds disappeared and Traci could only hear her heartbeat.

After, Herb helped her clean up. They didn't say much, but Traci was still feeling tingly and lightheaded. "You're going to be late for work," she said. "I'll finish up here."

"Sure?"

She nodded.

"Is something wrong?"

She opened her mouth to say no, but closed it.

"It's the show tomorrow isn't it? You're worried."

"Yeah."

"We can cancel. Even this late, we don't have to go."

"I want to. I want to let everyone know."

"Okay. Good. I'm proud of you."

He gave her a quick peck on the cheek and was out the door.

*   *   *

The past few days had gone by in a blur. Last Saturday, at the Thruway Mall, Traci had paused for a quick taco snack at the food court, when the young man in the fancy suit had approached her. At first, she thought he was one of those mall survey guys, the ones that ask you the silly questions about God-knows-what. But he had quickly put that idea to rest when he handed her his card.

Len Spinkle – Mona Day Productions

"Mona Day?" Traci whispered.

"Yes, Ma'am, do you know who Mona Day is?"

He had Traci's full attention now. "Do I know?! Are you kidding? I watch her every day practically. God, she's so nice. Like the time when she had those twins on the show; you know, the one was a nun and the other a transves..."

"Yes, that's super," Spinkle politely cut her off. "I see you do know. How would you like to come on the show?"

Traci felt like she was going to wet her shorts. "On the show?"

"As a guest. I'm sure you've seen Mona's guests?"

"Yes, oh, of course, but how ...?"

"Well," Len gave Traci a full tilt smile, revealing snow white teeth, "I noticed you're wearing a wedding ring. May I ask how old you are, Miss? My guess would be about twenty-seven."

Traci blushed furiously, a shade of red so deep it matched her hair. "I'm eighteen."

"Really?" Len was all surprised. No one had ever mistaken Traci for somebody that old.

Traci quickly piped in, "But lots of people say I act much older than I am, like Herb."

"Herb?"

"He's my husband. We just got married in the summer."

"And Herb is your age? Quite a young marriage, eh?"

"No, Herb is forty-two."

Len stood there looking at her for a full minute. Traci thought something was wrong with him. "Are you okay?"

"Okay?" Len whispered. "Are you kidding? I'm great. This is perfect. God, Mona will love this."

"What?"

"What?" Len snapped out of his thoughts. "Uh, what I was about to say is that Mona is doing a show on exactly this, older/younger marriages, and we'd love for you to be on the show."

Traci fainted.

When and how did you and _____ meet?

I went to Cleardale High in the heights. One day, late in my senior year, Herb needed to come to school to fix one of the bathrooms. Somebody flushed a whole roll of toilet paper down and everything backed up. Herb, my husband-to-be ~~was~~ is a plumber so he was at the school. He came out of the bathroom and ran right into me. His first words were, EXCUSE Me. Later, after school, there he was with his plumbing truck waiting for me. He asked if I wanted to go to a Penguins game so I said sure. That's how we met.

What attracted you to your husband?

He ~~was~~ is really cute. He doesn't have a lot of hair, but I think that makes him cuter. He has wide shoulders and brown eyes and very nice teeth. He's very gentle, even though he looks like he means business. Right from the start he treated me like a woman.

What has the reaction been toward your marriage to _____ from your family and friends?

Awful. My family practically disowned me and it's torture to let Herb near anyone like my father, who's the worst. Most of my old friends are just jealous I think. I say old friends because they hardly don't talk to me anymore. Jenni is going to Penn I think. I mean what's their gripe? Cause I'm happy and they're not?

Where do you see yourself twenty years from now?

I'd like to have children of course. I think I'd be a good mother and Herb is certainly willing. He didn't have any kids from his first marriage and it makes him sad sometimes and I don't want him to be sad. He has a great job that he loves. He owns his own plumbing firm. We have an apartment now, but are saving for a house. I've been thinking maybe of doing some craftwork, like needlepoint. It would be fun to try and sell some things down at the local flea market. Herb has encouraged me to do that.

Is _____ the first person you had sex with? How is your sex life with _____ ?

Herb is the first MAN I've had sex with. I mean I let Jimmy Gratton feel me up at the junior prom, but i thought he was gonna puke cause i think he was drunk. Sex with Herb is a wow! Sometimes I feel like I'm on cloud. It's like one of those movies on Cinimax late at night, one of those foreign movies where the woman meets an incredible lover. Well, I met one.

Herb had a slightly different set of questions, Len explained, and Mona would prefer if they didn't share their answers just yet.

"It makes for better television," Len said. "You understand, don't you Traci?"

She did and she kept to her side of the bargain, but one night in bed Herb told her some of his questions. They weren't all that different from Traci's except the ones about Herb's first wife and something about being a father figure, which neither Herb nor Traci understood.

After the questions were all filled out (as well as release papers and proof of identity and copies of their marriage certificate) both of them had to meet with Len again to confirm things and get times and such. It seemed to Traci that Herb and Len didn't get along very well. She figured Herb was about ten years older than Len, but Len kept talking to him like Herb was a boy—like he didn't understand. Herb got steamed, Traci could tell, every time Len asked, "Are you with me?" Traci just squeezed Herb's knee under the table and that pretty much settled things.

On the way home, Herb explained that he ran up against those types all the time.

"What do you mean?" Traci asked.

"I'll go into a house, a real fancy one, out in Oakland someplace. These people don't know squat about pipes, about how their very own three-million-dollar home works. And they give me attitude, you know, like I'm lower than them."

"You ain't, Herb, you're higher than anybody."

"Not to people like that Len guy. He's just another suit, that's all." Herb called anybody who made more money than him "a suit".

"Well, it's not Len we'll be talking to, it's Mona."

Herb smiled. "I know, baby, I know. This is special to you so it's special to me."

Traci beamed.

*   *   *

There was a time, in fact only last year, that Traci had a crush on Chris Bronski, the star running back of the Cleardale Cougars. Actually, he might have been the tight end, but Traci was never able to figure that out. Anyway, sometimes she'd come home after school and just sit and cry in her room and think of Chris Bronski. If anybody asked, she'd tell them how physical her hurt was, how much her chest ached every time he passed her in the hall. Of course, nobody asked and she wouldn't tell them if they did.

This crush she had—Traci called it love back then—was everything in the world to her. For a while, her life revolved around it. She'd develop elaborate fantasies involving Chris Bronski; them going to the prom, for example. One year ago, nothing could have been so important.

Now, however, when Traci was wrapped in Herb's arms, she understood how far she'd traveled in such a short amount of time. She felt so ... grown up. Herb made her feel this. Just a few weeks ago, in fact, she'd heard that Chris Bronski had been arrested for stealing a car. She wasn't surprised or sad or angry. She just shook her head because he was still so young and Traci wished he had the chance to grow up like she had.

* * *

Her mother called Traci a slut. She laughed at Traci and said that Traci was going to end up face down in a bottle or a ditch. This wasn't really new. Gladis had been calling Traci a variety of names now for about five years, ever since the judge had asked her to choose between her father or her mother. Traci picked her father, not really because she loved him more, but because he was a drunk and Traci felt he couldn't take care of himself.

"And besides," Gladis reminded Traci over the phone, "I don't suppose you've lost any weight since I saw you last, did you?"

"Weight?"

"You know, the stuff between your eyes and your feet. And I heard the television makes you look ten pounds heavier."

Despite this, Mona Day was the one thing Traci and Gladis had in common, so Gladis agreed to be in the audience for the show. Traci understood her mother would be there only because her mother watched the Mona show even more religiously than her daughter, but Traci thought it might be a good chance, perhaps, to heal some past wounds.

Traci was a healer. It was a title she picked for herself and she carried like a cross. Her family was a mess, always had been. Just another dysfunctional family in the great primordial dysfunctional family soup. Her brother died when Traci was two. He drowned at a hockey practice—just crashed through the ice and slipped out of Traci's life along with the current of the mighty Allegheny River. They never found his body, and sometimes Traci imagined her brother's ghostly form, still out there, skating. As near as she could tell, all her uncles and aunts were either drunks, criminals or perverts, so Traci never exactly had a role model around the house.

When Herb stumbled onto the scene, he seemed like the perfect knight. The shining armor was navy blue overalls and the sword was a plunger, but after eighteen years of abuses, Traci wasn't complaining. Herb had a steady job, something her father never held. Herb was close to his family, and Traci felt wanted by someone, finally. Now she was the matron of her family, the responsible one. She was going to take care of them all and the Mona Day show was going to be like Traci's coming-out party. The new Traci would emerge—the Traci that was a woman.

*   *   *

The drive to the studio was unbearable.

"You're squirming like an octopus," Herb said and laughed.

Herb looked good today, Traci thought. He looked like a businessman in his dark red tie and black suit. Even his nearly bald head shined almost elegantly. Len had made it clear that there was no dress code, but Traci had insisted they wear good clothes. Traci had decided on a nice two-piece outfit, abandoning a dress for blue slacks and a matching coat. She wore on her lapel an ancient brooch, given to Traci by her grandma Nelli years and years ago. They made a fine couple, like they were important—maybe even going to dinner at a fine restaurant.

The television studio was a massive hanger-like place with pipes and scaffolding and all sorts of wires and God knew what else. Traci watched the Mona Day show nearly every day, but the actual studio looked very different in person. Len met them as they made their way down toward the stage. The audience wasn't assembled yet and technicians were running this way and that. It was like an ant colony, all those people with wires sticking out of their ears moving like they had important places to go. Even Len looked frazzled. Herb grunted when he saw Len in jeans and a sweatshirt.

"Herb, Traci! You two look fabulous! And so early!"

Len vigorously pumped Herb's hand. "The makeup people aren't here yet so just relax for a few minutes. Look around if you like, but don't get tangled in any wires."

He flashed them a giant smile, winked and disappeared. Herb and Traci walked around a bit, but finally, having no place else to go, they settled into a row of seats near the front of the stage.

"I can't believe we're doing this," Traci whispered.

Herb nodded. "It does seem funny. I mean to be on the other side of the television, you know?"

"It's like we're the stars," Traci said.

Herb smiled. "Stars for the day. Everyone will be interested in us. Just us."

Traci poked him in the ribs. "Just us!"

＊   ＊   ＊

The other guests started showing up after a while. There was a couple from Wheeling. The man looked to be in his forties and was tall, thin and pale. His name was Tommy. His wife, Georgette, outweighed Traci by at least fifty pounds and she physically pulled Tommy around by the ear when she wanted him to move in a certain direction. Traci learned that Georgette was nineteen. The other couple were two bikers from Johnstown, Hank and Denise. They both wore leather from head to foot and Denise was so round, Traci thought of a giant, black beach ball. Hank had tattoos all over his arms and neck.

One, a green and black snake, slithered around his chin and disappeared into his leather vest.

Len led all six of them to the back room, a place called the green room—called this, Traci found out, because the floor was covered with a rich, green astro-turf like you'd find at a miniature golf course. In the green room, Len explained to them that most of the show was going to be spontaneous, that Mona had read all their surveys so she knew what to ask and that the audience would ask them questions at various times throughout the show.

"All Mona wants," Len said, straightening his tie, "is that you all be honest. Everyone will be interested in your stories and there's nothing to be embarrassed about. You may get asked some hard questions, so keep your chins up and answer as best you can. I'll be back in five."

He left them standing there, looking at each other.

"Well, uh, nice to meet you all," Traci said pleasantly.

Everyone nodded. Hank grinned. Georgette picked something from under one of her orange fingernails.

Traci turned to Herb and he only shrugged. "I know, baby, I know."

"Do you think Mother is here yet?"

Herb shrugged again.

"Is your mother going to be here?" Tommy asked. It was the first thing he said all day.

"She said she was," Traci replied. "At least I got her a ticket."

Tommy nodded. He looked at Georgette who was still lost in her fingernails, before continuing. "I would have liked for my mom to come."

"Why couldn't she?"

"She's dead," he said with so little emotion Traci didn't know how to respond.

"Tommy!" Georgette shrieked. "Nobody wants to hear about your dead momma!"

That ended the conversation as Tommy lowered his eyes and went back to staring at the green floor.

At exactly five minutes before the show was to start, Mona walked past the open door to the green room.

"Mona!" Traci leapt up and shouted before she even knew what she had done.

Mona Day, dressed in a smart, dark blue pant-suit and concentrating on reading the sheet of paper on the clipboard in her hand, was the portrait of a successful television personality; from her deep concerned eyes to the startling whiteness of her teeth. From her full, red lips hung a brown cigarette. Traci's shout so startled the host of the Mona Day Show that Mona jumped a full foot off the ground, losing the clipboard in the process. A small "poof" of ashes floated up off her cigarette and landed squarely in the crease at the beginning of her cleavage. She shouted something intangible and clutched frantically at the front of her suit, now spotted with gray and black ash marks. The last Traci saw of Mona Day was of the host running for her dressing room, surrounded by stage hands all trying to put out the smoldering fire now growing under Mona's shirt.

*   *   *

The show started ten minutes late, and Mona was now wearing a light blue dress. Her cheeks looked slightly flushed. Traci had been apologizing to everyone she could, but no one seemed very concerned. Traci even apologized to the other guests, but Hank and Denise just laughed, Georgette clicked her tongue and Tommy stared at his shoes. "It's not a problem, doll," Herb assured her. "We'll be able to speak to Mona later and we'll all have a good laugh."

That's not quite how it worked out. As Mona warmed up her audience before the cameras actually started rolling, the show's host would look in Traci's general direction every so often and narrow her eyes. When Mona met her guests finally, she didn't shake Traci's hand.

So, when the familiar theme music for the Mona Day Show started and the audience was clapping and Mona Day was flashing that big smile of hers and walking up the stairs to signal the beginning of her show, Traci was already apprehensive and worried. Traci spotted her mother, but Gladis turned away. The cameras rolled and Traci tried to steel herself.

Mona turned to the camera with the red light and in a loud, concerned voice said, "Women who marry their fathers and men who love overweight women! Today on the Mona Day Show!"

For the second time in a week, Traci fainted away.

*   *   *

Later, much later, Herb and Traci sat at home. Traci hadn't said a word since they had left the studio. They had begged her to pull herself together and go on. Mona herself had knelt beside Traci and with those warm, caring eyes Traci knew so well from television, Mona had pleaded with Traci.

"The show must go on, kid," Mona had said. Traci couldn't believe Mona had actually used that line. "The audience wants you, Traci," Mona said. "I want you."

Traci looked straight through her.

Finally, after twenty minutes of everyone from the stage hands to the other guests trying to comfort her, Traci looked up at Herb.

"It's your choice," he said.

"Take me home."

Mona clicked her tongue and stood abruptly. "Oh fuck it. We're burning studio time. Cut the section and restart the theme. Find me some replacements." Without another word she walked away.

Back at their apartment, Traci sipped from a mug of hot cocoa Herb had made for her. He didn't say anything. He just sat and waited.

"She isn't really a nice person, is she?" Traci asked.

"Who's that, doll?"

"Mona Day."

"No, I guess not."

"I didn't really marry my father Herb, did I?"

"No."

"And I'm not fat?"

"No."

Traci knew she would be barraged with calls tomorrow from her mother and friends. She knew that tomorrow, like so many other days, she'd have to defend herself. She knew that Chris Bronski was a fantasy, no more real than Santa Claus, and she knew she'd never understand the pipes which rattled under her feet. Also, Traci knew that tomorrow she'd try to get through her afternoon without Mona Day.

※

Dan J. Szczesny is a journalist and writer. His fiction and nonfiction has appeared in The Buffalo Spree, The Union Leader *and the* Princeton Packet. *He lives in New Hampshire, where he is busy climbing mountains in an attempt to join the 4,000-footer club.*

DAN SZCZESNY

❧

I, THE CHILD

by Lois M. Hendricks

MY NAME IS BRENDA. I live in Florida. I remember when I was in kindergarten, I really liked school. It was when I was in kindergarten. My teacher was really neat; her name was Miss Anderson. She told us, "Don't ever be afraid to ask if you don't understand something. I want to make learning fun.

And she did. Every day was like a game. She showed us something new—the alphabet and their sounds, rhyming words, matching words with pictures—every day we played a new "learning game," as she called them. It was fun.

There were only ten students in our class, and we all knew each other's names, so it was almost like having another family. I especially liked it at school, because that's when Momma and Daddy began having their "troubles" at home.

I have one sister, Earline, who is two years older than me. She is named after Daddy, whose name is Earl. She even looks like Daddy, with dark, curly hair. My hair is lighter, like Momma's, and straight as a stick. Momma usually braids it for me. Earline is very pretty. I'm kind of plain looking, but Momma says I have a nice smile.

We always walk home from school together (Momma told Earline she had to wait for me). Our house isn't very big so Earline and me sleep in the same bedroom. We share a dresser, but we each have a drawer for our stuff.

One night when we got home, we went right to our room, because Momma and Daddy were yelling at each other, real loud. We didn't know what to do, so we snuck up to our room and closed the door. The noise still came through the door. We both love our Momma and Daddy, but we don't know what to do when they fight and yell at each other. We just cover our ears until it gets quiet again.

That night it took a long time and, when there was no more noise, we went downstairs. Daddy was gone and Momma was crying. I hugged her and told her I got a star on my paper at school. (I thought that would make her feel better.) She smiled a little, then told us to sit down 'cause she had to tell us something. It wasn't good.

Daddy, she said, had a new "girlfriend," and she didn't think he was going to live with us anymore. Then Earline and me started to cry too. We couldn't imagine what it would be like not to have Daddy around.

I remember how he carried me on his shoulders when I was little, and on Sunday mornings, he would take me and Earline to the diner and would order doughnuts, whatever kind we wanted. "nothin's too good for my girls," he'd say to the waitress. Then he'd smile his big smile. But now he was gone, and he hadn't even told us "goodbye." I couldn't stop crying.

"Did we do something wrong? Something to make him mad?" I asked, and Momma shook her head. "It's nothin' to do with you girls."

Then Momma said she had called Gran in North Carolina and asked her to come down for a few days to help her figure out what to do. Gran was Momma's mother and was real special. That made us feel better. Maybe Gran could get everything back to normal.

When Gran came, we were all so happy to see her, but I guess even she couldn't fix the trouble. We had a family meeting (that's what Gran called it), and she said Momma and me and Earline would have to live alone from now on. She said when Daddy decided he needed a new girlfriend, then he didn't need a wonderful family like us. She said maybe someday he'd come to his senses, but for now, we'd manage just fine, thank you.

Gran made us feel some better, but I looked at Earline and she looked as scared as I felt. "Who'll pay the bills?" Earline was older and knew how we often ran out of money before Daddy got his next check.

"Your Momma talked to the manager of the restaurant where she's been working part-time. They'll give her extra hours. That will help until I talk to an attorney. Your Daddy's going to have to help out too, or he'll answer to me." Gran looked angry.

"Can we stay living here?" I didn't want to move away and miss school.

"Why, 'course you can, and I've got a little extra put away to help you if you need it. But I know you'll do just fine." Gran smiled and hugged us, like everything really was going to be fine. My stomach was feeling kind of sick. I guess it was scared too.

"There's only one thing," Momma said. "I have to go in to work early to help with the breakfasts, so I won't be able to get you two off to school, like usual."

"Now we're not talking about babies here," Gran said. "These two big girls can get themselves up and off with no trouble. Right?"

Earline and I both nodded, but my stomach still felt queasy. Momma always made us breakfast and braided my hair and made sure we had everything. I was worried; I didn't feel like a big girl at all.

"I can help Brenda," Earline offered, and Momma got tears in her eyes and hugged her. "Of course you can. And if there's any problems, you can always phone me at the restaurant."

So Gran went home, promising she'd return just as soon as she could get away to see how we were doing. Momma started her new work schedule, and Earline and I were all alone. We always had to keep the doors locked, and NEVER let anybody in. At first it went pretty good, but Earline got awful bossy, and when I told Momma, she said we had to get along with each other. "I have enough to worry about without you girls fussing." So I didn't complain any more.

One morning, we both slept through the alarm, and had to run for school without any breakfast. I didn't get my hair combed, so I went to the bathroom when I got to school. I wet my comb and slicked my hair down straight, as best I could. It didn't look very good and Miss Anderson gave me kind of a funny look when I came in the room, but she didn't say anything, thank heavens.

With Momma gone so much, school became even more special. Miss Anderson seemed to see I needed extra attention. (I guess I looked sad a lot, thinking about Daddy leaving so quick-like.) She had me do extra work on the board, because she knew I really liked that, and then she would tell me what a good job I was doing. She always gave me a hug when I came to school and when I left. Most of the time those were the only hugs I got. I don't think I would have been happy at all except for Miss Anderson.

Momma never got home until almost six o'clock. She usually was very tired and said she hurt all over. "You'll have to make your own supper, and please do it quiet so I can get some sleep." So Earline and me learned to cook, but it was usually hot dogs or canned soup. We had to keep the dishes washed and the house straightened too.

We took turns. Momma didn't want us going anywhere, so we stayed in the house. Earline liked to watch TV, especially the kissing shows (UGH). I usually went to my room and drew pictures or wrote in my workbooks.

Once in a while Momma would surprise us and bring us some food from the restaurant where she worked. It was like a real special party, and we'd laugh with delight when we saw her coming in with an armful of little, white, carryout boxes. Those nights were our best times ever. It was almost like it used to be—before Daddy left.

Then pretty soon it was summer. Me and Earline took the bus up to see Gran, and she took us to the beach. We had a wonderful time. When I came home, I was going to be in the FIRST GRADE. I was really excited about that. Miss Anderson had talked about all the new stuff we would learn. I knew I'd really miss her, and when I told her that, she said the first grade teacher was very nice and I shouldn't worry.

When school finally started, I hurried to the first grade room. I was surprised. All my kindergarten classmates were there, but there were two other kindergarten classes there too. Our new teacher, Mrs. Dempsey, had thirty students to teach, all by herself. I was bashful with all the new faces I didn't know, but Miss Anderson was right. Mrs. Dempsey was very nice, so I thought everything would be fine.

It wasn't the same though. Because there were so many students, Mrs. Dempsey had to divide us into groups, so I was with about ten students. Most of them were new people so I tried to learn their names. First grade was different. We had to figure out a lot more stuff by ourselves. I missed Miss Anderson. I never could learn as fast as the other kids, even in kindergarten.

Mrs. Dempsey told us to raise our hands if we didn't understand something, so I was raising my hand a lot. I noticed a couple of the new kids put their heads down and snickered when I did that.

My face got red; I was embarrassed. Mrs. Dempsey didn't notice, and I didn't want to tattle, so I stopped asking questions. When Mrs. Dempsey asked if we understood, I'd watch the rest of the kids and shake my head "yes" like they did, even though I didn't.

I guess it was about then that school wasn't much fun anymore.

I finished first grade, and then I was in second grade. Our class was about the same size, so we had groups again. Each had a bird's name. Ours was the "seagulls."

One day, out on the playground, one of the students asked me which group I was in. When I told her, she said, "Oh, that's the dumb group." When she saw my face get red, she said she didn't mean that I was dumb, but I sure did know what she meant, especially when I saw her and one of her friends laughing and pointing at me. I was angry with them, but at myself too. I wondered why I had to be so stupid.

Our teacher wanted us to be good readers. She said we should take a book home every night and read it to our parents or a big sister or brother. I asked Earline if I should ask Momma to listen to me read, and she said I better not bother her. She got in a real bad mood if you asked for something special, so we tried to stay out of her way. Earline said she'd listen to me read a story that night, but she had a lot of homework to do too, so she couldn't help me every night.

When I went back to school the next day, the teacher said we should raise our hands if we had read a book to someone, so I raised mine real tall, but I didn't know what I'd do the next day. That's when I got the idea to read to my doll. So every night after that, I'd read to my teddy bear and my doll. Earline said I was telling the teacher "kind of a fib," but I knew I'd be in trouble if I said I didn't read every night. So I kept reading to my doll and teddy bear. They couldn't help me with any hard words, but they sure smiled a lot.

Gran surprised us one day. She came down on the bus to see us.

That was the day we got our report cards, and Momma was not happy with mine. The grades weren't very good, and she said it didn't look like I was trying.

She showed the report card to Gran who shook her head, "What's goin' on here, child? Doesn't look like you're working very hard."

"Yes, I am, Gran. I really am. But I'm just not as smart as most of the kids and they have help at home too." I was crying by now.

"I don't want to hear about other kids," Momma said. "You gotta know by now that all kids ain't equal." Her voice was rising. "I didn't plan on your Daddy running off and leaving me all alone. I ain't got it easy, Lord knows, and if you girls want to make something of yourselves, you're going to have to work day and night, just like I do."

Gran looked sad and put her arm around my shoulder. "Your Momma is doing a good job. She's keeping a roof over your heads and food on the table. You've got to ask your teacher for more help if you need it."

"There's too many kids for her to help." Sobbing, I ran up to my room, tears streaming down my face. They just didn't understand. It was especially hard to have Gran unhappy with me, too. I didn't know what to do. I don't think I ever felt so alone. Earline wasn't one of the best students, but her report card was lots better than mine so she wasn't in trouble like me.

I guess I finally cried myself to sleep, because soon Earline was waking me, and it was time to go to school again. Gran had left. Momma took her down to the bus depot on her way to work. I didn't eat much breakfast because my stomach was hurting again.

After that, things seemed to get even worse. I couldn't concentrate at school. I just couldn't forget about Momma and Gran being so disappointed in me.

One day my teacher, Mrs. Morgan, asked me to stay after school. She said I had been looking very sad and wondered if something was troubling me. I told her my Momma and Gran weren't happy with my report card, but I really was trying as hard as I could, but I just didn't understand a lot of the work, and I didn't know what to do. By that time I was crying, and Mrs. Morgan looked like she was going to cry too.

"I think I can get a tutor to help you," she said. "Mrs. Emily is a grandma, and she comes in and helps students if they're having trouble with their studies. She's a very nice lady and the children love her. Would you like to meet her?"

I wasn't sure what a tutor meant, but I sure needed something. "OK." I nodded my head, wiping my tears.

"I'll have her come in tomorrow and introduce you," Mrs. Morgan said. "I'd like to see that smile back on your face." She gave me a big hug.

I went to meet Earline and asked her if she knew what a tutor was. She said some of the kids in her room had tutors to help them. She said the tutors work alone, just with one student at a time. She said I was lucky, because they never have enough tutors, and she wished she could get one to help her with math. So I felt better; maybe this tutoring would help.

The next day I met Mrs. Emily. She was really old and small and kind of humped over with pure white hair and thick glasses. But she had a big smile for me, and that made me feel better. We just sat and talked for a while, and I told her about Momma having to work all the time, and Daddy leaving and not saying goodbye. She said that would make her sad too. I talked more than I had for a long time.

"You remind me of Miss Anderson, but you're older," I said.

She asked me how old I thought she was, and I said, "About 100." Then I felt bad I had said that because I knew nobody was that old.

Mrs. Emily just laughed. "Well, I'm not quite 100 yet, although I sometimes feel that old." Then her eyes twinkled. "That's why I enjoy working with students like you. You make me feel young again."

I smiled. I liked her already.

So on Tuesdays and Thursdays, every week, for one hour, Mrs. Emily and me would work on reading or grammar or anything I was having trouble with. It was one of the happiest times I can remember. She was very patient and I soon learned that I could ask her any question and she wouldn't think it was stupid. She kept telling me how much I was improving and my grades were getting better, and I was smiling a lot more now. For the first time since kindergarten, I began enjoying school again. And Mrs. Emily always gave me hugs, too. I guess that's why she reminded me of Miss Anderson.

When I read, she'd say real loud, "That was simply splendiferous!" I asked her what that meant, and she said that was our special word for when I did something REALLY good.

I looked forward to going into that special tutor room twice a week. When I walked in, Mrs. Emily was always there, with her big smile. "What kind of splendiferous things shall we do today?" I would giggle.

All my classes were easier now. Mrs. Emily said it was because I was gaining more confidence. I didn't really understand what that meant, but I knew it must be good, because my stomach didn't hurt at all anymore.

Then it happened. One day I came to school and Mrs. Morgan said she had bad news for me. Mrs. Emily was in the hospital and was going to have surgery. No one knew when she might be back. There were no available tutors to help me, but if she found one, she'd let me know.

"Can I go see her?" I had tears in my eyes. She is my very best friend in the whole world."

Mrs. Morgan sat down next to me. "You can't see her, but why don't you make her a card, and I'll be sure she gets it."

So I made the prettiest card I knew how, with flowers on it. Mrs. Morgan helped me with it and checked my spelling. It said, "You're my very special friend, and I'm sorry you're sick. I don't ever want any tutor but you, so this card is instead. I love you. Brenda."

A few days later Mrs. Morgan gave me a card. It was from Mrs. Emily's nurse. She said Mrs. Emily was too weak to write, but my card made her smile and smile. Mrs. Emily said she wanted me to know that the card was really "splendiferous!"

I was happy to get the card, but sad too. I knew Mrs. Emily wouldn't be coming back.

School continued about the same, year after year. I discovered that if you just stay quiet, and don't make waves (as Earline says), you don't get a lot of hassle. And I was doing better. Momma wasn't upset about my report cards anymore.

Earline said she is going to quit school as soon as she is old enough. She said she's going to get a job and help Momma with the bills. I know there's another reason too. She likes boys a lot and wants to get some new clothes. I'll probably quit school too, soon as I can.

We never did hear from Daddy. Gran said he had moved to California and had a new baby. So I guess he's forgotten all about us by now. I'll never forget him though. I keep his picture on our dresser, the one where he's holding me on his shoulders. I look at it every morning when I get up.

Momma is doing OK. She seems happier lately, probably because she has a new boyfriend. He seems nice, but is kind of loud. I think he's trying too hard to make us like him. I'll like him if he makes Momma happy.

And I'll do OK too. Maybe some day I'll get married. But I'll have to be awful careful. I sure wouldn't want to make my children sad, like Daddy made us. "Life ain't easy," Gran says, "you have to roll with the punches," whatever that means.

I just hope there's something "splendiferous" waiting for me somewhere.

❦

Writing has been a lifelong, enjoyable passion. Minor successes, such as a weekly human-interest column, sustained me until retirement offered the time to more diligently pursue this craft.

The emotions of tutoring, another retirement pursuit, prompted me to write "I, the Child."

LOIS M. HENDRICKS

THE APPLE TREE

by Rob Kerr

E MMIE SMEARED PEANUT BUTTER on the white bread. She started to lick the knife, changed her mind when she noticed I was watching, then rinsed it off in the sink. She packed her lunch sack with the sandwich, chips, and a shiny red apple, and by the way she mumbled to herself and brushed back the stray wisps of her hair, I could tell she was anxious.

"Too bad Mommy's left for work already, Emmie. She'd love to see you leave for your first day of high school."

"It's no biggie."

"It seems like only yesterday she was making your lunch in this same kitchen for your first day of kindergarten."

"We'd better get going, Dad. It's raining really hard."

Before I could respond, she darted out the side door and raced through the rain the few steps to my silver Volvo. I grabbed an apple to take with me, put it in a brown lunch sack, and followed her out the door.

The rain was pouring as it seems it can only do in Houston in August. The streets were not flooding yet, but if the thunderstorm had started earlier, the opening day of the 1999 school year might have been postponed. It doesn't take much for these flat urban streets to flood, and the water on ours was already beginning to rise as we backed out of the driveway.

A flood of memories welled up in me, too, as I returned to the school I had graduated from 25 years earlier. I wanted to tell my daughter about my experiences there, about my teachers and friends. I had told her some of these things before, as she was growing up, but I had never told her about the apple tree or my friend, Andy. I suppressed the urge to do so now. This was her day, not mine. I looked out at the dark skies, hoping the rain would let up before we reached our destination.

"Are you nervous?" I asked Emmie as we drove down our street.

"Kinda."

"Well, it's only natural to be a little apprehensive on the first day of high school."

"I know."

Water swirled around the tires as I drove as far away from the curb as I could. The car's headlights illuminated sheets of rain against the darkened sky.

"Every ninth-grader's going through the same thing you're going through today."

Emmie took a brush from her backpack and brushed her thick brown shoulder-length hair. "I know, Daddy, but what if none of my friends are in my classes?"

"You'll make new friends. I was new at Lamar once myself, and I didn't know anyone there on my first day."

"Sure, Dad," she said distractedly, as she examined her face in the visor mirror. "Do I look all right? I don't know what everyone else will be wearing."

I glanced at her. She wore new blue jeans with a pink cotton shirt tucked in. A soccer ball key chain dangled from the zipper of the green backpack resting on her lap. Despite the darkness, her hazel eyes reflected brightly in the mirror.

"You look just fine, honey."

We drove in silence for a few blocks. I looked again at my daughter, who was shoving her lunch sack into her backpack. My thoughts returned to my days in high school. I usually brought a brown bag lunch, too, to eat with my friends under the apple tree on the front lawn of the school.

* * *

It was actually an oak tree. A very old, stately live oak, one of eight or ten scattered around the front lawn. All the trees were about the same age and size, but this was the one where we gathered on pleasant days to eat our lunch. If it was rainy or cold, we ate in the cafeteria, but normally most of our loose-knit group of friends wandered out to the apple tree with our brown lunch bags for C period lunch. Some trudged out alone, lost in thought. Others sauntered in gregarious groups of two or three, laughing and hailing those more distant, calling each other the names by which we were known. We were all juniors, sixteen and seventeen years old. On any given day there would be 15 or 20 of us, mainly, but not exclusively, boys, some close friends, others more on the periphery. A few, like me, were new to the school.

It must have been either Susan or Tommy who dubbed it the apple tree, but it was Andy who started the tradition. Every day Andy's mother packed a bright shiny red apple in his lunch bag. He hated apples, but had given up his futile effort to convince his mother of that fact. Evidently it assuaged her maternal feelings to include the fruit in this lunch bag, though she knew her son would never take even one bite of it.

Early in the school year, Andy simply gave his apples away or left them in the bag when he tossed it in the trash barrel. But one day in November, he improvised a humorous pantomime, and it met with such success that it quickly became a ritual. At some point during lunch, sometimes early, sometimes just as the fourth-period bell spurred us to our feet, Andy would theatrically produce the apple from his sack.

"Here's another ripe one for the tree," he would announce as he breathed on the apple and polished it against his chest. Sometimes he would toss it behind his back or roll it down his outstretched arm, before the inevitable denouement. He would assume a baseball pitcher's position with his lanky frame, a position he knew well as the best pitcher on our district championship team. Then he would nod to the imaginary catcher, check the runners on base, kick high his long left leg as slowly as he could without falling over, and fire a blazing fastball square into the live oak's trunk. Our gathering place for lunch became known as the apple tree, and as it grew in popularity, I felt silent pride at having been present at the birth of this new and unique tradition. And I basked in Andy's reflected glory as we drove to and from school each day in my white Volkswagen bug.

My family had moved to Houston just a few weeks before the eleventh grade school year was to start, and I didn't know anyone my age in the city. I met Andy on our block, shortly after we had moved in. That summer, he mowed yards in the area to earn spending money, and one day he dropped off a flyer in our mailbox and stopped to chat. Andy was quite a salesman. He stood in our doorway pitching his services, with a broad smile and tousled jet black hair, and it was impossible for my dad to tell him no. Andy stood on our front porch in the waning daylight, hands gesturing wildly, laughing loudly at my father's modest jests.

"Yes sir, Mr. Wallace, that Saint Augustine grass will be mowed just right. Not too low so it dries out, and not too high so I'd have to keep coming back to take your money like those other yahoos like to do."

When Andy learned I had a car and would be attending Lamar High, the full court press was on. He offered to take care of me at school, show me the ropes. And all I had to do was give him a ride each day. I resisted at first. What if I didn't like him? I would be stuck. But he had such an irrepressible personality I couldn't refuse. And though he was incorrigibly late, running daily to my honking bug with his books under one arm, socks and shoes under the other, and his shirt invariably unbuttoned, I soon realized I couldn't have made a wiser decision. Within the first few weeks of the new school year, Andy had drawn me into his ever-expanding circle of friends and admirers. I quickly became a member of his loose coterie, and some of the friends I made through Andy—like Tommy and Susan—I count among my closest today. He even used that word for us—coterie. He had a special bond with our elderly English teacher, Mrs. Greenwood, and loved to popularize vocabulary words everyone else learned only for tests.

"You guys are members of a select class," he would say dramatically. "You're members of Andy's coterie, a special and exalted group."

Andy gave everyone a nickname, and it was on one of those first car rides to school that he gave me mine.

"You have to have a nickname, but we can't get anything very original out of Christopher. We'll work on your last name, Wallace. I think a good name is 'Wally.' But only if you want it, Wally."

Then he laughed, and I laughed. And from that day to this, Wally has been my nickname.

*   *   *

The windshield wipers beat furiously, barely keeping pace with the driving rain, as Emmie and I stopped at a red light down the street from the school. I watched her changing stations on the radio, the music punctuated by static from the electrical storm outside.

My old bug would have been leaking by now. It had a sunroof with a hand crank that was out of kilter, and no matter how tightly

I tried to close it, water always poured in during a heavy rain. The leaking began when Andy and I drove through a car wash and neglected to shut the sunroof. When the wash water suddenly began streaming through the opening, we both lunged for the hand crank. He grabbed it first, and frantically cranked it shut, laughing uproariously, his black-rimmed glasses flying into my lap. After that, the sunroof leaked when it rained hard, and it sagged permanently from the residual water in the cavity. I was always suspicious that Andy knew the sunroof was open when we entered the car wash. The glint in his blue eyes belied his strenuous denials.

"C'mon, Andy, you planned the whole thing," I had accused him. "You got me messing with the radio so I wouldn't notice the roof was open."

With mock gravity he replied, "Would I do a thing like that, Wally? But weren't you just a little bit curious to see what would happen? And it makes a dang good story, doesn't it?"

I've told my daughter that story before, and some others about Andy, though I don't believe I've told her about the apple tree. As we drew closer to the high school, those memories washed over me like the torrential rain beating down on the hood of the car.

Emmie and I pulled into the Lamar parking lot. Its entrance was on busy Westheimer Street. I vividly remember entering and exiting the same parking lot when I had been a student at Lamar. The school day ended at three o'clock, and it was always difficult for the long line of departing cars to merge into the traffic of the busy street. This was maddening to Andy, whose fast metabolism seemed constantly revved up.

"I've got a plan," he announced one day, and the next day he brought a crossing guard's vest and a whistle. "I was chief student crossing guard in sixth grade, and that's just what this school needs."

After school that day, Andy strode into the middle of the street blowing the whistle, arms outstretched. He stopped the traffic and let the grateful students out of the parking lot. When my car arrived, he jumped in and away we went. After a few days his procedure became more sophisticated. He would let seven or eight cars out and then allow the street traffic to resume for a while, and he told me to wait and be one of the last cars out.

"Just cool your heels, Wally, until it's your turn. If I'm gonna do this right, I have to be fair about it," he explained.

I expected that any day the school authorities would put an end to this vigilante crossing guard, but they never did. They had to have known he was doing it, but it helped the traffic flow so much they must have looked the other way. When the school yearbook came out that year, the frontispiece was a full-length black and white picture of Andy, standing in the middle of Westheimer, directing traffic.

*　*　*

It was still raining ferociously as my Volvo crept across Lamar High's asphalt parking lot.

"Let me out as close as you can to the side door, Daddy. It's really coming down."

"Some of the teachers I had when I was a student still teach here, Emmie. Maybe you'll have one of them."

"Maybe."

"One nice thing about this school is they let you eat your lunch anywhere you want, as long as you stay on campus."

"I know, Dad. That'll be cool."

"Our group always ate under the same tree, out on the front lawn."

Emmie laughed. "Not on a day like this, though."

"No, not on a day like this."

Our car was idling in a long queue, waiting to get close to the side entrance in the driving rain. I could see the apple tree briefly between each swipe of the windshield wipers, clearly visible, then rapidly melting away in the rain until the wipers swiped again.

"Do you see that tree over there, Emmie? That's where our group used to eat."

"That looks like a good place. One of the limbs is so long it's almost touching the ground."

"Yes, two or three of us would sit on it while the others sat on the ground. We called it the apple tree."

"It's not an apple tree, though, is it?"

"No, it's an old live oak." Seeing Emmie's puzzled expression, I just said, "I'll tell you about it later."

"Sure, Dad. Later."

It was still raining hard and we were several cars away from the front of the line when Emmie put on her backpack and opened the door. "I think I'll get out of the car here, not by the door."

"Be sure to call home if you have any problems today."

"I'm sure I won't have any."

"Be careful where you set your backpack down, Em. There are over 2,000 students at Lamar and you don't want someone to walk off with it."

"No *prob,* Dad."

"Okay then. Good luck. You know, it doesn't seem so long ago I was driving you to elementary school."

She laughed. "I remember when I put on my backpack you would always say, 'Don't forget your parachute.'" She kissed me briefly on the cheek and got out of the car.

I watched her as she ran with her jacket pulled over her head the 20 yards or so to the walkway covered by corrugated tin. She quickly blended into the sea of students arriving from various parts of the parking lot. I squinted a tear and rubbed it with my sleeve, watching through the rain my little daughter enter such a grown-up school.

*   *   *

It rained hard like this on the day of Andy's funeral, but it was also bone-chilling cold. It must have been January third or fourth, I suppose, because he died in a car accident on New Year's morning. It was in all the papers and on television as Houston's first traffic fatality of the year.

It was one of those gut-wrenching tragedies that there's no making sense of; not then, not now. One of our friends, a boy Andy didn't even know well, had an extra ticket to the Cotton Bowl and asked Andy to go. The friend's older brother from college, a boy Andy didn't know at all, was to drive them up to Dallas on the morning of the game. The brother had a history of reckless driving, but Andy didn't know it. Before they had even left Houston, the brother sped his car down Westheimer Street—past the high school—headed toward Interstate 45. It was only seven-thirty on New Year's morning and few cars were out. According to the news reports, the brother's car was traveling over 90 miles an hour. As they approached an intersection, the light turned red. The brother tried to stop, but wasn't even close to doing so before he collided with a car crossing in front of him. Amazingly, no one was hurt except Andy. The brother's Camaro split open on impact and Andy, riding in the back seat, flew from the car. He landed on the pavement and died instantly.

We all cried at the cemetery, in the rain. Tommy and Susan cried a lot. Andy's younger sister Nancy, his only sibling, cried the most. They had been close. He always included her in everything we did, and I never saw them fight or bicker the way most siblings do. I don't have a clear memory of Andy's parents at the funeral. I guess I was at the age when friends seem all-important, and parents are considered extraneous. But now I can only shake my head in sorrow at what they must have felt. Their darling smiling adopted son, friend to all and destined for a college baseball scholarship, snatched from them on the first day of a new year.

Andy's parents are deceased now, and Nancy lives up North— Michigan, I think. A few years ago, after a visit to Andy's grave, I wrote her a letter. But she never responded and I regretted sending it; I can think sentimentally about Andy, but she probably cannot face thinking of him at all.

The first day back at school following the holidays was just a few days after Andy's funeral. It wasn't raining, but it was still bitterly cold. That morning I asked my mother to make my lunch, even though everyone would probably be eating in the cafeteria. I picked out the reddest, plumpest apple I could find in the fruit basket on the counter, and walked to my white Volkswagen bug to drive to school.

I thought of altering my regular route that day but decided resolutely to go the way I always did, past Andy's house, and imagined him running from his front door, arms flailing and half-dressed. Often I would pretend jokingly to leave him behind, reversing down his drive as he chased my bug.

Laughing, I would shout over my shoulder, "I can't wait any longer, Andy! Coach will bust me if I'm late today!"

But on this morning, there was no joke. I paused in front of his house and thought fleetingly of honking in tribute, but decided not to disturb his family. I downshifted gears and depressed the accelerator in the closest approximation of pick-up my bug could muster.

On that early January day, students filed into the classroom building from the parking lot, hunched up and breathing on their hands for warmth. Inside it was cold, too, as the building's sluggish heating system was just waking after the long holiday season. When it got close to lunch period, the air had warmed slightly, but the temperature still hovered around the freezing mark.

I was seated at my desk by the window in Mrs. Greenwood's second-floor English classroom, gazing aimlessly out on the front lawn.

In the cold, the lawn was deserted during both A and B lunch periods. From time to time, I caught Tommy's eye and together we would glance over our shoulders at the empty desk behind us. Lovable and scholarly Mrs. Greenwood, with her white hair and rosy cheeks, provided the class with literary allusions suitable for the occasion. *We will meet, but we will miss him. There will be one vacant chair. We will hasten to caress him, as we breathe our evening prayer.* Mrs. Greenwood had been one of Andy's biggest fans, always cajoling and prodding him to produce work beyond what he thought himself capable of.

After class, I walked along with Tommy and Susan down the stairs and outside through the big front doors for C period lunch. Some of the others were already at the apple tree by the time we arrived. Eventually there were 30 or 40 of us, the only ones on the front lawn. I sat with Tommy and Susan on the low tree limb, which had been tacitly reserved for Andy's closest friends. We ate in silence, heads down, avoiding each other's glances. Susan shivered in the frigid air.

As the bell rang, Tommy climbed off of the limb and took an apple from his sack. He looked at it for a moment before heaving it against the tree. The others formed a line, and one by one threw their apples against the tree. I went last. I reached back and threw my apple as hard as I could. I wanted to knock the tree over, to make it disappear.

*   *   *

The squeaking of the wipers on the dry windshield lifted me from my reverie. As happens often in this city in August, the storm had halted abruptly and had been replaced by steamy sunshine. Before I left for my office, I pulled over on the side of the parking lot nearest the apple tree. I saw Tommy and Susan sitting on the low limb with

Andy on a pleasant Fall day, and I saw myself there with them. We were shooting the breeze, discussing school, music, sports, general things and particular people, joking and laughing out loud.

The sun was bright now, and the sky was as piercing blue as Andy's eyes had been when I first met him on my front doorstep. The tree was just as I remembered it, the low limb perhaps hanging slightly lower than 25 years before. How long had it been there? One hundred years, maybe longer. Possibly it was there before the city of Houston was even born. And still it stood. Proud and solid, unchanged and unchangeable.

I looked across the front lawn at the imposing high school building. I could see students through the windows, seated at their desks in the first class of the new school year, the school year that would begin in one millennium and end in a new one.

I could almost hear Mrs. Greenwood's mellifluous voice through one of the windows, reciting Shakespeare. *But if the while I think on thee, dear friend, All losses are restor'd, and sorrows end.*

The building looks today pretty much the same as when I had been a student in the 1970s, probably not much different from when the doors were first opened in the 1930s. It was a new school then, full of hope and excitement and dreams, and to the students, like my daughter, sitting in their first high school classroom, it still is.

I took the apple from my sack and bit into it. "Don't forget your parachute," I said softly.

❦

I began writing last year and have been working on two young adult novels as well as writing short stories. My work has appeared in Renaissance Online Magazine. The Apple Tree *is my first story to be published in print. I live with my wife and four daughters in Houston.*

ROB KERR

A FEW TENSE MOMENTS

by Steve Kucinski

I**T WASN'T SUPPOSED TO** turn out like this. I was supposed to be at home with my wife and son, not in this bank with a 9mm Glock. Then again, the heathens at the bank weren't supposed to send my account to collections a week after I paid it up to date. They weren't supposed to make my wife cry when she talked to them. I like to think that I'm a rational person—not the type to resort to violence.

When I would see news reports of people going nuts and holding car salesmen hostage, I would wonder how they could blow a gasket like that. Well, in the case of a car salesman, I could understand. In fact, I might even have cheered them on. Generally though, I thought I was being as diplomatic as the next guy. Now the bank manager at whom I'm pointing the gun, and, who has recently wet himself, might disagree. Not just now, you understand, but under normal circumstances, he would say I was a psycho.

What don't these people understand? How much abuse should normal human beings be expected to take before they lash out?

How many lies, deceits, overcharges, and scams must one take before being expected to snap? I have to tell you I lost count in my own case. I guess all that matters to the bank manager in the wet boxers is that this is the time that put me over the edge.

All I really want is someone to listen to me. That's all I have ever wanted from the beginning. I really don't think that's asking a lot. The majority of the people that I couldn't get to listen to me held positions whose job it was, was to listen to me. Go figure.

Okay, I admit it. I lost it. Now I've crossed the point of no return. I walked into this bank today fully expecting to speak my mind and have my problems solved for me by the gracious bank manager, Mr. Fisher. Only when I got there, Mr. Fisher apparently had forgotten our conversation. That's a pretty important detail, especially considering that I agreed to drive all the way out here. And to be rude to me when I shared my displeasure in the entire situation. . .big mistake.

So the doors are locked, and everyone has left except for me and good old Mr. Fisher. I bet this is the worst date he's ever had. I have so many decisions to make in such a short time. I mean, the police will be storming in soon with tear gas and pepper spray, guns trained on my poor melon. The question is, am I going to go out in a "blaze of glory?"

What about my wife and son, you ask? How can I leave them like this? A better question might be how could she leave me and take my son like that. I've been alone in that cold house for two months. Two months to stew and get angry and finally boil over.

"Mr. Clark. What do you intend to do to me. You hear the sirens, don't you?"

Should I answer him? Nah, I'm just going to give him a blank stare. I think that will be more upsetting than threatening him. Actually, it's a good question. I'm not sure what I'm going to do with him. I don't think he deserves to be hurt but, then again, I didn't deserve any of the garbage they put me through either.

He's definitely looking at me differently than when he was telling me he couldn't help me—looking down his nose at me. When I think of that face, I do want to hurt him. But right now, he's looking at me as if he's well-aware of the gun aimed at his belly. He's sitting in that chair across from me and he must face the indisputable fact that, in the next few minutes, I am going to decide if he lives or dies. I feel a little bit like St. Peter at the Pearly Gates.

The phone across the lobby at the main desk is ringing, but I'm not going to answer it. I don't need to be talked down or have my psyche examined by the local police shrink. I'm just going to ignore them. I hear car doors slamming outside. They're probably mapping out what doors they'll storm first and how to give themselves a tactical advantage. It doesn't matter—whatever happens will happen.

"Mr. Clark. I have a family, you know. And I'm sorry about how things went for you here."

Okay, now I'm just laughing at him. Does he actually think that he's just going to talk his way out of this? Does he really believe that he could step on my private parts and then just say "oops, sorry"? Major screw up mentioning family, too. Fisher's really striking out in this little hostage crisis situation we have going here.

I think I hear people on the roof now. I wonder if the newspaper and television reporters are here yet. They bug me, too. They're always trying to capitalize on other people's pain. I'm not even going to tell them my story, even though I want people to know why this happened. I know there's a lot of other people out there just like me.

Fisher's still shaking over there in his nice plush office armchair. I wonder what he's thinking. He's careful not to make too much eye contact or talk too much. I'm sure that he's been trained how to act in this type of situation, but who the hell really expects it to happen to them?

Things are going to get crazy here pretty soon. I think it's time I messed with Fisher's head a little.

"How much is your life worth to you, Fisher?"

"What do you mean?"

"Which word didn't you understand? How bad do you want to live?"

"I want to live. I already told you I have a family."

Cha-chank.

I chamber a round in the gun on that second painful mention of family. He's really pissing me off. Now the gun's up and pointed at his head. I think he senses exactly how delicate the situation is. I think I like that.

"Fisher. Whatever you do don't mention your family again."

"Okay. I'm sorry. I just didn't understand your question. I still don't."

Fisher's looking towards the windows hoping that a SWAT officer comes leaping through to save the day. I think he should be more concerned with answering my question.

"So Fisher. Since we only have a few minutes left here, how about answering my question."

"But I don't. . ."

"Fisher, don't say you don't understand the question. You're an educated man; figure it out."

Look at that bastard sitting there looking so stupid and witless. Now he knows how it feels. I doubt it will make a difference, though.

"Let me help you out, Fisher. Do you want to live badly enough to kill me?"

Now, granted, if I end up dying here today, since it was Fisher who brought me here in the first place, you could say he killed me in the first place.

"How can I kill you? You have the gun."

"Jesus Christ, Fisher. Are you trying to get me to shoot you?! I know you lie for a living, but can't you just answer the damn question?"

Now I know what he's thinking. It's probably the same thing I would be thinking in his place. What's the right answer here? Do I risk telling the truth and say "yes" (Heaven forbid!) or do I try to placate him by saying "no"? Glad I don't have to make that decision.

"Yes. I want to live badly enough to kill you."

I look at him. He's scared. It was a good answer. I'm not going to give him the satisfaction of telling him I think so. But a good answer, nonetheless.

"Well, I tell ya, Fisher. I'm no expert on SWAT team etiquette but I have a feeling that they'll be coming in any minute now. The only problem is that there's a good chance you'll be hit the same time as I am. All the confusion and adrenaline. Wouldn't that just suck?"

For the first time, Fisher looks worried about something other than what I might do to him. Another glance towards the windows, then back to me.

I'm gonna make you a deal, Fisher. And don't take too long to think about it because, like I said, I think we only have a few more tense moments left here."

Fisher can only sit and watch me with frightened and tired eyes.

"I'll lay my gun down on this table that's between us. It's loaded and you heard me chamber a round earlier. Then I'll sit back in my cozy little red armchair just like yours. You guys should really take some of the money you rip off of people with ATM charges and returned check charges and get some new furniture."

I think Fisher almost wants to smile at that one.

"Then the gun will be right between us, eh?"

"So what?"

Fisher is getting braver by the minute.

"So, since you want to live bad enough to kill me, I guess you'll want to grab the gun up off the table. Then you can do what you want—walk out, kill me, whatever."

"And what if you get the. . ."

"Fisher, don't say 'what happens if you get the gun first'?"

It was going to be settled just like the Old West. If someone swindled you out of your hard-earned money, you took care of business out in the street, giving everyone a sporting chance.

The phone continues to ring and I hear voices on a bullhorn outside as I wait for Fisher to start trembling again. I so enjoy watching that.

"Are you ready, Fisher?"

I leaned over toward the table, ready to lay the gun down.

"I don't know."

"Remember. . .SWAT team bullets spray the area."

I give him a smile just to piss him off and goad him into doing what I want.

"Do it."

"You're a piece of shit, Fisher. Nothing that happens from here on out is gonna change that. Just so you know, I did more for you here than you were willing to do for me. I gave you a fair shake."

I set the gun down and ease back into my chair. Fisher locks eyes with mine and tries to figure out what I'm thinking. We both hear glass breaking in the outer lobby and we know that it's almost over. Almost.

Fisher lunges forward for the gun and I don't even flinch. He points it at me, shaking almost uncontrollably. Hot tears of anger, relief, and tension stream down his face. I actually don't know if he's going to kill me or not. I don't really know if I care.

I wish I could read his mind in those few tense moments that he holds the gun on me. I wonder if he even sees the SWAT team sniper's laser sight on his head. I wonder if he ever considers that they might think he is the assailant. I wonder if it hurts when the bullet enters his head and he slumps over to the side of the chair and his blood flows into the doily. I wonder if he wishes, even for a split second, that he hadn't screwed with Justin Clark.

* * *

"Mr Clark? Mr. Clark?"

"Yes? I'm Justin Clark."

"Hi. Jeff Fisher, bank manager. Sorry you had to wait so long out here. Surprised you didn't nod off. I hope the chairs were comfortable. Mr. Clark, I'm afraid I'm not going to be able to help you out. You see. . ."

ADMIRATION

by A. Price

I WATCHED HER AS SHE walked. It was towards me. Her gait was comfortable. Fluid. Supple. Her movement started at her hips, as if she was flinging her legs forward from her middle and her knees were an accessory. It was a glide, really. Very smooth.

Likewise, the sidewalk was agreeable. Level and straight, newly poured cement. She had plenty of room to herself, as if her essence told others to yield a little more space than usual. They always did so she walked alone in the crowd.

Or maybe it just seemed that way to me, for my focus was dialed on her alone. I had been waiting for a while. She was late. I was patient. I didn't know where she had been and I wondered if I would ask.

My glass was half full, but the ice had melted and the tea sank to the bottom. The empty lemon slice was in the ashtray next to the vase. One pink and one yellow gerber daisy stood just high enough to allow my viewpoint a little camouflage. From this distance it looked like she was small enough to stand right on top of them.

"No thank you," I told the waiter.

She kept walking. I kept watching.

The big orange hand in the box must have said she couldn't cross the street, because she stopped at the corner and stood. Passing cars made the air turn beside her and her hair flew in front of her face. It was auburn. Shoulder length, thick, and dark. But when the sun hit it as it did on that corner, you could see the red. I liked the red. I was grateful to the big orange hand in the box.

As she crossed the street, she moved her bag to her left shoulder, then raised her right hand and pulled her hair back into place. She ran her pinky by the corner of her mouth pulling a few strands from between her lips. She was closer now. Just half a block. She saw me.

I felt a twinge and had to shift in my seat. I cleared my throat. Her glance turned away knowingly. I'm sure I saw a sly smile.

I watched her as she walked towards me. Jeans, and a white t-shirt like a man wears. V-neck tucked in tightly so the fabric was taut from her breasts to her belly.

She wanted to be kissed. I could tell. She needed to be kissed well.

She was getting closer, just a few steps away. I could already smell her. Vanilla soap and musk.

She took one more step and was at my table. She took another and passed by without breaking stride. Our eyes did not meet. We did not touch. But I could feel her just the same.

I stood up and moved to the chair on the other side of the table. I watched her as she walked. I watched her as she walked away, just like I did yesterday. Just like I will tomorrow.

RED BREASTED ROBINS AND SHINY BLACK BOOTS

by Larry E. Scott

". . . A husband . . . a father . . . a soldier . . . a friend—by all earthy measures, a very good man . . . ."

Rain pit-patted against the tent. It smelled as only wet canvas smells—and cut fresh flowers—and March in Kansas—all of it mixed with death. We sat in rows of folding chairs, collars raised against the wind—a bitter wind from the north.

". . . And, so, oh Lord, we lay him to rest on this most hallowed ground . . . ."

When I was young and it was summer and the windows were open to catch a breeze, I lay on his chest on the living room couch and watched our black and white television set—mostly boxing matches. He smelled of white shirt and *Old Spice* cologne and *L & M* cigarettes—the safest smells I've ever smelled—all of it mixed with the scent of him.

"The Lord is my shepherd, I shall not want. . . ."

"Mommy! Mommy! Why is he dead? Why's that man dead?" the child blurted in the middle of the prayer from several rows behind me.

"Shoosh . . shoosh," the mother whispered, trying to quiet her little one.

And what, I thought, would the world be like if we carried such innocence through every day, through all our questions, and into the grave? What if we blurted our way through life, asking but honest questions?

The rain trickled down a crease in the tent and gathered in a rivulet and streamed from the edge of the tent to the earth. It hit the grass—the green, green grass—with a hissing sound, gouging the earth from beneath the green, exposing the white of the roots.

"Was he old, Mommy? Old like Grandpa?"

"Shoosh . . . shoosh."

". . . he leadeth me beside the still waters. . . ."

I wonder how I could love him so . . . yet never feel that I was enough—never enough for him? Why did I have to prove and prove and prove and prove and prove and prove. . . ? And why was it never good enough?

The ashtray I made from clay in school and gave to him one Father's Day—the ashtray he never used. . . .

Mostly "A's." But—why that "B"? . . . .

Football captain. . . .

Honor roll. . . .

Fraternity president. . . .

Teacher and coach. . . .

Attorney at law. . . .

I remember thinking that he would be proud when I told him I wanted to be a lawyer. I remember him saying, "Why be a lawyer? Too many lawyers. Cause more problems than they solve. The world would be better without them."

It hurt. Hurt a lot. I remember saying, "Well, then, I guess I'll try my best to be a good one." That's the only time we spoke on the matter. Yeah, it hurt. But I tried. I tried real hard. And I think I was good. But never quite good enough.

"*. . .Yea, though I walk through the valley of the shadow of death. . . .*"

I wonder who sent those pretty red flowers? Don't know what you call them. They sure are pretty. Prettier than all the others. . . .

Off in the distance a siren wails. I wonder what happened . . . who's hurt . . . who's dead . . . whose lives will be changed by the siren. Never the same. Never the same. The siren wails and lives are changed—never for the better.

"Mommy! Mommy! I gotta pee!"

"Okay, Sweetheart. Just a minute."

"No, Mommy! No! I gotta go bad."

A few heads turned. Some scowled. Some grinned.

"Okay, Sweetheart. Just a second. Let me find the keys."

I hear the jingling of keys being drawn from the woman's purse. I hear her whisk her daughter away. And then from afar a car engine starts. I watch as they drive away.

"*Dust to dust . . . ashes to ashes. . . .*"

From high, far away, atop the next hill I hear the bugler play taps. Nothing on earth—except, maybe, bagpipes crossing the heather through the mist—captures the lonely, the empty, the loss as does this simple tune in brass. Nothing on earth is so final.

I lean to my mother. "Are you okay?"

She looks straight ahead. Her lower lip quivers. Stoically, she nods. I touch her hand. She doesn't respond. I pull my hand away.

"*Aa-tten-hut!*" the officer barks. The honor guard, like razor strops snapping, comes to a crisp and perfect attention. The flag is folded and brought to my mother. She rests it gently on her lap, placing her gloved hands on it.

I watch as she slowly and absently strokes it—knowing somehow she's touching him. His cheek? His hair? Perhaps his lips, when they were young and the sun shone brightly on his uniform and she wore a ribbon in her hair as he waved to her through the open window as the train chugged off to war.

She stares unfocused and far away as though mesmerized by an empty blackboard waiting for someone to write something on it—*anything! anything!*—on it.

"*Aa-tten-hut!*"

Slap! the guns rise from the ground to the soldiers' chests.

"*Present Arms!*"

Slap! the guns fly from their chests to the soldiers' shoulders.

"*Fire!*"

The guns explode.

"*Fire!*"

The guns, again, explode.

"*Fire!*"

One last time . . . then silence.

The soldiers' boots, in perfect row, glisten like polished obsidian. They turn. They march. They go away. We're left to do whatever comes next—whatever that may be. Mostly just going on, I guess. Whatever it takes. Keep going on. That, I suppose, is what he would do. That, I suppose, would be his advice. . . .

I wish they'd come back—the marching boots. I miss the comfort of their sound . . . marching . . . marching . . . marching. They sounded of power—of something brave—of something strong—of something eternal. And I miss the sound of him.

The sun breaks through a crack in the clouds. It isn't warm. It's only bright. Hard and cold and it gleams too much upon the raindrops gathered in beads on the green, green grass and the winter wheat fields at the edge of the Kansas town.

A robin chirps. The first hint of spring. Its red breast glints against the sun. And then the clouds close up again and swallow the world in gray.

❧

Father, son, fly fisherman, oilfield worker, railroader, teacher, lawyer, counselor, writer—lives in Sarasota, Florida with a tank of goldfish. A well-spent day, a well-cast fly and a well-written poem are among his greatest passions.

LARRY E. SCOTT

SCENES BLOCKED FROM VIEW

by Michael S. Smith

The trees that bled and drooped in rills
Beside the highway as we ran
Around Cape Cod on red road Six
Blocked our view of dunes and ocean

Like blinds that hide the girl next door
You stay up late to spot in the light.
We wasted a rainy day for this,
And everything hid from sight.

We expected post card vistas
On either side, sailboats and gulls
And dramatically swaying grass
Dancing around red and yellow hulls.

But the road went up the middle
As if to bar satisfaction—
Like her father, who bundles her
Body and blinds your distraction.

INCOMING

by Michael S. Smith

I love to watch the white slip in,
The black espresso turning tan
Camouflage when the caffeine jolt
Alarms my clock, the night's alert.

The hushed hours of pre-dawn détente
And peaceful solitude sustain
My sanity till time for work,
When lights flared on sharp furniture

Pin me down again. I get high
Those coffee hours of real work life
Before the job and the boss surround
My land-mined compound, firing rounds

Out of range. Fire fights invade my soul
And ship it, after hours, back home
In a body bag of boredom, zipped
To bloodshot eyes, clasped with a silver clip.
 Booze evacuates the stiff mind

While we drill and practice pretense,
Targeting our shelter to save
Our lives for one more night's reprieve.

※

Over 30 of Michael Smith's poems have appeared in over 150 journals and anthologies, most recently The Chattahoochee Review, Writers Forum, Connecticut River Review, Chiron Review, The Ledge, *and* S.L.U.G.fest. *Red Dancefloor Press published his first mini-chapbook* Holiday Arrangements *in its "prime poets" series this year. He supports his writing with a job managing the insurance department of an international agricultural cooperative.*

MICHAEL S. SMITH

THE CHALK THEFT

by Marion Vaughn

I WENT TO THE school yard once, the summer I played with Gingie May. I wasn't allowed to play with her, because her mother drank gin and fed the children out of a can. I went anyway, because it was exciting. Her big brothers needed haircuts and laughed at everything I said. I never knew what was funny, but I laughed, too.

One afternoon, when I went to their house, the boys were walking on the porch railing, pretending it was a circus high wire, and Gingie May was eating Cracker Jack for lunch. Her feet in the pale dust made a dry wake like a boat does, as she rocked back and forth in her tire swing. We sat and talked and laughed for a little while; then she jumped up.

"Let's go to the school yard," she said, giving herself a shove to twirl on one foot. The brothers laughed and leaped to the ground, whirling with her until they all fell down.

We stayed on her street so that my mother wouldn't see us. At the next block we crossed over to the school.

We walked to the boiler building, past Mr. Gregor the janitor's open door, and sat on the smoke stack ledge, where we used to eat apples at recess. The bricks were hot against my back, and I leaned to wrap my arms halfway around it. I hung my head so low that my spine hurt and stared at the leafless weeds like thin, brown snakes.

Gingie May raised her arms over her head and scratched her fingernails down the bricks.

"Wanna get some chalk?" she said. "There's nobody in there."

"Sure."

"There's nobody around, and I'd like some of that colored chalk in Old Fat Slanafin's bottom drawer."

I liked Miss Slanafin. She came to our house for dinner before school was out. And when I had pneumonia, she brought my homework and played checkers with me in my room.

"I have chalk at my house that you can have." Gingie May jumped down and scooped up a handful of cinders, cupping them back and forth like packing a snowball.

"You're scared," she said in her ghost voice. "You wouldn't dare." And she jumped and laughed and threw the cinders in a shower over our heads. She always acted so smart.

"All right," I said. "Let's go."

*   *   *

Inside the hall the bare coat hooks were waiting for the kids to come back. Heat bumped us like warm balloons. We walked into the third grade room, where the desks were arranged in ten rows of pairs, five on each side with an aisle down the middle. The bottom blinds were fastened beneath the sills, and the tops were stretched into long wrinkles, making the room yellow like a golden world.

I sat in my last year's seat and wished it were like this everyday, so quiet and lovely and soft-looking. Gingie May went to Miss Slanafin's desk and opened the bottom drawer that was twice as deep as the others. She slid the wooden lid off the box and reached for the chalk.

"Gee, what swell colors," she said, lifting out a handful and tossing back the broken sticks. She took one of each color and made long streaks down her arms.

"Boy, these are pretty," she whispered, smiling at the ribbons she drew. Gingie May looked pretty, too; I never saw her look like that before. She held up one arm, and very softly brushed the marks together to make new colors, slowly turning her arms until her skin was covered.

"You look so pretty, Gingie May. I wish my mother could see you." Quickly, she turned her back, and stuffed the chalk into her pocket.

"Want some?" she said.

I went over and dipped into the box. Blue, yellow, purple, red—all the colors we used to draw our holiday scenes on the blackboard. The powdery sticks were slippery, smooth, warm, and brighter than my colored chalk at home. Mine was hard and wrote best on sidewalks. My mother liked mine, because it was dustless.

I made long streaks down my arms like Gingie May. She slid the lid across the box and closed the drawer.

"Let's go," she said, rattling the sticks in her pocket. Her bare feet made hard little heel sounds across the floor, louder than my shoes.

At the doorway the sun yawned like a tiger.

"Run!" she yelled.

"To my house!" I hollered, and we raced across the playground, holding our pockets to keep the chalk in.

My mother was sitting on the front porch, sewing. I tried to catch my breath.

"Here's Gingie May, Mother. She looks so pretty." Mother put down her sewing.

"What is that on your arms, Marnie? She brushed cinders out of my hair.

"Chalk. Here's Gingie May." Mother drew me to her, looking only at me. For a moment Gingie May stared at her, then whirled and darted down the street.

"Where did you get the chalk, Marnie?" I looked into her eyes and could see two me's standing side by side.

"At the school. We just walked in and took it. And, Mother, isn't Gingie May pretty?"

"Took it? Do you know what you have done?" The two me's rocked their shoulders to let me know they were there; then they disappeared, and there was only my mother. I wasn't there at all.

"When you take something that doesn't belong to you, that is stealing," she said. "Now go upstairs and wash and then return the chalk." My mother wore the look she had for arranging flowers. "There," she would say, "It took a little bending and snipping, but it looks nice now." She took my hands to turn me around toward the stairs, and I could feel my arms growing long like flower stems.

I went upstairs and ran water over my arms. The colors began to blur and a dirty rainbow dripped from my fingers. I rubbed with soap and it all turned into grey foam that wouldn't go down the drain. My arms were red with pore dots, and ached from the cold water. I felt like that inside, too.

*   *   *

I took the chalk back to the school. There was no one there except some flies buzzing behind the window shades. The room was yellow like before a storm, and I could hear my breathing. My long arms put the chalk back into the box, and I knew something was watching me.

I slammed the drawer and turned and raced past the hall hooks curved like knives. Outside the sun scratched its eyes with its paws. As I ran past the chimney, Mr. Gregor came out of the boiler building.

"Hello, Marnie. Where's the fire?" he said. He saw me! I tripped on the leafless weeds that felt like dry snakes.

"I put the chalk back, Mr. Gregor. I won't do it again," I cried. He helped me up and looked into my face.

"I know all about it, Marnie. I know you won't do it again. Go home now."

At our corner the sidewalk moved with shadows where the leaves blinked at the sunlight shining through. My mother had turned on the lawn sprinkler. I stood near the spray of tiny drops until my pounding heart slowed down and my stem arms grew smaller again. It looked so clean and fresh and pretty, like my mother. I went up the steps and sat beside her.

"I'm sorry, Mother. I won't do it again." She put her arm around me.

"I know you won't, Marnie." I leaned against her, and her arm tightened to hold me close.

"Mr. Gregor saw me." She looked into my eyes.

"Someone usually does," she said.

The porch swing moved like a lullaby.

Marion Vaughan was an education writer for many years, and now is turning her interest toward fiction and poetry writing. This is her first published short story.

MARION VAUGHN

JUST BELOW THE SURFACE

by Enrico B. Wallenda

I T'S ALREADY HOT AND it's only about ten in the morning. It's going to be one of those summer days that the heat just keeps creeping up until the air is so thick that you can't stand to breathe, like trying to inhale water. Perspiration started rolling down right after sun up. By this time of day I just stay soaked in my own sweat. The kids are playing ball over in the lot by Gray's store. Old man Gray doesn't like it, but he's too old to stop them. All the yelling going on is probably Mack trying to steal the ball again. I don't play ball any more, not since I got hurt. Besides, I don't like to be around those knob heads anyway.

I prefer to spend my Saturdays alone. I tolerate the others all week long in school, and then I am afflicted with the likes of those goons. Most people do everything they can to keep from spending time alone. I don't mind the solitude. It gives me time to think, and try to make sense of my world.

I hope Mack gets away this time. They can't catch him, or whip him if they do. Mack is just a little guy, but no one at school can take him. I admire Mack, but I don't like him. In many ways he's like me. He doesn't fit into the prim and proper world any more than I do, and we can never categorize him. Yeah, by the way everyone is screaming now, he must have gotten the ball this time. Serves them right. Now they won't be able to play either.

Mack is bounding through the brush growing over the ditch between the back yard and Gray's field. I see him, but he doesn't see me. He is hiding the ball down an old gopher-turtle hole that hasn't been occupied since we ate it. I am not moving, I just stay stretched on the old '66 Impala seat in the scrub oak in the back yard. Finally Mack looks over and sees me.

"Hey, what are you doing there, Buckey?"

"Nothing."

"Where's your mama, fat boy?"

I smile because I know I can't catch him. "She's inside aiming the BB rifle at your backside." He looks over to the porch real quick, and when he doesn't see her, he smiles.

"Want to play some ball?" he asks with that look that just tells me he doesn't mean it. I already know what he's up to, so I just keep my eyes on him as he abandons caution and comes within range. ZZZZZZZZthwap is all I hear when the BB hits his cut-offs just about on his thigh.

"I told you never to set foot on my property again, Mack Aldredge."

Mack jumps about ten feet back to the ditch that marks the edge of safety.

"No need to get all stoked up, Mrs. Buckwald. I wasn't going to steal any eggs. I just came to pay my respects to Buckey. I know it's been about a year since . . . ."

"Well, you just keep your distance, and remember I got this Daisy full of a whole pack of BB's!"

Mama goes back into the house, and Mack stops rubbing his leg.

It still hurts, but he doesn't want me to know.

"Hey Mack, you ever going to give back that ball?"

"When I think I've punished them enough."

"What did they do this time?"

"Same old stuff."

"How come they don't like you, Mack?"

"Maybe I have something they don't."

"I know you have the ball, but what else?" He just smiles. Mack is smarter than they are. His grades are always up there, but he never does any homework.

"Go get that ball and let me see it." I used to throw a pretty good fast ball, and I want to see if I can hit Mack in the head before he gets back to the ditch. I'm not sure he'll fall for it, but I see him going for it. He's reaching into the hole, but he has this look on his face like he has just been bit by a rattler, and then a dazed look. I know there's no rattler in there, or anywhere, because we've already eaten all that were around here. He pulls the ball out first, and then this thing next.

I can see the thing glowing from where I am. Mack looks at me to see if he's dreaming or something. We both stare for a minute, and then he starts towards me. It's not a far drop, but I roll off the car seat to the ground landing on my good leg. Mack is holding the thing out for me, and with his eyes he's asking me what it is. I have no more of an idea than he does.

"What do you think it is?" I say.

"I was going to ask you. You've never seen it before?"

"No, and never seen one like it either. Come on, bring it into the fort." Dad and I built a fort in the oak the summer before the accident. We used to spend some nights there together.

For the next ten minutes we sit in the fort without a word. We just stare at it. Once in a while one of us asks something like, "Where did it come from?" or "Do you think we should tell anyone about it?"

Just then I hear all the boneheads by the ditch. They are saying things like "Is this where he came through?"

"Hey you guys, come here and look at what we found," I shout, and they look over at Mack and me standing in the doorway of the fort.

They see me and Mack together, and just look bewildered. None of them likes us, or we them, but they had never seen the two of us together until right now.

"No, really, man," Mack says to them. "This is really cool. Here's your ball, just come and look at this thing."

The ball convinces them that it's not another of his pranks. Slowly they are all coming toward us.

"Let's see from here," Bobby finally says. I can see that they don't yet believe we aren't going to ambush them or something. Extending my arm toward them, I hold the thing up so they can all see that there is no treachery involved. As soon as they can see it, their faces soften like stone turning to bread, just like I saw Mack's do.

The thing seems to have a power over us, and all the anger we usually show for each other melts like ice cream on a hot day. We all just look at it, wondering what it is.

This is the first time I don't feel any anger since the accident. That old car seat was all that was left of Dad's Impala, so Mama let me keep it. My leg got pinned between the dash and the tranny, and the steering wheel went right through Daddy. My leg hasn't healed up right yet, but the doc said one more operation, and I would be able to play ball again. Mama was like a protective bubble of strength through it all. She kept us fed, and kept the bill collectors away. I don't know how she did it, because our lives were amazingly fragile. Mama didn't have a social life. Everything she did was for the family to survive. Besides, there was too much gossip in the town, so she just stayed to herself.

"Wow, can I hold it now?" Joey Mcfadden asks. We all share that thing one at a time. We all touch it. No one tries to take it away from the others, or claim it's theirs. It's so peaceful I wonder why Mama hasn't come out to ask us why we aren't fighting.

"Let's take it to Grandpa Rex, he knows everything. I bet he'll know what it is," Mack finally says.

"But he lives all the way out in Crawford's swamp," Frank reminds us.

"Yeah, but he'll know," I say. "Let's go."

The thing is round, and smooth, and glowing with sparks of lightning, but not like a light bulb. I look right at it, and my eyes don't burn or anything. It seems to be an energy of some kind. It almost looks alive. It vibrates gently like a cat purring in my hand.

"Hey, it's a long way to Crawford's. I'm going to need some help," I say.

Mack reaches for my crutches, and with eyes that are full of concern, he hands them to me. I exchange the thing for the crutches. None of us is greedily grabbing for the thing or saying any of the sarcastic things that usually dominate our contact with each other. Mack just looks up at me. His face is so gentle it glows with the gratitude of a lamb rescued from a burning barn. Is this the same Mack that darted across Bent Pine Road on his bike and made Dad's Impala swerve and roll into the ditch? Am I the same boy that is now trusting him to get me back home safely?

My leg seems to be fine as we're walking and sometimes running. We get to the swing rope across Turtle Creek, and I stop. They are all crossing without hesitation. The water is too deep this time of year to wade across; besides, I am still not allowed to get my leg in brackish water. When they are all across, only Mack stops to make sure I am okay.

"Come on, Buckey."

"I can't. My leg, and what about the crutches?"

"Leave them. You can do it. Just try. I'll help."

As Mack steps toward the creek, he reaches out to me, and I feel a confidence that I haven't felt in a long time. With one hand he holds the thing in the air, with the other he reaches toward me. I have the rope in my hand, the water below is not running fast, but it's further down than I want to fall. I feel the surge of adrenaline just when I let go of the crutches, and fly across the span. Mack grabs me as soon as I am in reach. The friendly arms of a fellow outcast are more than welcome.

We are in Crawford's swamp. It's not far now. The others are just ahead, moving slower now that there are things to watch for. Things like snakes and swamp creatures might be in the path. I used to spend a lot of my time in the safety of these woods. I felt insulated from the craziness of the world around me. I am more at home here than the others are, but this is the first visit since the accident. Even Mack is looking to me for leadership now. We have all been here before, but I have spent more time in these woods than any of the others.

"Don't be scared, it's too hot for gators to be up out of the swamp, and snakes prefer not to come in contact with humans."

"I'll lead the way with the thing. Maybe it has power to protect, too," says Mack.

For the next half mile or so we are silently making our way through the palmetto path. The blazing sun seems to have no effect because we are on a mission. Mack is holding the thing out in front of him as if it is our guide, even though we all know where Grandpa Rex lives. About that time I notice that my leg has not bothered me since Turtle Creek. No pain, no limp, and I am keeping up with the pace.

"There it is," I say as we reach the clearing where his shack is. He's been here as long as any of us remembers. He isn't anyone's grandfather for real. He's just an old man who is helpful to any who need it, and he likes us calling him "Grandpa." There are a lot of stories about this old man that have been told around campfires. I have not known any of them to be true, but I have spent a lot more time in these woods than the others have, and I know Grandpa Rex.

Society has never welcomed him. The townspeople have often told these tales of him to keep us away from him, but he seems to be the most sane person in town. Grandpa Rex has the ability to look just below the surface of the townspeople's facade. He once confronted them in church over the difference between their behavior and their words. The men of the town all go to church on Sunday morning after the poker game at old man Gray's Saturday night. The ladies all gossip about Mom, and Sunday morning they smile and say pretty things. Mom tells the story that he stood and pointed to each of them individually and named the wrong they were doing, including the preacher spending too much time pretending to "minister" to Mama. When confronted, the townspeople gave him so much trouble in town that he sold his place and moved out here to be away from the hysteria. He chose to live on the fringes of society, rather than in the thick of the hypocrisy.

"You go first, Buckey. You know him," I hear one of the others say. Mack extends the thing toward me as if for me to stand beneath its protective cover. I just walk past him.

At the edge of the clearing are some pines just beyond the shack. To the left is a little glen of oaks, and I see a stack of firewood. The palmetto's create the rest of the perimeter. No one is unwelcome, but only those who want to learn the truth would venture beyond these walls of safety. They feel safe if they stay outside of the old man's symbolic reach. The boundary represents safety for those who fear the penetration of his real words into their plastic lives.

Grandpa Rex rarely leaves his compound. He goes to Gray's store and trades an occasional gator skin or tail and to pick up his social security check. Old man Gray doesn't like Grandpa Rex, but loves the fresh bass he brings, so they formed a trade agreement. Mama is especially close to him. He has come to our house for dinner sometimes, but when the rumors were hurting us, he stopped.

I see a stream of smoke rising above the shack from the other side. "Grandpa Rex," I call out. I begin to walk toward the shack. Mack follows, but the others hesitate. I think they are waiting to see if I fall down dead or something. "Come on," I say. Mack gives them the hand signal to come out of the palmettos.

"Grandpa Rex. Where are you?"

"Over here, Buckey," I hear from the other side of the shack. "What are you doing all the way out here, and without crutches? How's your mom, is everything okay?"

"Yeah, everything is okay. We all just came out to ask you something," I say. Then he notices all the other boys.

"Come on over, boys, I just made a new batch of swamp juice."

Mack extends the thing, and I say, "Grandpa Rex, we found this thing, and want to know what it is."

"Oh, um, well, I'll have to look at it a little closer," he says with a curious grin and disappears into the shack.

"Are you crazy? You aren't going to drink that stuff, are you?" Tommy whispers.

"I drink it all the time, it's the best thing on a hot day."

"My mom told me he poisoned a whole bunch of kids at her school when she was in fifth grade," Joey tells us.

"You know that stuff they tell us is because they don't like him. Besides, if he did that, he'd be in jail. This stuff is the best thing when you're thirsty."

"That's right, Buckey. Swamp juice is a formula that I found by boiling pine needles, swamp cabbage, some wild berries, and orange peels in swamp water," he says as he reappears with some old tin cans.

"Now let me see that thing."

With the expression of the shrewdest old carnival storyteller he says, "I used to have something like this once." He raises an eyebrow and glances away from the thing, now resting in his hand, toward all of us as we sit with our eyes fastened on his weathered face. He pulls up a stool, and we all gather round, sitting on the ground before him. He holds the thing in one hand just far enough from his face that we can see he is focusing on it with his aging eyes. The other hand is stroking his beard. The thing is between us and him, so, as we look up, we can see his face studying the object just beyond the thing in his hand. His brow wrinkles in deep thought, and his glance strays from the thing to all of our faces.

"How's the swamp juice, boys?"

I am just finishing mine, but the others haven't yet touched theirs. I ask, "Can I have some more?"

There is a small wooden barrel beside the shack that is always full. It never stands long enough to ferment and become something other than a thirst quencher. That's why old man Gray won't allow it to be sold in his store. He prefers moonshine, and Grandpa Rex won't have anything to do with liquor.

"Boys, I've noticed none of you have lit up a smoke since you arrived. Have you given it up? Well, I know your answer will incriminate those of you who do enjoy a puff. Actually, I was surprised to see so many of you here . . . together. No fighting today, boys? You know I've noticed something different about all of you, but I can't put my finger on it just yet. Drink up your swamp juice and I'll tell you what this thing is."

"Hey, this stuff is pretty good," Mack says. One by one they all finish and make a second, and third trip to the barrel.

Grandpa Rex continues, "So you all came here together, without fighting or smoking? Any cussing along the way?" Everyone shakes his head. Grandpa Rex is smiling through a well-worn face. "You think this globe had something to do with it?" Everyone's eyes are now fixed on him.

"I remember an old man gave me something just like this once. I never knew what made it glow. It had something to do with the chemical reaction inside when the thing felt any vibration—like one of those glass bubbles that makes snow inside when you shake it. Well, this old man was a chemist, and he made it. I found it one day, and went to him. I learned a lot that day about free choice, and how we choose what we are going to do. Nothing can make me angry; I choose to be angry, or not angry. Sometimes a common goal will bring people together, and they can lay aside anger and bitterness. There is no power that keeps me from being angry, and none that can make me angry. It's all in the power of free choice."

We are all just staring at him now. Did we just choose to lay aside our hostilities?

"Boy, Grandpa Rex, the stories we have heard about you sure were wrong. You are nothing like the weirdo we expected."

"Well, Joey, you can't always tell what's inside by looking at the outside. Like these old soup cans you drank out of. They look like trash, but the swamp juice on the inside is sweet, all natural, and quenches like nothing on this earth, and it's good for you. A man, or a boy, can be the same way. You can dress up the outside, but you can't hide trash that lives on the inside. It's what's below the surface that matters, and it's all a matter of choice. Make your choices count, boys. Now drink up and get on home. It will be dark soon, and I don't want you jumping Turtle Creek in the dark. By the way, Buckey, there's a lesson here for you, too. Your leg? All you needed was a little confidence to get on it again. Tell your mother I'll bring her some fresh gator in a few days."

"Bye, Grandpa Rex," we all say—almost in unison.

"Grandpa Rex, can we come and visit again?" Mack asks.

"You boys can come any time you want. There is always swamp juice for visitors. If you just want to stop in and have a cool one with me, you can do that, too."

"I'll be back more often now that I know I can make it alone, Grandpa Rex. Thanks."

As we are leaving, Mack grabs the ball from Frank and takes off running through the palmettos.

❧

SHE WORE SPECKLED CHICKEN FEATHERS IN HER HAIR

by Ronald L. Anthony

T HERE WERE TWENTY-FOUR pigs of each sex, thirty-five plump chickens of various colors, twenty bows with over a hundred bamboo arrows, five hundred white cowrie shells, six stone axes and five straw baskets of yellow and purple sweet potatoes. The marriage of Nakalis Kalakmabin, the youngest son of Worgorak, to Pidokopuk Uropmabin, the youngest daughter of Inggikaret, had been arranged and the dowry was supposed to be delivered to the Uropmabin hut on the morning of the wedding day.

A full year had passed since the Easter Sunday when Pidokopuk celebrated her twelfth birthday and, according to the Ngalum's tribal custom, she make the transition from silly little girl to coveted woman of marriageable age. Her older sisters, Bidjendik and Apkwikmu, used the ocherous mud from the river to paint large rings around Pidokopuk's beautiful brown eyes and around the nipples of her pubescent breasts. The contrast between the yellowish mud and Pidokopuk's ebony skin created a look of erotic mysticism. Long strands of polished boars' teeth dangled from holes in her ears, and a necklace of cuscus fur, cowrie shells and dried nuts hung from her neck. Then, just before they left for church, Pidokopuk's mother did something that was considered very extravagant for an Ngalum family. She placed a crown of speckled chicken feathers on top of Pidokopuk's curly black hair. Everyone applauded in agreement. Pidokopuk was now a beautiful woman. She was God's black angel of Easter.

Pidokopuk was sitting on the dirt floor of the church, listening to the missionary pastor tell the story of the resurrection, when her concentration was interrupted by the stares and smile of a young warrior squatting in the section reserved for clans from Mabilibol. Trying to hide her embarrassment, Pidokopuk covered her face with her hands but, as she peeked through her slightly spread fingers, she couldn't suppress her urge to giggle. Pidokopuk had never met the young man; but, after one glance at his sinewy black body, glistening from a recent rubdown with rancid pig fat, she knew who he was. Stories of his strength and skill as a hunter were repeated throughout the valley, and it was said that he could catch a *cenderwasi,* bird of paradise, with his bare hands without rumpling a feather. He was the most handsome warrior in the valley, and his name was Nakalis Kalakmabin.

Pidokopuk was pleased when Nakalis became a regular attendee at the mission's Sunday services. As soon as the closing hymn had been sung and the final amen had been mumbled, she would run outside to meet Nakalis in a secluded corner of the church yard. At first she just held his hand and talked about trivial things, but as the weeks passed by, she began to accompany him on long walks along the river. Then, on one special Sunday morning in late summer when the sky was a baby blue and the air was filled with the scent of orchids, Pidokopuk spotted a pair of sulphur-crested cockatoos mating in a eucalyptus tree. Convinced the birds were a sign of God's consent, Pidokopuk followed Nakalis into the forest and they made love for the first time.

* * *

Snorting pigs, squawking chickens and a gregarious group of young Nduga warriors, carrying baskets of over-ripe sweet potatoes on their heads, comprised the groom's early morning wedding procession on the path from Mabilibol to Yapimakot. Nakalis was in a merry mood as he and his three older brothers supervised the transport of the valuable dowry demanded by Inggikaret, chief of the Uropmabin clan and father of Pidokopuk. The brothers were having fun, teasing Nakalis about his virginity and offering him all sorts of manly advice on how Pidokopuk should be entertained and where she should be touched, on this their wedding night. Then, suddenly and without warning, a strange whizzing sound emerged from a cluster of sago palms on the right side of the path. Unable to duck in time, Nakalis screamed with pain as the poison arrow entered the right side of his neck and exited just below his chin. With blood filling his mouth and spouting from his jugular vein, he fell to the ground. The pigs and chickens were eerily quiet. Nakalis Kalakmabin and his brothers were dead.

* * *

Pidokopuk was weaving *bunga bunga ungu,* purple flowers, into her fresh grass wedding skirt when she overheard her father talking to some tribesmen. They were standing in front of the family hut. Thinking that Nakalis and his brothers had arrived with the dowry, Pidokopuk was relieved. But then, from the aggressive tone of the tribesmen's voices, she sensed that something was wrong. It wasn't the voice of her Nakalis.

When she went outside to investigate, she saw the huge dowry. It filled the entire schoolyard. There were forty-eight pigs, seventy chickens, forty bows, hundreds of cowrie shells, twelve stone axes and ten baskets of yellow and purple sweet potatoes. Why had everything been doubled? Then, with fear in her heart, Pidokopuk recognized the short, pot-bellied and pock-faced man arguing with her father. It was Ebenetus Oktemka and his brothers from the village of Dabolding. Why was her father talking with these sons of the devil?

Rushing to her father's side, Pidokopuk pulled on his arm and asked, "*Bapak. Dimana Nakalis? Saya harus membicara dengan Nakalis.*" She was not prepared for his answer.

Without any hint of sympathy or remorse, Inggikaret pushed his daughter away and said, "*Nakalis Kalakmabin mati.*" Nakalis Kalakmabin is dead. Warriors from an enemy tribe, the Ungarakuru, had murdered the Kalakmabin brothers on their journey from Mabilibol.

Pidokopuk knew that her father had to be lying. Nakalis and his brothers did not have enemies and the Ungarakuru lived many valleys away. Pidokopuk's impulse was to run. She had to find out what happened to Nakalis. Unfortunately, she hesitated for one moment too long. Ebenetus grabbed her by the hair. As he pulled her face within an inch of his wet lips and pock-marked nose, Pidokopuk gagged at the smell of his sour breath.

Ebenetus whispered into her ear, "Don't you dare to resist me, my little whore. I know what Nakalis did to you in the forest on Sunday afternoons. I hid among the trees and watched you, eagerly making love. But your strong and courageous Nakalis is dead now and your father is giving you to me."

Pidokopuk strained to free herself, pleading to her father for help. It could not be true.

Inggikaret struck her across the face and told her to shut up.

The crown of speckled chicken feathers fell to the ground.

Pointing to the schoolyard, Ebenetus said, "Can't you understand, Pidokopuk, you're not wanted here. You are dirty. The pigs and chickens are more valuable to your honorable father than a daughter who is a whore."

Pidokopuk fought back her tears. She kept asking, "Where is Nakalis? What have you done to him?"

Grinning through his discolored and rotting teeth, Ebenetus said, "After I told your father that Nakalis had been fucking you every Sunday afternoon, he wanted Nakalis dead."

"No! No!" Pidokopuk cried. "It can't be true. Father, tell me it is not true."

"It's true," Inggikaret shouted. "I promised my good friend Ebenetus that if he killed Nakalis and doubled the size of the dowry, he could have you. I must honor my promise."

"But what about me?" Pidokopuk screamed, "I can never marry him. He's the son of the devil." She tried to break away, but Ebenetus' grip was too strong.

Tiring of the struggle, Ebenetus released his hold on Pidokopuk's hair and forced her down onto her knees. Then he put his scab covered foot on the back of her neck and pushed her face into the dirt.

Pidokopuk waited until her father and the Oktemka brothers walked away to inspect the double dowry. Their laughter and boasting was disgusting. When she was certain they were at the far side of the schoolyard, she lifted her head just high enough to find her crown of speckled chicken feathers. She stood up slowly, put the feathers back in her hair, and without looking back, she ran into the forest.

She kept running, deeper and deeper into the forest, not looking back and not knowing what she was going to do. She did not even know in what direction she was going. She ran blindly for what seemed like hours, slipping and falling on the rotten vegetation that carpeted the jungle floor. Her chest was heaving from exhaustion and her bare feet and her ankles were coated with the slime from blood-sucking leeches. But, the only pain Pidokopuk felt was the ache in her heart. Her only thought was to get far away. She had to escape from the evil that would consume her home, the village of Yapimakot.

And Pidokopuk was right. On the next day, before the sun came up over the mountains, Worgorak, father of Nakalis and chief of the Kalakmabin tribe, avenged the death of his four sons. It was the bloodiest tribal uprising that ever occurred in the valley of the Ngalum people. By midday, the men, women and children of the Uropmabin and Oktemka clans had been slaughtered and the villages of Yapimakot and Dabolding had been reduced to piles of charred bones and smoldering ashes.

Many years later, a team of mining prospectors from Australia landed their helicopter deep in the interior of Irian Jaya, Indonesian New Guinea. While they were prospecting for gold, they came upon a beautiful highland valley surrounded by snow-capped mountains. Frothy rivers cascaded down over limestone cliffs to the fertile valley floor. The Aussies agreed that God must have created the valley on a special day for a special people. But the only inhabitants they found were a beautiful young lady and a handsome young boy. The Aussies never discovered who they were or how they came to be there, but they said they saw the boy catch a bird of paradise with his bare hands without rumpling a feather, and the lady wore a crown of speckled chicken feathers in her hair.

❦

On the faculty at the University of Maryland School of Medicine for twenty-nine years. Since his retirement in 1994, he has been a part-time consultant in Clinical Pathology at the American University of the Caribbean in Saint Martin.

RONALD L. ANTHONY

MY DIET

by Jack Bartler

Dieting is such a bore
Going out to dinner
Expecting to get thinner
As our host trumpets
"Have some more!"
Of course I say
With thought oblivious
"It certainly is delicious"
(Even though
It may not be nutritious).
What?
The scale is up again?
Incredible!
I've been buying diet food
Oh, it must have been
Dinner last night
That caused this awful plight.
But it would have been rude

To turn down such scrumptious food.
Not my fault you know
That I can't say no.
It must be a con
This stupid diet
I'm on.

✤

A retired trial attorney who has been writing for his own amusement and catharsis for many years, but never submitted anything for publication before this. Besides enjoying the Florida sun in every way possible, he continues to write, act and teach literacy.

JACK BARTLER

THE OLD SWING TREE

by Linda Damron

SEEMS TO ME THAT when a person reaches that special age, most of their time is spent reminiscing about the past, and remembering special things that bring that old feeling of sentiment to their hearts. I'd pretty well served my usefulness around the farm and was content to sit and rock on the front porch, watching my children and grandchildren carry on the work and play necessary around a farm. I'm not saying I'm completely useless now; in fact, I happen to be the best whittler in the county and also the best darn storyteller to be found anywhere around these parts.

Last night I'd told the children about the time my Pa cut down my swing tree. I guess I wasn't much older than seven or eight, and I'm sure I was probably the devil to put up with.

That day, many years ago, I'd finished all my chores and had been swinging on my rope tied to the big tree out beside the house. The rope had a big knot in it that Pa had tied so I could sit on it. Ma had called me in to lunch and I was eating like wildfire so I could get back out and play. About midway through my meal, Pa came in and said, mostly to Ma, but I knew it was meant for me, too, "We're goin' to cut down the old tree today. Luther's brought his saw over and we're goin' to start directly."

Pa looked at Ma and then Ma looked at me. I was staring at Pa with my mouth wide open. He turned and walked out the door. I jumped up and ran after him. "But Pa, you're not goin' to cut my swing tree down, are ya?"

"Yep," he answered.

I ran along behind him out to the tree. "But Pa, you can't!"

"Son, the tree has to come down. It's getting too old and it might fall on our house if a strong wind comes."

"It won't fall. I promise it won't!" I cried.

Uncle Luther was standing by the tree with his big saw and Pa walked up to him.

"Please don't, Pa."

"Now boy, it's not all that bad; there's plenty other things to do," Uncle Luther said, trying to calm me.

"I don't want to do anything else."

"Son, I've told you what's got to be done. Now stand back out of the way."

They stood on either side of my tree and raised the big saw between them. I stood there glaring at them both, clenching my fist and feeling the water rise in my eyes. They started sawing and I turned and ran. I stumbled out across the pastures, tears flooding my eyes and streaming down my cheeks. I ran and ran, past the cows I usually stopped to talk to, past the baby calf born last week, and on to the creek where I finally collapsed. I sat and stared at the brown water and watched a snake move slowly into the water on the other side. A rabbit hopped past me a little ways off and stopped to sniff the air, then moved on. Birds were singing and jumping about, but none of these special things that made the magic of the creek made me feel any better. I couldn't see the house from the creek because it was up pasture and over a little rolling hill, but I heard a voice yell,

"Timber!" and a loud final thud as the tree hit the ground. I cried like I'd never cried before. I laid my head down on the ground, and sob after sob broke from my throat. The sobbing shook my whole body. I felt sick. I felt like my best friend had been killed and by my own Pa! I was tired and cold and when I raised my head, it was dark all around me. I was sure to get a whippin' when I got home. I'd missed dinner for sure and probably the fire lighting. It was my job to bring in the kindling.

I was hurrying across the pasture towards home, which is a particularly dangerous thing to do at night when you can't see where you're steppin'. That'd be the end if I stepped in a pile 'cause Ma wouldn't even let me in the house then. The back light was on and I checked my shoes before reaching the back door and they were alright so I opened the back door real slow and peeked in. Ma was drying dishes and when she saw me, she put them down and ran to me and grabbed me right up.

"Where have you been? We've been so worried about you. I bet you're just starved. Here, set right here and I'll get you some food. Pa, Jamie's back!"

Ma was wiping tears from her eyes and bustlin' around the kitchen, and Pa had rushed in and was standing in the doorway. I look up at him, almost afraid to see him. "Where have you been, Son, me and your Ma was right concerned about you."

"I was at the creek and I guess I fell asleep. I didn't mean to miss dinner, though," I answered, staring down at the red tiled floor.

"Well, next time try to be on time or tell us where you're goin' so we can come and fetch ya."

"Yes sir."

I ate my dinner and it sure tasted powerful good. Ma's cookin' was always good. After dinner Pa asked me to come with him. He had the lantern and we went out the front door.

"I want to show you something, Jamie."

I followed him to where my swing tree lay on its side. I felt a funny choking feeling in my throat and all warm inside my stomach as I looked at the old tree. Pa boosted me up on his arm so as I could see the stump of the tree.

"Now, Son, see all those rings startin' from the very center of the trunk?"

I nodded my head. There were a lot.

"Each one of those means that this tree has lived one year. Now, if you count all the rings, that's how old the tree would be. See right here though?"

I looked where Pa was pointing and saw a dark spot where the rings had been broken.

"Right here your Uncle Luther and I found a bullet in your tree."

He pulled the bullet from his pocket and showed me how it fit right in that very hole. Then he handed it to me. I looked at it in my hand and felt the smooth edges.

"That bullet killed your tree and it was dying from the inside out. Jamie, everything has to lay down and rest after it's been standing for so long. It was time for your tree to lay down or else it would have rotted and fallen on our house, and we wouldn't have a place to live. You know your tree wouldn't have wanted that to happen to us. That's why your tree had to lay down and rest. Do you understand that?"

I nodded my head and then wrapped my arms around Pa's neck and he carried me in to bed.

Now I know Pa was talking about more things than trees that night. As I sit here rocking and whittling my wood, I also know there will come a time when I'll have to lay down and rest just like my old swing tree.

❧

MURDER AT GETTYSBURG

by Dale W. Hagen

CAPTAIN CLARION DOWNING, SWAYING on the buckboard seat, grimaced and rubbed his knee—painful reminder of sporting days on the fields at Yale. Bouncing over wheel ruts carved in blood by Robert E. Lee's retreating caissons, he studied an OFFICIAL REPORT OF THE UNITED STATES ARMY (July 15, 1863).

"Old friend," Clarion said to Cicero, his ebony-colored driver, "a first for us." Not looking up, he continued, "We have never investigated the murder of a General."

"Wind is blowing lonesome," Cicero replied. His fierce eyes and flared nostrils put Clarion in mind of one of his favorite paintings: a guardian lion on the wall of an Egyptian tomb.

Looking past the field (dotted with isolated Union and Confederate equipment, like droppings from the Devil's herd), Clarion pointed to a farmhouse shimmering in the sun. "Corps Headquarters?" he asked.

"Dry bones rise up; they fight forever." Cicero reined a blaze-faced black gelding. "Shadows are walking."

Clarion was accustomed to his ageless servant's oblique answers. His father had sent Cicero to college with him to insure that he would act "sensibly"—as a third generation Yale man should.

By now close enough to the stone farmhouse to hear gruff talk and laughter of men drinking ardent spirits, Cicero slid the buckboard to a stop. He shuddered, as if he had looked over on the other side, and seen terror. "Be careful, Mister Clarion," he said. "Someone here does not want us to find out who killed that General."

2.

"Come in, Captain Downing. General Benedict will soon join us." Unsmiling, Major John Gaunt ushered Clarion into the living room, pointedly allowing the door to close in Cicero's face. "Have a drink, Captain? Coffee?" he asked.

Ignoring the Major's glare, Clarion opened the door and motioned Cicero to a chair. "Forgive me, Major," Clarion said, stooping to whisper in Cicero's ear. The room had been improvised to look like a courtroom; rows of field chairs faced a table with three high-backed wicker chairs. The room was scattered with relaxed Union officers.

A baby-faced officer in disheveled blue uniform caught Clarion's eye. Hand-cuffed and leg-manacled, he sat in a corner, guarded by a teen-age soldier. Clarion studied the officer's face: By God, that boy looks familiar; can't recall where we met. Bothers the very devil out of me.

Major Gaunt noted Clarion's stare. "Bastard killed one of our best men," he said. "General Livermore, fine officer, brave as . . ." Just then, Brevet Brigadier General Alexander Benedict invaded the room.

3.

"Clarion, my friend, good to see you, splendid, splendid." Clarion exhaled from General Benedict's bear-hug. "By the Saints, you're handsome as ever."

Clarion escaped his grasp: Benedict in an earlier time would have worn a toga and overwhelmed the Forum. "Good to see you too, Senator," he replied warmly. "How are you?"

The General shook the roof timbers. "The better for having seen you, my boy . . . Well, then, let's get on with this beastly murder business." He spread his arms as if he were back introducing dignitaries at a political rally. "All the men who might know something about the murder of poor General Livermore," he said.

"Thank you, General." Clarion sat, flanked by the General and Major Gaunt. Pausing briefly, he announced, "I will ask each of you to tell us everything you know about the crime. Now if . . ."

Major Gaunt, leaning forward like a greyhound at the gate, interrupted, "As the officer in charge of this proceeding, I shall report . . ."

"No." Clarion's voice was firm. "Forgive me, but I have my own way of doing things."

Major Gaunt's ferret eyes were malevolent slits. "Captain Downing, proceed as you would in one of your New York court-rooms," he said.

The spare built prisoner, chains clanking, struggled to attention. "I am a Lieutenant in the Army of the Potomac. Innocent, I beg of you . . ."

"You are out of order, sir." Major Gaunt motioned to the stripling guard. "The killer must not be allowed . . ."

Clarion's voice split the air like the sound of river ice breaking up in the Spring. "Forgive me—you mean the accused. Not the killer. This is my investigation."

Major Gaunt turned as red as an open wound. "I must protest this . . ." General Benedict put a hand on his sleeve.

"Major, please. Lincoln has sent Clarion from Washington to investigate. I suggest we let him handle it as he sees fit."

Cicero and Clarion exchanged a quick glance. Looking at Gaunt's eyes, Cicero mouthed, "Be careful, Mister Clarion."

"Have a seat, Lieutenant. We will hear from you later," Clarion said. He lit the ivory pipe which a grateful client had given him for solving a vexing legal problem before the war. "Please proceed, gentlemen," he said softly.

4.

Next morning, Clarion gulped his chicory and ground acorn coffee. "If it is not too much trouble," he said to the officers seated around the oak table, "I would like to look at the body." No one moved. "Forgive me, gentlemen. Now. Please. Now."

Major Gaunt slammed his cup. "Out in the Spring house. Brigade Surgeon Malloy will accompany us," he said, brushing past Clarion on his way out, sword clanking, boots clicking.

Water trickled from the table where General Livermore's puffy remains were packed in ice and sawdust. The room smelled of alcohol and mortifying flesh. The body lay on its stomach; its skin felt like clammy bread dough.

Clarion quickly noted that the ball had entered the General's back above the middle of his left shoulder blade. "Kindly turn the body over, Surgeon Malloy," he said.

"The ball came out here," Malloy said, indicating a circle the size of a mole hole just under the left nipple.

Clarion then inspected every inch of the bloated body. Major Gaunt drummed his fingers on the scabbard of his gold sword, smoking a cigar: "Mask the smell," he said. Just under the General's ear, Clarion felt a hole which barely admitted the tip of his little finger.

After a few more moments, he patted the cold, bulging stomach. "God rest you merry, General," he said, "your duty is done. Major Gaunt, kindly assemble the men on the battlefield to re-enact the crime."

5.

The officers of the Corps, some on horseback, whispered fitfully on the green hill. The air smelled of death. "And, General Livermore was located here?" Clarion asked.

"Yes, Captain," Major Gaunt replied. "I stood here, in front of the General. General Benedict—then Colonel Benedict—sat on his horse at Livermore's right."

"Just so." Benedict stood in his stirrups, and said, eyes misted over, "Cemetery Ridge is over there, see? General Livermore directed his artillery from here. Like a rock. Still can't believe he's gone."

Clarion jotted notes. "And the Lieutenant?"

"Just where the traitorous dog now stands." Major Gaunt pointed a gloved hand at Drayton, who stood, guarded, on a bald knoll behind the horsemen.

"Anyone else?" Clarion asked, scanning the tree line some two hundred yards behind.

"Three officers and two enlisted men. Sent down for Pickett's charge—poor devils, all killed." Gaunt's eyes accused Drayton. "That's it, except for a couple of niggers." He glanced at Cicero seated on the buckboard. "Officer's servants, I mean."

"Now, just what happened?" Clarion looked to General Benedict. "Everything, if you please."

Benedict drew a deep breath. "Like I said, Johnny Rebs counterattacked; bloody graybellies tore up the hill like a spooked herd, rebel-yelling like all mad. Sound like a damned bunch of geese, if you ask me." He hesitated. "We tried to . . . move back . . . in an orderly fashion. But, there was a good deal of confusion."

"Did General Livermore retreat with you?" Clarion caught the brief flash of anger, regretting his blunt words.

"No, bless his soul, he stood firm. When we returned, General Livermore lay bleeding—shot dead—through the heart. Lieutenant Drayton was gone."

Clarion perused THE REPORT. "Drayton's revolver was found near the body?"

Benedict indicated with his sword. "Scoundrel must have dropped it in the confusion."

Major Gaunt handed a revolver up to Clarion. "Here it is," he said. ".36 caliber. Drayton admits that it belongs to him. Ball from the General's body is .36 caliber. No question about the murder weapon." Surgeon Malloy nodded.

"No rebel got close enough to hit us with a pistol," General Benedict added. "Drayton shot the man in the back; ran away like a chicken coop weasel."

Clarion hefted the revolver. "Feels like a Colt," he said, turning the barrel toward his eye. "But, not quite. Southern manufacture, I believe. Lieutenant, what were you doing with a Confederate pistol?"

"Sir." Lieutenant Drayton braced his thin shoulders. "Took it off the body of a secessh bastard at Antietam Creek. But it weren't with me. Sounds like I'm lyin', but someone stole it off me before the battle."

"Then how did this revolver find itself on the ground near the dead man?" Clarion clicked the empty cylinder.

Lieutenant Drayton eyed the Union officers surrounding him with suspicion. "Don't know, swear I don't . . ."

"Don't be afraid, son. Just tell me the truth." Clarion stared, still trying to remember where he had seen Drayton. "The truth without doubt and without error."

"Well, sir, wasn't exactly the way the General just told the story.

General Livermore and I held our ground, that much is true. But, you see, when the Johnnies came charging up the hill, things got right smoky and confused. General Benedict, he and the Major they sort of got crazy scared; ran like the very devil was . . ."

"Lying rascal. I'll shut your . . ." Major Gaunt raised his sword.

"Let that man alone, or I swear to God, I will see you arrested." Clarion stared until Gaunt's sword dropped to his side. "Go on, Lieutenant."

"I stayed on this hill 'til I just couldn't hold on no longer. I got hit myself. Just grazed, but sent me running."

"That's why the pickets found you a mile away, heading for Southern lines?" Clarion looked at the REPORT.

"Don't know where I was, Captain. Dazed like, I was."

"Is that all?" Clarion felt hot hostility from the ring of muttering officers. "Holding something back?"

The young Lieutenant rubbed angry lines around his wrists, looking to the sky. "Well, I guess General Livermore is dead and can't be brought back anyways." He sighed deep in his chest. "As I high-tailed, blood running down my head, I heard a shot. Turned. Saw General Livermore fall from his horse." He stopped, looking at Gaunt.

Clarion dismounted. "Do not be afraid," he said.

Lieutenant Drayton sucked in his breath, and pointed at Major Gaunt. "Was him. Pistol in his hand—standing there with a pistol in his hand—smoking it was, too. Swear it on my . . ."

Gaunt bolted over the grass like a wild boar. He spun Lieutenant Drayton to the ground and circled strong fingers around his thin throat. "Lying dog, I'll kill you for this!"

Cicero jumped from the buckboard. He disengaged Gaunt's hands from Drayton's neck and lifted him in the air as easily as if he were a bag of new picked cotton. "Let go of me, you damned savage. I'll have your ass."

Drayton added to the din. "Swear to God, don't know how my pistol got there," he wailed, fingering the bruises on his neck. "On my mother's grave."

Clarion stepped forward. "Everyone be quiet. Quiet, I say." The yellow knoll stilled. He looked at General Benedict. "Clearly, someone here is lying. We shall find out who it is soon enough, soon enough."

General Benedict cleared his throat. "Surely you will believe the word of the Major, Clarion?"

"I'm not here to believe. Proof and facts rule my judgment." He walked toward the buckboard. "General, I suggest that we place both of these men in custody as . . ."

Major Gaunt struggled to twist free. "General," he said, "don't believe that killer. He has every reason to lie."

"The Major is right," Benedict said. "Gun is the only evidence we have. No reliable witnesses."

"Not quite so, Senator," Clarion said, motioning Cicero to release Gaunt. "You have forgotten the Negro servants who were here the whole time. They will throw much light on the whole affair, I believe. Much light."

6.

Clarion's writing hand jiggled as the buckboard rolled down the hill. Handing some papers to Cicero, he said, "Ride into town and send this message by telegraph to our old friend Sam Colt in New Haven. Send the other to my father at his church in Boston. Wait for replies."

Cicero tucked the messages in his starched shirt. "Should I interview the servants first? Couldn't find them last night."

"I know, don't bother," Clarion replied, testing his tender knee. "And don't forget to check those trees."

"Birds flying free to the drinking gourd, I think," Cicero said, looking at the sky.

Smiling faintly, Clarion flexed his knee. He now clearly remembered where he had met young Lieutenant Wilson Drayton.

7.

Late that night, Benedict and Clarion met privately in the library, which was surprisingly grand for a farmhouse. Clarion peered at a crackling fire through magenta liquid in a crystal glass. "Damned fine Madeira, Senator."

"Prefer the Port myself." Benedict poured another glass. "Now, Clarion, I do hope you have this matter in hand. My officers are skittish. Can't blame them," he said, lighting a cigar from an ember. Dense white smoke filled the air.

"Precisely why I asked you to meet me tonight."

Benedict pulled his chair close. Clarion lit a pipe in self defense.

"Tell me, then, just why did Lieutenant Drayton kill the General?" Benedict asked.

"Allow me to proceed slowly," Clarion said, pausing to sip his wine. "Cicero spoke to the servants earlier this evening. Moses and Charlemagne, I believe. One is your manservant, is he not?"

"Why, why, yes." Eldridge spilled a few drops of his Port and tried to flick the stain from his uniform. "Charlemagne is my servant's name, yes."

"We will get to them." Clarion removed a paper from his pocket. "Incidentally, I was right about the revolver. Sam Colt telegraphed. Leech and Rigdon .36 caliber is a precise Confederate copy of the Colt Navy-model."

"Drayton doesn't deny that it was his pistol."

"Quite right, but, don't you see; the .36 caliber ball could have come from Drayton's revolver, or from any Colt Navy-model. That sidearm is carried by many Union officers." Clarion re-lit his pipe. "Carry one myself on occasion."

"So does Major Gaunt, but it's absurd to believe that the Major would have killed Livermore."

"He didn't, Senator."

"Well, then, I guess we'll never know. Could have been any soldier who picked up an officer's weapon in the battle." Orange light from the fire speckled Benedict's forehead.

"Forgive me, but I know." Clarion's voice could scarcely be heard over the sputtering fire. "I know."

"I, sure as Hell has sinners, don't know. And I won't play hide the ball. Either tell me, or I shall take my leave and retire." Benedict flowed toward the door like a battleship clearing port, smoke swirling behind.

"One moment, please. Hear me out. The bullet which killed General Livermore traveled at a downward angle, from his upper shoulder blade to a spot under his heart." Clarion slanted his fingers toward the plank floor.

"What the hell difference does that make?" the General asked, hesitating, puffing energetically.

"Well, it means that a man on foot could not have fired the shot." He angled his hand upward. "That rules out both Lieutenant Drayton and Major Gaunt, doesn't it?"

Benedict bolted his Port, stepping closer. "Then, you think it was someone in a tree. A bushwhacker?"

"Cicero checked every tree—none close enough for a pistol shot."

Benedict's hand trembled slightly as he tipped the decanter. "Well then, how in thunder was the man shot?"

"By a man on a horse," Clarion said evenly, poking the sparking logs. The close air smelled of pine and cigar smoke. "A tall man on a tall horse." His gaze fixed on Benedict.

Benedict paused. Face crimson, medals on his chest quivering, he smashed his glass against the wall. "Surely. Surely—God damn you—you don't suspect me?"

"More than suspect, I'm afraid." Clarion pointed the poker like a teacher at the blackboard. "Forgive me, I hate this. But, I must arrest you for murder."

"Can't prove anything, damn you. Just as easily been one of the officers; the ones killed in battle."

"Could have been, but they all carried Remington side arms." Clarion patted the REPORT which sat on the table. "Your men did a thorough job of investigating. Drayton's .36 caliber, which you left at the scene, was the murder weapon, wasn't it?" Benedict slumped into a chair. "If there was any doubt," Clarion continued, "the fact that Charlemagne has disappeared convinced me it was you."

Benedict's voice reminded Clarion of an ungreased wheel. "Son-of-a-bitch ran off. Means nothing. Proves nothing. Darkies always running off."

Clarion slipped a telegraph from his pocket. "From my father. He says Charlemagne has been with you for twenty years. Just up and ran off? After all those years? Unlikely. You didn't react when I mentioned seeing Charlemagne, even though you knew he was gone. It all fits, I'm afraid."

Clarion looked into the barrel of Benedict's Remington revolver. "General, you don't want to do this. Don't do anything you will regret." Clarion's voice was calm.

Benedict's booming voice had reduced to a rasp, like a shovel scraping ice. "Leave me no choice, it will be my word against . . ."

"Put the gun down, General." Cicero's sharp voice ricocheted off the stone walls. "Not worth dying for." It was Benedict's turn to look into a gun barrel.

8.

Benedict dropped the gun. "I apologize for the Hamlet scene," Clarion said as Cicero and Major Gaunt emerged from behind a curtain. "Always prudent to take precautions, no?"

Major Gaunt's mouth foamed like that of a rabid dog. "You would have let me hang, for a crime I didn't commit. Bastard! Why? Why?"

Clarion stepped between the two men. "Wondered the same thing. Why? Years of public service. A long and distinguished career. Gone. Why? Some of the answer may be here." He held the telegraph and read it by the light of the fire. "Dad says your friends back home are rounding up support for a run at Lincoln in the '64 election."

Benedict burrowed down in a leather chair, hissing, his shoulders hunched. He reminded Clarion of a cornered badger. "I couldn't let the war end, sitting here as a no-account Brigade Commander. Had to get Livermore out of the way so I could command a Corps, an army maybe, become a hero."

Despite everything, Clarion felt sorry for the man. "All is ephemeral—fame and the famous as well," he said, remembering his Marcus Aurelius.

"Damned Grant gets all the press. Don't you see, I had to do something." Benedict shook violently; tears finally came. "I would have been a great president."

"Easier to be bribed by power than by money." Clarion put his hand in the man's heaving shoulder. "Pride goeth before destruction, and a haughty spirit before a fall."

"Now I'll be hanged as a murderer," he said between sobs. "God knows I deserve it."

A smile flickered over Clarion's face. "Forgive me, you deserve to be hanged—and likely will be—but not for murder. Cicero, please bring Lieutenant Drayton to us."

9.

"Well?" Clarion looked puzzled. "Where is he?"

Cicero had returned alone, holding a piece of paper. "Looked all over. Drayton's gone over the hill. Left this."

Clarion shrugged, saying nothing. He took the paper, glanced at it for a few moments, and then, read out loud:

"Dear old friend Clarion,
I could tell from your eyes that you would eventually remember my older brothers."

In a roundabout way, Clarion had been reminded of his meeting with Drayton by his Yale knee injury; the Drayton boys of Edisto Plantation, South Carolina were fire-breathing slavers who attended Princeton. Clarion had recalled the Draytons had come to Yale to compete—fifteen years or more ago. Their youngest brother, Little Willie, tagged along. Clarion had heard that one brother now commanded a battery defending Charleston; the other was home, blinded at the Second Battle of Bull Run. He continued to read:

"When you did remember, you would certainly suspect me of being a Confederate spy—an ugly word for such a grand calling! No one else would notice, but I figured it would dawn on you that the little hole under General Livermore's ear had something to do with me.

When my Confederate brothers got too close on the hill, I took off. But, I tripped; turned to see that blowhard Benedict double back and shoot Livermore with my pistol. Alas, Livermore, probably the best young general the North has, (or had), was not dead. Finished him off with my derringer, as I'm sure you surmised.

When I got caught, I hoped to kill two birds with one stone by sticking Gaunt (Obnoxious as hell, but another good officer) with the murder, but we can't have everything. Had no wish to see Benedict discovered. We see it as a plus for the Cause to have an incompetent blowhard politician like Benedict as a Union Corps Commander, but—like I said—we can't have everything.

Clarion, after this damnable war is over, I shall treat you to a partridge and woodcock dinner in the best dining room in Charleston. GOD SAVE THE SOUTH.

Wilson (Little Willie) Drayton, CSA"

※

Northwestern University: B.A. 1959
Yale Law School: LLB 1962
Practiced corporate and antitrust law, New York City: 1963–89
Publications: Non-fiction articles in Saturday Evening Post *and business journals*
Recently completed Civil War novel
Short play produced as one of Best Short Play series at Florida Studio Theatre

DALE W. HAGEN

THE STARS WONDER

by Cristina Lopez

Dance, song moon, dance.
Rise, high sun, rise.
Dusk is almost gone.
Where we come from
Another moon, another sun have gone by.
Stars nestled in the sky spell out our names
and cry for us, for years gone by,
and wonder when we're coming home
or if we'll stay to wander.

ODE TO THE MODERN AGE

by Cristina Lopez

While the digital ads debut their daunting success
I sleep a long sleep
And dream of roots taking shape and soaking up their liquor
For no water can be found in the showroom desert.

I fall prey to associations and networks of copy-fax-telex-modems
Where the only true font is my very pen
And I don't have to be on-line, in-line or feline to have a thought.
I just do.

Where were you during this revelation?
Painting outdoor ads in elevation?
Or merely sleeping the sleep I slept
Once
Before all this began
And my cable was hooked up.

SPELLING

by Cristina Lopez

These letters I
These thoughts I
Sound
Out
Slow.

These names I
These ideas I
Spell
Out
Loud.

I cast letters to make words
That I say to make you laugh
You cry
You think
You know what I'm going to say next but you don't so
You argue.

My letters are mystic
Syllables entrancing you to
Hear me speak,
Touch my thoughts with your ears,
Close your eyes and see my sound.
I transform my thoughts to yours
My spell is magic,
My spelling power,
My language weapon.
Hear me.

I'm an up and coming author, currently working on a non-fiction book about finding someone I haven't seen in eighteen years. In addition, I write some short essays, but mostly poetry because it keeps me sane. I have appeared in the on-line journals Switched-on Gutenberg *and* Cherrysucker *and am featured in the anthologies* In Our Own Words, Volume 2 *and* Showcase 2000. *I most recently was awarded Third Prize in the National League of American Pen Women's International Free Verse Poetry contest for 2000.*

I'm a huge fan of the X-files, Little House on the Prairie *and my nephew.*

CRISTINA LOPEZ

PERK ASBURY

by Robert Magill

L OOK AT THAT. They're everywhere," he muttered, half aloud. "I knew it. I knew it would be like this."

As he had anticipated, his private spot had not been disturbed. It was as it had been in prior years when he had come here.

A shoot, he mused confidently. A real bug shoot.

It was now just a matter of harvesting a crop. His only challenge was to avoid alarming the mob below until he had cleaned out the place. He maneuvered into a better position so as to be directly above the scurrying forms on the sandy sea bottom.

The hunter turned slowly and scanned the area reached by the beam of his helmet-mounted spotlight. The water was inky and the only natural light filtered down from a wan sliver of moon. Seeing no other predators, the diver turned his full attention to the scene below.

This little known reef was home to hundreds of fat Florida spiny lobsters in prime condition. It was now just days before the start of the annual open season for divers. In the Florida Keys, the last Wednesday and Thursday falling together in July was set aside for the sport season.

109

Perkins Asbury adjusted his face mask, gripped his mouthpiece firmly and prepared to begin the slaughter.

Got to keep up a good steady pace, he thought to himself. Slow, slow, real smooth now, like you always done it, Perk boy.

Carefully he brought the long-barreled spear-gun up to aiming position and gently squeezed the release. The heavy bolt slashed the water and went to the mark. A three-pound "bug," as the locals called the spiny lobster was impaled cleanly through the upper body, the carapace. The Hunter was careful to avoid piercing the tail segment which would mar the succulent meat and lower the market value.

Asbury quickly retrieved the struggling creature, drawing stealthily the long cord attached to the keen projectile. With a practiced motion, he wrested the hapless creature free from the point and transferred it to the mesh bag at his waist. He then began to seek his next target.

Good. They never spooked, he gloated. It'll be cake, tonight.

The only legal way to take Florida lobster during the sport season was either catching them by hand (a difficult task with these wary creatures) or by using a long, thin wand, a "tickle stick," to prod them out from under the coral into a net. Spearing lobster had been outlawed years ago when the practice threatened to diminish the fishery. But Perkins Asbury was a dedicated and relentless poacher.

A fifth generation Key's native, known commonly as a "conch," he had little regard for these legal niceties. Tonight's quarry was the spiny lobster. On another safari it might be giant grouper or some other large reef denizen. On occasion even the rare and protected queen conch was harvested with gusto for its prized shell.

He regarded, as did many old time Key's residents, fish and game regulations as applying only to outsiders and not to himself. Chronically fatalistic, these Key's natives were resigned to a lifetime awaiting "the big one," the monster hurricane which would sweep their islands clean of the interlopers and tourists who didn't understand their ways and whose presence drove up the property taxes. This long anticipated killer storm might also even old scores which festered and simmered for generations among the sea-girt inhabitants.

For years Perk Asbury had haunted this and other secret spots which were unknown to the newcomers. To take the sea bounty in any manner he chose was the only way Perk Asbury knew.

With a swift and determined efficiency this silent predator cleaned out the reef population starting with the biggest of the still unwary crustaceans. Countless loads were transferred from his holding sack to a special compartment rigged for this purpose on his dive boat which rode at anchor nearby. Perkins knew he had little to fear from his fellow "conchs," many of whom knew or suspected his unlawful activities. The threat of the Water Patrol always existed, but most of them were recruited from among the island boys. Lately, unfortunately, some outsiders filled the ranks and, therefore, were now a concern to him.

The penalties for harvesting lobster in this manner and in these quantities were significant. Asbury was well aware of the risk, but had prepared for it.

She's about three-quarters full, he decided. One more go should do it.

Perk removed the last of his take from the catchbag and shoved the creature into a narrow, spring-loaded hatch built into the end of the dive platform which lay behind the cruiser. To any onlooker, this was a commonplace device found on the stern end of many boats. But this sinister contraption, of his own design, was intended to thwart any possible detection of his nefarious collecting activities.

Perkins Asbury had replaced the original dive platform with a carefully constructed holding chamber for his illicit cargo. It was six inches deep, almost two feet wide and spanned the full ten foot transom of the craft.

Although resembling a single entity and appearing solid, this spacious compartment was actually of two parts. What had been the top of the original platform was replaced with a laminated fiberglass panel containing a thin, but powerful, electromagnet. An electric conduit, concealed within the starboard platform hanger, ran into the hull and connected to a strong storage battery. Below this false top and held securely by the powerful force of the magnet was a metal tank which was the holding container for his contraband. Painted all of a color, it was impossible to tell the platform was not a single piece.

Below the dashboard of his cruiser, out of sight but readily accessible, was a single-pole toggle switch. Any threat of discovery could be countered by switching off the current to the magnet. Thus released, the tank with the incriminating evidence would head to the bottom of the sea in an instant.

Not far from where Asbury was hunting lay a flat shelf that banked sharply from the shallow sea bottom—then dropped into a deep ocean trench.

The creature was a stranger to these waters. Its home range lay far to the warmer southern seas. This year a series of early spring and summer storms had risen up from Africa and driven the waters westward along with its normal prey. For months the leviathan had slowly moved away from its home waters and followed the bait into the shallows of the Florida Straits.

It sought refuge in the cool deeper trenches during daylight hours, but never rested from the eternal search for the crabs, fishes and other small creatures which it needed in huge quantities to assuage its gargantuan appetite. The waters around this particular reef were teeming with blue-bottle jellyfish, a prized delicacy.

Although not having reached its full mature growth, the youngster was still almost forty feet in length and weighed many tons. The giant's most impressive feature was its terminal mouth with thousands of small, pointed teeth set in each mammoth jaw. It cruised with its mouth open wide, taking in everything in its path. The great fish was as black as the nighttime sea except for odd whitish spots and vertical markings on its back. Its small eyes were almost useless in the failing light. As it swam, the horizontal ridge on its vast back eddied the warm waters it traveled.

The creature swam lazily through swarms of the floating jelly-fish, gulping everything into its maw, then filtering out the great quantities of sea water taken in. The monster, although the largest creature on earth—save some great whales—was entirely harmless.

While not a danger to man or beast, its presence in the area had caused all the large predators to keep a distance. Nowhere to be seen were the big sharks and barracudas which normally infested the reef. Even the solitary jewfish, those giants who had no enemy save man, abandoned their coral homes. All preferred to avoid the stranger.

Although miles from others of its kind, the great beast was not alone. A large colony of small striped fish, the remora or sharksuck-er, traveled with it constantly. Throughout their lives they lived attached to its huge bulk with rubber-like suckers growing from their heads, only darting off briefly from the host to feed and breed. These slim opportunists fed from the leavings of a continual banquet.

When the sun came close to the horizon and the waters began to cool ever so slightly, the great fish rose from the depths to begin its nighttime foraging.

Perkins Asbury was closing the compartment of the stash place on his boat, preparing to head for shore. Satisfied with the night's work and contemplating the money it would bring in, he felt the presence before he saw it. The immense bulk of the creature created a pressure wave which preceded it.

"Oh my God! Oh Great God," he gasped.

The whale shark was almost upon him. Its enormous head and gaping jaws glistening with tiny baleen teeth filled the horizon. Perkins was raised in the Florida Keys and had no knowledge such a creature existed. A wiser man might have known what he was encountering. A gentler person would have considered other options.

Perkins was neither.

His entire nature spoke in one voice. Kill it. Kill that thing, Perk.

In one motion he drew his spear-gun to position and fired. Perkins Asbury was a true hunter. Even through the livid fear and near panic he was experiencing, his instincts ran true. The bolt pierced the creature's small eye and went deep into its brain. Death began at once.

A violent shudder ran the length of the mammoth bulk. The whale shark rolled over and over convulsively. One reflexive lash of its great tail carried away the entire stern section of the cruiser. The same force drove the diver, tumbling him backward and downward as he barely missed being smashed against the rapidly sinking craft.

Asbury struggled frantically, feeling for his lost mouthpiece as the air was forced from his lungs. The light from his helmet darted about aimlessly in the dark water, but he caught a glimpse of the tank filled with his ill-gotten catch spiraling downward, along with a torn piece of what had been the aft section of his boat.

The dying creature could still be seen through the roiled waters. Asbury witnessed its last feeble thrashing and then it disappeared over the edge and into the abyss. He was just regaining a portion of his senses when he became aware of the rapidly approaching shape.

At first he thought the creature had reappeared, but even in his extreme confusion, he realized it was not the awful demon he had encountered.

A large colony of sharksuckers of various sizes were carried about on the body of the great fish. Now some arcane intelligence raced throughout the colony signalling that the host had perished.

As one, they fled the hapless comrade with whom they dwelt in close association throughout their lives. Desperate for another large creature with which to bond, the school rushed en masse to where the diver still struggled.

They covered Perkins Asbury completely. At first the hunter tried to avoid the flashing forms that were all about him. Soon he could no longer raise his arms as dozens of the squirming fish suctioned themselves firmly in place.

They attached to his legs and body until every portion was occupied with the swarming horde. Many were forced to make do with a purchase on his dive equipment. They gathered on the tanks, the hoses; two smaller ones even found a place on his face mask. He could clearly see the rubbery disks on the heads of the fish before their thrashing tore loose first his mask, then his light and then his breathing apparatus.

His still form settled to the barren sea bottom. Nearby, the twisted remains of the storage tank lay where it had fallen. The small door had been forced open by the blow and, one by one, the lobsters emerged and walked slowly toward the coral reef.

❧

Author of a novel, Michael's Cut, *published in 1994; a short film,* The Lift, *featured in 2000 by the Sarasota Film Society Kine-Vision and currently on the web at ifilm.net. He is, with his wife, Mary Providence Magill, filming a documentary and has a screenplay,* Not With a Bang, *being considered for production in Australia.*

ROBERT MAGILL

KISS AND TELL

by John McCafferty

L ET'S TURN THE CLOCK back to an important moment in everyone's life—well, almost everyone. I'm talking about the time we experienced our very first kiss.

Actually, I want to tell you about my first kiss, but now that I've raised the subject, you probably are thinking about your own first kiss. And who can blame you? A first kiss is a once-in-a-lifetime experience. If you were a boy, as I was when it happened, you realized—perhaps for the first time—that girls are different. You may have concluded that kissing girls was neat, though they weren't much fun when it came to playing football.

I don't know what girls think about their first kiss. My impression is they see it as a memorable moment—something to look forward to, to dream about and to tell other girls when it finally happens. Sort of like a boy thinks the first time he finds a frog, climbs a tree or hits a home run.

So, let me tell you now about my first kiss. You'll have to stop thinking about your own first kiss to appreciate my story.

I don't know exactly when it happened—probably when I was

nine or ten years old. Somebody in the neighborhood had a party and I was invited. Before I knew it, we were involved in a game called spin the bottle—or was it post office? It doesn't really matter, because the object of both games was to kiss a member of the opposite sex.

If I'd known what was coming, I'd have made a dash for the door to play marbles or try a new trick with my yo-yo. Unfortunately, I was caught off guard and suddenly face-to-face with this big, fat girl with outstretched arms and a determined look. She was no Miss America, no Julia Roberts. More like a sumo wrestler with patent leathers and pigtails.

It happened quickly. She put a hammer lock on me, then her beefy arms encircled me like a bear. Her lips bore into mine. I couldn't breathe. I tried pulling away but she wouldn't let go. Her neck veins bulged. The pressure increased. I began to panic and worried whether I'd get out alive. I was about to faint when I spotted her ankles. Finally, I got one foot behind them, grabbed her shoulders and pushed as hard as I could. That did it. She relaxed her grip as she fell backwards. Whew! Free at last!

The big moment had passed. I had just experienced my first kiss. Now, let me sum up what this young lad thought about it.

Yuck! No. Make that . . . Yuck! Yuck! Yuck!

It took me a long time to get over the experience and obviously this girl and I never eloped. Eventually I healed and, as time passed, I had other opportunities to kiss other girls. One could easily see that they were much better at this game than I was. In fact, I'm probably enshrined in their Kissers Hall of Shame.

Along the way I suffered various battle scars. I learned that some girls love to bite when they kiss, and others have breath that would chase a crocodile at midnight. One girl apparently thought kissing's objective was to have her tongue snake past my lips and through my gastrointestinal system until it reached my kneecap.

Now I hope your own first kiss and subsequent smackers produced more pleasant results. As for me, don't worry. Many years have passed since my childish adventures. Eventually, I realized how dumb I was in the art of puckering up.

Finally, I met a girl who kissed me like no other could. Her offerings were soft and sweet and made me feel great. When she kissed me, my heart pounded and my head said, Don't let this one get away. Well, I didn't. I married her and I'm glad. When I kiss her, I forget my childhood disasters. And I hope the girls who put up with me years ago will do the same.

For 43 years now, my Queen of Kissers has been giving me lessons, and by now I've learned a thing or two about the art. I enjoy kissing her as much today as I did when we first met. Come to think of it, we never did kiss on that first date. When it came time to say goodnight, we looked lovingly into each other's eyes and shook hands.

IF RANDOMNESS EXISTS

by Pegi Clark-Pearson

If randomness exists, I choose March 20, 1989.
Can I put a space around it? Yes.
Glass and wood and a glimmer of the river.
I give it emotion: excitement, nostalgia, regret.
Tuesday, March 20
Glass house in the woods.
Excitement. Nostalgia. Regret.
Want to keep the first emotion foremost.
Not dwell on what didn't happen
in that house of stillborn dreams.
Stay positive. Keep packing.
Nine crates of playbooks for the town library.
Our common love for Albee, Checkov, Miller
not enough to bind us, while we each searched
for a star part. The role's the thing, or was.
Sewing machine hummed and a cake in the oven
while the decade cracked like a house on the Andreas fault.
Friends died from bad livers and lack of vision.

Divorce. The first shook the ramparts but soon
as routine as Friday night poker.
You knew how it would play,
friends choosing, his side or hers.

A Tuesday. Not a special day.
No visitors. Just me and my cartons.
Let the kids decide about kid stuff
They're gone and so am I, nearly.
I've sold antiques. My lack of sentiment energizes me.
The money's real. Banked in an account marked "new life."
But I keep stuff too. No white wicker dream for me in Southland.
I keep Honey's beds and Andy's library chair.
I keep the walnut table and the "Baron" dining chairs
I keep the double bed I slept in as a kid. All over again.
Excitement. Nostalgia. Regrets. In that order.

POINT OF VIEW

by Pegi Clark-Pearson

Think of Crow or Bear looking at you
where is the hair?
where are the feathers?
This one's ripe, this one's plucked.
On the other hand imagine
a crow without feathers
a hairless bear.
We cover our selves not from modesty
as much as vulnerability.
Why then are we endlessly at war?
Of all the species we seem
most designed for peaceful existence.
We celebrate nudity
call it art
the guards warn, do not touch
touching's a thing punishable by death in the nineties.
Keep it behind glass or latex
better yet take a picture to bed or watch on video
would Darwin have a take on this today?

Think of a crow. Think of a bear.
Think of them watching three hundred and twenty two of us
climbing aboard a DC6 and lifting off.
A penny for their thoughts
This skin we're in shows every blemish, sag and wrinkle
age is a varicose topography of time
vulnerability underlined
youth's joke that can't be true for long.

❦

A widely published prize-winning poet. She has three chapbooks of her work. She performs frequently at cafés and bookstores. Ms. Clark-Pearson is a painter and has had twelve solo exhibits. She also writes prose-fables, fiction, travel essays, and teaches.

PEGI CLARK-PEARSON

IDENTITY

by Virginia Schaaf

This poem is about me
Hanging on to my father's little finger
Having my face spit-cleaned by my mother
Watching my Grandmother fall asleep
  while reading me a bedtime story.

It's about eating cold, creamy, crunchy Tin Roof Sundaes
  at the Ice Cream Store with my Grandfather.
Rainy days with dolls and books
The excitement and anxiety of school
Twelve years in a cocoon of belonging.

My poem is about longing for the independence of college
The pride of having my own earned money
The giant step from a daughter to a wife
The frightening responsibility of being a mother.

The joy of family
The sorrow of losing a mother
Experiencing the sweet and the bitter of living
The devastating emotions from the loss of an only child.

My poem is about growing older as a couple
Saying goodbye forever to Fathers, Grandparents, Aunts, Uncles,
    and friends
It's about retirement and
The making of new friends, exploring new places.

The quiet feeling of everyday contentment
The numbing shock of my love's sudden death
This poem is about the loss of my identity
This poem is about finding myself.

THE BOY ON THE BUS

by Patricia Richards

"NANA, WHERE ARE WE GOING?"

"On the bus, Luv."

"Where on the bus?"

"To America."

"You can't go to America on the bus."

"Sean, you weary me with questions."

"I want to know."

"We take the bus to Galway. Sail on the Shamrock to Boston."

"Will I like the boat?"

"I'm sure I don't know. 'Tis a rocky bit. My sister, Margaret, was sick all the way."

"I won't be sick. I'm strong and mighty."

"A mite you are, but a good lad."

"Why can't we stay? Grandpa said, 'Never sell the farm.'"

"Grandpa's gone. It's time to leave. Ireland eats boys."

"Like bits of cheese and ham," Sean laughs.

"No, they drag them into English hating, to throw rocks, hide . . ."

"Won't I ever see Jamsy or Uncle Pat?"

"I don't know, child. Hush! Take these pence, buy a scone, fill your mouth with it, now."

"Are you sure you want to go?"

"Michael Gorman, what are you doing here?"

"I met Pat. He said 'Delia is leaving today.' Why didn't you tell me?"

She shrugs.

"Why are you going?"

"Irish women in Boston make lots of money raising the children of the rich."

"If I had money, I would ask you to stay."

"Ahh, it's not money. It's Ireland."

"I wish I could go to America."

"And what would The Cause do without you?"

He lowers his head; she fidgets with her rosary beads.

"I'm sorry, Michael. I mean no offense."

"It's the boy."

"Yes! The boy. The Cause can't have him."

"His father was a patriot. He should know."

"He'll know childhood, school books, a night's sleep without being afraid."

"And what the English did?"

"His father died of influenza."

"You can't run away, live a lie."

"He'll not be a messenger. Get killed for The Cause."

Michael shakes his head, and turns away. "God Bless, Delia. Have a safe journey."

"Nana, why is your face so red?"

"Sure, 'tis warm in here."

"Who was that man?"

"Just a man I knew when I was a girl."

"Is it almost time for the bus?"

"Soon Sean, soon."

"I think I've seen the man standin' outside the play yard. He always smiles."

"He has a smile like the divil himself. Come, the bus is here. Help me with the soft bag, there's a good boy."

"May I have the window seat?"

"Yes, I've no need to look back."

"Nana, the man . . ."

"Mr. Gorman."

"He's watching us. Should I wave?"

"No."

The bus pulls away.

"Sit back and relax. We'll be in Galway in an hour," the driver says, and clears his throat. "I have sad news. It's just come over the radio. The United States has declared war on Germany."

Delia gasps, "God help us!"

"Will I go to war, Nana?"

"God forbid. It'll be over long before you're old enough to go."

"I think not," says the man beside her.

"I'm going to war," says the boy.

※

Mother, retired school teacher, writer and storyteller, with credits in Catholic Digest, Family, CWFI Newsletter, Doorways, The Upper Room, Yesterday's Magazette. *Weaving is her hobby.*

PATRICIA RICHARDS

RHYME TIME FOR CHILDREN OF ALL AGES

by Carole F. Scutt

THE ABC'S OF BEES

My body's big, my wings are small,
they say I shouldn't fly at all.
I spend the days among the flowers,
my wings stay strong for many hours.
If you should meet a bee that stings,
remember, females do those things!
Say, "Buzz off bee, get out of sight,
and fly away like Orville Wright!"

FLOWER POWER

Am I to presume you don't like my perfume?
You say it's just not for you.
It's hard to be friends when someone offends,
but what is a poor skunk to do?
I've tried all my power to smell like a flower,
oh that is a hard thing to be.
So all I can say is I'm hopeful today
tomorrow I'll be "Odor-free."

TAKE ME TO YOUR LITTER

My friend and I went to the pound,
and there we found a hairy hound.
A dog in need, no name or breed.
Just a friend, love's dividend.

PEEP IN TOUCH

We're four little chicks in a nest of sticks,
but where can our mother be? Peep Peep
She finds us grub in a leafy shrub
and returns to our "family tree." Peep Peep

PLEASANT PHEASANT

See all those feathers in the brim of that hat?
They came from my tail where I normally sat!
I need those for beauty to get me a mate,
but cooked under glass is a worse kind of fate.

NIGHT OWLS

We nap and doze the whole long day
and plan on how to catch our prey.
We have no neck to rest our head—
it slid onto our chest instead!
We fly at night with silent wings
to find our meals of mice and things.
You'll think this is a funny diet.
I have a hunch you'd never try it.
With big round eyes we see quite well,
but where we hunt we'll never tell.
If you should find us, please don't shoot,
'cause then we couldn't "give a hoot!"

CLEARLY I'M A JELLYFISH

I'm a gorgeous amorphous kind of shape
as I pulsate my way through the sea.
I'm not well designed for a fast-type escape
yet you'd better be wary of me.
My skirt is adorned with beautiful thread
as I silently swim through the deep.
My beauty deceives when a sting you receive
or a rash should develop instead.

Carole Scutt has been published in five volumes of the National Library of Poetry. *Received 1995 Editor's Choice for Outstanding Achievement. Associate Member of the International Society of Poets 1994, 1995, 1996.Semi-finalist in North American Open Poetry Contest 1995, 1996.First Prize in the Philadelphia Book Show 1997 in Juvenile DivisionLiving in Sarasota, Florida*

CAROLE SCUTT

❧

MY DAY AS A CROCODILE

by Joseph Carter

ONE DAY I WAS walking and thought, *what if I could be a crocodile?* So I went to a fortune teller to check my future. She saw that I could change into a crocodile for only one day. All I had to do was believe in myself and I could do anything. I thought, *what if there was a hunter just waiting for me?* Anyway, I sat on the floor and believed in myself for more than an hour.

When I opened my eyes, I felt very weird. I moved around. I looked behind me and all I saw was a long, green tail. "Yes!!!" I bellowed. I was a crocodile.

I went to the lake but I scared people half out of their wits. When I got to the lake I was starving. I looked around for some fish to eat. I managed to find some and was very full after the feast. I fell asleep right when I was done and rolled into high grass.

When I woke up, I saw a human with a gun right beside me. He didn't see me from the protection of the grass. I couldn't do anything but stay still.

I waited for two hours and my patience grew very slim. Soon I would have to do something or I would die of thirst, so I lunged out and bit off his foot. He was running like greased lightning after that. He never came back either.

Soon night came and I had to turn back into a human. So I went home and went to bed.

MY ADVENTURES AS A DOG

by Evan Feely

HAVE YOU EVER WANTED to be an animal? You haven't? Well, this must be your lucky day, because I'm going to tell you how it went when I was turned into a dog, and how I spent my day.

It all started when I was at my house. I was just strolling along in my back yard when a hole started swirling under me, and rays of light started pouring down, and electric sparks were flying around. I felt like I was in Frankenstein's lab. Then, all of a sudden I started shrinking and getting smaller. I felt myself get furry and grow paws with claws. I grew a stubby tail, and my snout grew long with a black nose. My ears went up, and I discovered I was on all fours. It couldn't be, I thought, I've transformed into a Doberman.

With that, my adventures began. When I looked around, I saw it was morning. I decided to be a good dog and get the newspaper. I trotted to the driveway and snatched the paper up in my razor-sharp teeth. So I went to the doggie door and head butted through. I saw my mom cooking breakfast and she saw me. She looked scared and puzzled, but she thought only a good dog would bring in the newspaper. So she threw up her hands in relief and cried, "Oh, Evan can finally have a dog!"

My father heard my mother's joyful cry and came out of the woods. He was wearing a red, patched shirt and faded jeans with his torn-up black-and-white sneakers. He came in the house with an ax over his shoulder. He thought I must be a good dog, too, and asked me to play fetch. We went out to our humongous back yard. He picked up a stick and threw it almost into the woods, but I soared into the sky and felt like Michael Jordan as I caught it in my teeth. After he was worn out from playing fetch, he said, "You can jump so high, I'm gonna name you Glider."

What was that? I thought I heard a faint meow off in the distance. I sprong up an ear toward the sound until, finally, I met an orange striped tomcat. I grimly sneered, "You're toast, feline." The cat ran off past the trees and I chased after it. I was about to catch it when it sped up a tree. I looked up at the cat and barked out, "If you ever cross my path again, I won't be so easy on you."

I went back to my house and saw that my folks had gone out. I thought that they must be out looking for me. I thought it would be a Doberman's duty to guard the house. Once a robber tried to get in by breaking down the door, but I bit his behind and he scampered off.

All of a sudden I felt a jumbly feeling and I started growing. I morphed from a clawing shape of terror into a normal human boy. Just then, my parents drove up in their Corolla and saw I had finally returned home. They hugged and kissed me until I had to say, "That's enough." They wondered where the Doberman had gone, but they figured maybe he had a master of his own.

These are my adventures as a Doberman. Maybe one day you might change into an animal.

THE MAGIC CARPET

by Jared Litwiller

ONE DAY CARLOS AND I went to a large stand with carpets. Carlos and I went to get a carpet. Carlos bought a carpet for five dollars. The carpet was rose red with golden yellow stripes.

After Carlos bought the carpet, we walked to my very light brown house with forest green shutters. Carlos and I sat down on the fabulous carpet in the green silk grass.

When we sat down on the marvelous carpet, the carpet started to float. The terrific carpet said, "Where do you want to go?" Carlos said, "To a jungle." I said, "OK." Then the incredible carpet started flying to a jungle.

When we got to a jungle, the wonderful carpet went slow so we could see the jungle. Then we heard a growl. Carlos and I stood still and looked around. Then we saw a jaguar. The jaguar had a golden yellow coat with light black spots. He jumped at us but he missed. Then we started going down.

Carlos and I saw that the jaguar had made a tiny hole in the wonderful carpet. I had a needle in my pocket and some string, so I started sewing fast. Then, when I was done, just in time, the magic carpet started flying again.

It took us home and we put the magic carpet in my room on the dark brown floor. Carlos and Jared learned to keep needle and string in their pockets so they can sew any holes, if there is a hole and they are flying. Carlos and Jared never told anyone about the extraordinary carpet. They did take more carpet rides to outstanding places.

IF MY LIFE WERE DIFFERENT

by Patrick O'Connor

HAVE YOU EVER WISHED your life were different? I do all the time. What do you wish you were? I would like to be a dog.

If I were a dog, I would do things like biting the mailman. I could even roll around in a flower bed. Or even lick my paws. That would be the life.

I would also be able to go more than two days without bathing. Wait, that wouldn't be good, because I'd smell bad. If I had a rich owner, I would probably get a nice dog house. Or if I had a movie director for an owner, he or she might put me in a couple of their movies. After that I'd be famous. I might even get a limo ride to work.

If I were a dog, I would be able to chew on dog bones. I've always wondered what they tasted like. I could also dig good holes. That's because I'd have strong front paws.

To conclude, I wish I could change my life to a dog's life. It would be fun being a dog. It would also be interesting. I wish I were a dog.

THE YUCKIEST THING IN THE WORLD

by Brittany Osborne

T HE OTHER DAY WE had a skunk in our clothes dryer. I thought the smell was just awful. It all started when my mom heard a scratching sound in the laundry room, "scritch scratch." We went to check it out. When we got there, we couldn't hear a thing. It was silent. My mom needed to dry some clothes and when she turned the dryer on, it hit us. The skunk smell was the yuckiest thing I had ever smelled. "Yuck!" I said.

We had to take some action so we called Pest Control. They came to our house and took care of the skunk, but the smell was still there. The next morning when I got out of bed, all I could smell was air freshener. "What a relief!" I sighed. That was better than stinky skunk.

That very same day, when I came home from school, that smelly skunk odor was there again, except even worse. I told my mom we needed a stink exterminator. My mom just laughed and told me there was no such thing as a stink exterminator.

That evening, I walked in the door with my gas mask on and about 25 bottles of air freshener. "Move out, Mom!" I said. I sprayed and sprayed until all the bottles were empty. "That should do it," I thought. Finally, all the stinky skunk smell was gone. Now all I will have to do is put a stink exterminator business in town. What a terrific business! I better tell Mom, Dad, and Sis that the stinky smell is over and out. "Mom? . . . Dad? . . ."

MY DAY AS AN ANIMAL

by Erick Swanson

ONE SATURDAY AFTERNOON, at twelve noon, I was in my front yard wearing a baseball cap, some black jeans and a white T-shirt. I was throwing my ragged old baseball up in the air and scampering to catch it. Suddenly my stomach felt weird like it does when I take a math test. Then I felt myself growing black hair around my body, my nose getting bigger and slimmer, and last, myself shrinking. I noticed I had become a grizzly black bear, just like what I wished for when I was watching "Animorphs!"

I quickly hid behind a big bushy evergreen tree. Pondering the problem of where I would go and hide, I thought of Jungle Gardens, because they have lots of trees to climb and plenty of fish to eat. I steeple-chased past our school and then I saw the sign "Jungle Gardens." I fled to the entrance, but did not go in the two front doors. I ran right into the jungle!

The first thing I did was to go to the tallest overgrown palm tree and climb to the very top. I seized the trunk of the palm tree and started to climb. After I got to the very last twig of the overgrown tree, I gave a roaring sound like a bear would do. My reply was some screams. I realized I would be in real danger if I got seen, so I quickly climbed down. When I reached the soft green grass, I was so hungry I could eat a horse. But I thought I could, since I was a bear. I slowly walked over to a shimmering blue lake and started to swat-out some fish, but could not get one. I finally got one! I looked at it, then, without thinking, I shoved it into my mouth! It was good so I had another, then another until I thought I would barf!

After all that eating and climbing, I was exhausted. I looked for places to sleep, but could not find one. I thought about where bears sleep and remembered bears sleep anywhere! So I nestled up some leaves and started to lay down. I closed my eyes and started to dream about being a boy again.

Suddenly, I felt the same way I felt when I was turning into a bear. When a black and brown monkey jumped from the tree and pulled my ears, I awoke and realized my dream had come true! I kissed my plain white T-shirt and black jeans. I was so happy I was a boy again, and I wouldn't have to make people scream, eat raw fish, or sleep in leaf beds.

I sprinted home and started to play catch again. This time I could not catch the ball, because I was not focusing on it, but thinking about what would happen if I wished I was an animal again.

❧

THE CIGAR MAKER

(EXCERPT FROM THE NOVELLA)

by Lester Ageloff

R ACHMAEL HAD BEEN APPRENTICED to a cigar-maker at the age of six, and cigar-making was all he learned. How much is there to making cigars? you ask. Using all his skills, he could eke out only a meager living to support his family. He bought bundles of tobacco leaves from the itinerant merchant who passed through his village and soaked, then twisted them into the misshapen ropy stogies he sold to the peasants on market-day. He was a poor man and couldn't afford the better leaves, and so his cigars were usually of the worst quality.

Some of his customers enjoyed a cigar with a bite—and Rachmael's certainly bit. Others said that they'd rather smoke grass or cabbage leaves, and occasionally did. When he tired of their complaints, he'd promise himself that he would buy better merchandise—bright Turkish leaves rather than the dark bitter ones from Astrakhan—and surprise them with a superior product. But every time he'd put aside a few kopecks for working capital, some family disaster would sweep away his resources. Disasters like a dying laying-hen that had to be replaced, or a window broken by village vandals, or a surprise visit from the tax-collector. Whenever the Unexplained depleted his meager purse, he'd console himself with the thought that his customers wouldn't appreciate life's finer things, anyway. And so it would go until the next time a customer's taunts motivated him. Then he would try again to squirrel away a few coins.

Every evening, he visited Velvl's Riviera—Nitely Entertainment, a thatched wooden dugout half-buried in the earth at the crossroads opposite the gilded onions of the Orthodox church, where the wooden sidewalk ended. Rachmael was not a drinker, but after he and Sonya put the children to bed, he would trudge the half mile in the mud to Velvl's tavern in hopes of peddling a few cigars. Velvl tolerated his presence because sometimes customers would tarry, waiting for Rachmael to turn up with his latest creations, and also because Rachmael occasionally paid him a cigar as rent.

On this particular evening, the entertainment advertised on Velvl's crude sign was actually taking place, featuring an aged wandering musician who sang sad ballads and violent battle-songs while accompanying himself on a battered balalaika. He wore a faded uniform and had only nine fingers—a wound from the Crimea, he once proudly proclaimed. Some suspected he'd shot off his own little finger to get out of the Czar's army, but no one really knew. He could play as well with nine fingers as he could have with ten. Of that, they were sure.

When his meanderings brought the old soldier to their village, Velvl would let him sleep on a pile of rags behind the stove and paid him with a few kopecks and a hearty breakfast of re-heated kasha and milk the next morning. Occasionally the patrons would toss a few coins his way. That's what kept him alive.

Rachmael arrived with his tray of merchandise to find a half dozen patrons in the establishment. Most were leaning against Velvl's bar in various stages of relaxation, depending upon how much of Velvl's libations they had so far consumed. In the Private Section (a corner table boasting four roughly-constructed chairs) sat a lone visitor, aloof and apart from the other customers. Rachmael didn't recognize the stranger, but he was obviously a man of some importance, because Velvl had spread his one table-cloth before him. And he was drinking wine, not Velvl's Special Blend, distilled from potatoes and aged at least one week, guaranteed! Rachmael was shocked. He never knew Velvl served wine. Of course, he had never asked, either.

Sensing a rare business opportunity, Rachmael approached the stranger and extended his display for inspection. "Would you care for a *seegara,* Your Honor?"

The stranger snorted. "Cigars? You call those goose-turds cigars? *This* is a cigar!" The visitor reached inside his tunic and extracted a snakeskin case in which reposed three perfect panatelas. While all eyes watched, he carefully selected one, bit off the end and lit it. He exhaled a plume of smoke in Rachmael's face.

"Smell it, smell it," shouted one of the bar patrons, almost falling off his stool with laughter. "Now you'll know what *real* tobacco smells like, not that rolled-up horseshit you sell us."

Rachmael was normally a mild-mannered fellow, but now the back of his neck reddened. Not only was his integrity being questioned, but he feared his livelihood was threatened. "You're right, Kalmanitzky, it *is* horseshit. You pay me horseshit prices, that's what you get. You wouldn't know *real* tobacco if you tasted it." The others at the bar howled with glee. Absent the balalaika player, a round of insults was their favorite diversion, usually accompanied by a round of Velvl's potent elixer.

"Maybe you sell better *seegara,* we pay you more," Kalmanitzky replied.

"Pay more?" interrupted his companion. "You? . . . Vera would kill you." Amid peals of laughter from the other barflies, Kalmanitzky glared at him, transferring his annoyance from Rachmael. "I'll get you for that, Sergei Petrovich," he growled. Velvl reached down behind the bar for his "enforcer," a stout club that was often brandished but seldom used—and never on regular customers.

While the others were trading insults at the bar, Rachmael lowered his voice and addressed the stranger. "With all due respect, Your Honor, that was not a very nice thing to do in a strange town. I have to make my living here. I know how to make cigars like yours, but I can't afford the *tabac.* Besides, this is a poor *shtetl.* My customers wouldn't buy them."

The stranger's eyes narrowed beneath the bill of his leather cap. He smiled through his dense black beard, displaying a row of perfect gold fillings. He patted Rachmael's shoulder. "Ah, a man with the courage to defend himself! I like that. My friend, you're right, and I beg your pardon. I assure you that your customers won't remember this by next morning. And to make it up to you, let me give you a little parting gift. If you use it right, it will help your business. Oh, yes, it will surely help." He laughed.

He reached into a pocket of his tunic and extracted a scrap of paper, folded many times. He unfolded it carefully to reveal a dozen tiny seeds. He handed the paper to Rachmael. "Plant these," he said, "and roll the leaves into your cigars. But never more than half a leaf, I warn you."

The fracas at the bar was becoming more boisterous. The stranger's gesture went unobserved. Rachmael pushed his hand away and drew back in horror. "I can't grow tobacco! I can't afford the grower's tax; I'd go to jail!. . . And the climate's wrong here, anyway."

The stranger smiled. "It's not tobacco. It's . . . ." At that point a roar erupted from the group at the bar as two patrons attacked each other and rolled together on the dirt floor. Velvl advanced from behind the bar with his enforcer and began to direct the two revelers towards the door.

Rachmael turned his head back toward the stranger. "I'm sorry, Your Honor, I couldn't make out what you said, with all this *shoom* going on. It sounded like *Marishka.*"

He smiled. "Marishka; yes, that's a good name for it." He stood and placed a gold coin on the table. "I must go now; remember, only half a leaf. And plant them *behind* the house." He made his way to the door past Velvl and the scuffling peasants. Foreseeing no further business that evening, Rachmael repacked his tray of merchandise. He stared longingly at the gold coin, but let it remain on the table. With a shrug, he refolded the paper and pocketed it. He edged out the door in time to see the stranger disappearing down the road on horseback in the bright moonlight.

Rachmael whistled as he approached his house. Sonya emerged and held a finger to her lips. "The children were restless tonight. I just put them to bed. Be quiet." She shivered and drew her tattered sweater about her as the early spring wind blew in from the Urals. Their house was similar in construction to Velvl's entertainment palace, half below ground level, but it had two rooms. Rachmael came up to her and set down his tray on the thatched roof. He removed his outer blouse and put it around her shoulders. Sonya pressed close against him as he put his arm around her waist. "Aren't you cold?" she asked. "No," he lied.

"Let's go inside and mess up the bed," he said.

She snuggled closer. "Wait, the kids are still awake. What's this in your pocket? Some *padrooga* sending you love notes?" She began unfolding the paper.

"Give it back!" he shouted, and snatched it from her hand.

She turned towards him, hands on hips. "Now, Rachmael Davidovich, now I *know* there's something going on. Here, take your *fahrshtunkina* jacket!"

"*Pajalsta, pajalsta* my pet," he said, as he held her arm. "Slow down. Who would want an old crock like me, other than you who are blinded by passion?" She smiled and put the cloak back on. "Here, I will show you, but be careful," he said. "It's supposed to be a great treasure." He slowly unfolded the paper by the light seeping through the oiled-paper window-pane. "There, this is supposed to make us rich!" He laughed bitterly.

"Rachmael, have you been drinking? It's just a few seeds. What are they?"

"You know I drink only on Purim, when it's required of us. Here, let me tell you the story."

When he had done, she asked, "If it's not *tabac*, what is it?"

"I don't know. He called it *Marishka*. Maybe a weed that gives it a better aroma; who knows?"

"Will you try it?"

"I have to; this is my whole night's wages. Can it make business any worse?"

She moved closer in the increasing chill. "Forget business. We'll always have each other."

He tightened his grip around her waist. "Think the little ones are asleep by now?"

* * *

The next morning Sonya planted all but three seeds at the far end of her kitchen garden, behind the blackberry bushes. On impulse, she took the last three seeds to a wooded copse at the border of the potato field behind their house and pushed them into the ground among some weeds. As early spring warmed towards summer, a row of little green seedlings peeped above the rich, black soil. Once they appeared, Rachmael would walk to the back of the garden every day to check on the progress of his experiment, as he called it. He watched impatiently as tiny leaves developed slowly into multi-fingered spikes, radiating from a center stem. Finally, he decided the day had come. He chose from among the largest plants, being careful to leave enough leaf surface for the plant to continue to live. He spread his harvest on their thatched rooftop, holding it down with small stones while it dried in the sun. By the end of the week enough leaves had dried out to be incorporated into his product. He soaked them and stored the remainder with the rest of his tobacco.

"Aren't you going to try one?" Sonya asked as he laid out a dozen cigars near the stove to dry.

"I don't know. Suppose it's poison? I never saw this funny plant before. It looks like the devil's fingers. I'll let my customers test it out first."

"Rachmael, I'm shocked!"

"You'd be shocked more if your husband lay down sick, or dead."

"But if a customer gets sick, they'll blame you."

"There are plagues, illnesses, diseases around here all the time. Nobody knows the causes. Bad air, bad water, swamp vapors. Bad *tabac*? How would they know? I'll hand out just one the first day. I'll choose my Official Taster, just like the Czar. Yes, just like the Czar." He laughed. "I think I'll let Kalmanitzky have the honor.

He's a *paskudnyock*. We have an old score to settle. . . Yep, he's the one, all right. . . Heh, heh, heh. The very thought of it makes me feel good!"

"Rachmael, this is a side of you I never saw before."

"I'm sure the stuff is harmless; it's been all over my hands from working it, and nothing's happened. Anyway, business is business. I'll take one or two over to the tavern with me tonight."

*   *   *

The troubadour had long since departed on his circuit, and the cabaret had become merely a saloon that evening. Four men sat around Velvl's one table, playing hearts with a greasy, dog-eared deck. They cursed the queen of spades in three languages plus the local dialect. Others watched over their shoulders, occasionally adding their own comments to those of the players. When Rachmael arrived and saw the coins on the table, he anticipated some good business, especially from the winners. Velvl stood behind the bar, towel across his shoulder, wearing a beatific smile. Rachmael sensed that the liquor and the kopecks were both flowing more loosely this evening. Good!

Kalmanitzky was at the card table. Since the devil favors the worst rogues, his was the biggest pile of coins. He caught Rachmael's eye and beckoned. "Aha! My favorite tobacconist is here! Rachmael, delight me with one of your best creations, if you please. The one with *tabac*, if you get my meaning."

Rachmael uncovered his tray and extracted the experimental product. He had taken great pains with it, even using one of his long-forsaken moulds to enhance its shape so that it resembled more a cigar than a piece of twisted rope. "I took your comments to heart, Aleksander, and bought a few imported leaves. I call this my Special Aromatic Metropolitan, and made it with you in mind. Do you want to try it?"

Kalmanitzky leaned back in his chair and reached for the cigar eagerly. "Let me see it."

Rachmael withdrew his hand just out of Kalmanitzky's reach. "Remember, you said you'd pay more for a better product."

"How much?" Kalmanitzky's chair was about to topple over as he extended his backwards stretch.

Rachmael quickly calculated the most outrageously high price he thought his customer would pay. "Five kopecks," he said. With Kalmanitzky's change of expression came instant realization that Rachmael had misread his eagerness. "That's the regular price, but for you, as an introductory offer, I ask only three kopecks," he continued almost in the same breath. Kalmanitzky swept three coins from the table and held them out to Rachmael. "You must think I'm a millionaire," he grumbled.

Rachmael put the cigar in Kalmanitzky's outstretched palm and removed the coins in a single gesture. Kalmanitzky examined his new treasure carefully. "I see you finally learned how to roll a good piece of merchandise." He sniffed it. "It even smells better."

"Imported leaves. And better materials deserve, no, *demand* better workmanship. At three kopecks I'm losing my shirt. Go ahead. Take a puff."

By now, all other conversations in the small room had stopped. Noting that he had everybody's attention, with great ceremony Kalmanitzky pulled a large knife from his boot and circumcised the cigar. He motioned to Velvl, who lit a piece of kindling in the stove and passed it across the bar. Kalmanitzky held the flame to the other end and took a deep draught. He exhaled slowly, as if chewing on the smoke.

A strong odor of tobacco smoke, plus a faint essence of—what was it?—filled the small room. Kalmanitzky coughed and spat on the dirt floor, and Rachmael's heart skipped a beat. Then a broad smile parted his beard. "Verry nice, Rachmael. It has a certain tang I never tasted before. Relaxing, too. What's in it?"

Rachmael's breath came back. "Imported leaves, like I said—trade secret. I've got one more with me, at the regular price, though. Want it?"

Kalmanitzky began counting out five kopecks from his pile of winnings, when a voice spoke from the other side of the table. "Six." He looked up. "Who said that?"

The peasant seated opposite him said, "Six, I bid six kopecks."

"Oh, it's you, Constantin," Kalmanitzky snarled. "Stay out of my business, I warn you."

"I'm his customer, too. I also have a right to try the new cigar." Constantin stood, his fully-developed belly resting on the table's edge. Kalmanitzky sprang to his feet, the knife in his hand.

Suddenly, Velvl jumped between them, brandishing his enforcer. "There'll be no blood spilled in my place, even if I have to break two skulls to stop it." Velvl was a huge man. Both combatants took a step backward. "Now let's settle this like civilized gentlemen, shall we?"

He turned and beckoned to Rachmael, who had withdrawn to the farthest corner with his merchandise. "Come here, my friend. Do you appoint me your auctioneer, for a modest fee, let's say twenty percent?" Rachmael, white as a sheet, nodded. "Good. Let me have the cigar, the Aromatic Metropolitan you called it, yes?" Rachmael silently handed it over and retreated.

Velvl displayed the cigar to all corners of the room. "Now, gentlemen, what am I bid for this rare piece of goods, eh?"

Rachmael finally found his voice. "It's not so rare, your honors. I can have half a dozen ready by tomorrow night."

"Shut up, Rachmael Davidovich. Who wants to taste this sensation—*tonight*?"

Puffing away at his prized specimen, Kalmanitzky said, "Five, that was what was agreed." The small room continued to fill with the smoke and the sweetish *essence* of his cigar.

"Six," Constantin stubbornly insisted.

"Seven kopecks," said a new voice from the gallery. Both antagonists turned to glare in his direction.

"Eight."

"Ten."

Fourteen was the final bid, Constantin was the winner. "Fourteen. Any other bids?" Velvl asked. "No? Congratulations. Here's the merchandise. Enjoy! Cash, please."

As Constantin slid a pile of kopecks over to Velvl, Kalmanitzky laughed. "Pay a little too much, Constantin Fyodorovich? You could have waited a day."

"No, my Grisha enjoys a good cigar, too. I'll take it home and surprise her, tonight."

Velvl handed Rachmael eleven kopecks, whispering, "I rounded it out; hope you don't mind." Rachmael nodded. Velvl then raised his voice so all could hear. "Gentlemen, I just earned three kopecks in that transaction. I'll use them to buy a round of drinks on the house." They cheered. "Of course, at three kopecks, I'll be losing money." They laughed.

Rachmael found his voice. He shouted, "I contribute two kopecks so Velvl won't lose any money, and I'll be back tomorrow night with more goods." Amid cheers and applause, he slipped out the door into the night and headed home to tell Sonya.

＊　＊　＊

A frantic knocking at the door awakened them just after dawn the next morning. Sonya sat upright in bed, clutching the blankets to her. "What's that?"

Rachmael's feet were already on the floor. "I'll go. It can't be good news. Get into the back room with the kids and bolt the door. Don't come out whatever you hear."

"Oh, Rachmael, I'm afraid."

"Go—quickly. I'll handle it."

The knocking continued. "Coming, coming," Rachmael shouted. He slipped into his under blouse and took a rusty old bayonet from behind the stove. Holding it behind his back, he went up to the door and invoked his fiercest voice. "Who is it?"

"It's me, Rachmael, your friend, Constantin. Let me in. It's freezing out here."

Rachmael glanced over his shoulder to see Sonya's ankle disappear behind the closing door. "What do you want, *friend?*" The front door remained shut.

Constantin was almost whining. "Please, Rachmael, I know it's early, but I must have some more of your Famous Metropolitans, before you sell them all."

"*Special Aromatic Metropolitans,*" Rachmael corrected him, as he unbolted the door. Constantin stepped down into the dark room. Through the open doorway, Rachmael could see his horse, breathing hard and steaming as if after a hard gallop. "You'll kill that animal one of these days, Constantin."

Constantin ignored the comment. "Those *seegara*—how many do you have? I'll take 'em all."

What is this? "Slowly, *pajalsta,* my friend. I know my cigars aren't *that* good. . . Oh yes, imported leaf and all that, but why can't you wait for tonight, or market day?"

"Rachmael, you don't know what you have there. When I got home, Grisha and I shared that cigar, and then we went to bed. Or rather, she *dragged* me to bed. She couldn't wait to get her hands on me; she practically raped me. It was like our first time in that haystack when we were both fourteen years old. I never had such a night!"

"No headaches?"

Constantin laughed. "*I* almost got a headache."

"Well, strange tobacco affects people in different ways. I can't give you *all* of them, because I have other customers to take care

of. . ." (Constantin's face fell.) ". . . but I *can* let you have three
or four. And don't worry, I'm expecting another shipment next
month." Constantin grabbed Rachmael's hand between his two
meaty paws. "Bless you, Rachmael. You're a prince. . . I hope it's
the same kind of leaf."

"Oh, it will be. Don't worry. But my supplier warned me that
costs are going up. You know how the market fluctuates. I'll have
to get seven kopecks from now on." He walked to the stove and
poked some life into the fire, inducing a flickering brightness
that cast elongated shadows on the whitewashed sod-brick walls.
"Is that all right?"

"No problem." Constantin removed a pouch from his pocket.
"Here's twenty-eight kopecks. I'll take four."

* * *

"Is he gone?" Sonya peered from behind the door, the children
clutching the skirts of her night-clothes. "What was that all
about?"

"The idiot! He was so anxious for some cigars that he couldn't
wait for sun-up."

"Rachmael, what are you selling? It must be more than just an
aromatic weed. Have you tried it?"

"*Nyet!* Before, I was afraid of being poisoned. Now I'm just
afraid, but don't ask me of what. There's something in my cigars
that grabs people. I can't let it take me over, possess me. *I won't!*"

"Will you keep on selling it?"

The awakening dawn was barely filtering through the paper
windows. Rachmael lit a candle at the stove. "Look at this
place—dirt walls, dirt floor, not a pane of glass, no shoes on the
kids! How can I *not* sell it! I made more money last night and this
morning than I do in a whole week. Don't you think I want to do

better for you and the little ones? How can I give it up?"

Sonya rushed to him and threw her arms about him, her head on his chest. "Have I ever complained? A dry crust is enough, if that's all you can give me. I don't want anything to happen to us, *to us.*" She sobbed, her body trembling.

Rachmael lifted her chin and kissed her tenderly, while the children grabbed both his and Sonya's skirts in alarm at their mother's outburst. "*Ketzelleh, ketzelleh,* my pussycat, don't be afraid. You cry because you think what I'm doing is somehow illegal, right? Will get us in trouble? Well, I don't think so. In Odessa, they sell hashish on the streets, openly, and nobody stops them. And that *kills* people! What I'm selling, whatever it is, just seems to give people a boost, make them happy. What's wrong with that?"

"If they drag you away, how could I live? It's wrong if it's against the law," she said, drying her tears with the edge of her sleeve.

"In Russia, it's against the law for people like us to make a living. What difference does it make?" He shrugged. "Does the Czar care if I live or die?"

"Come, children, let's get dressed," she said as she herded them into the back room. Over her shoulder, she added, "That weed, as you call it, *already* possesses you!" The door shut behind her.

Rachmael shook his head. *She's right, of course. This is the devil's work. It can't last forever. A runaway horse may win the race, but you have to be able to get off alive. Get off alive— that's the trick.*

※　※　※

Business certainly improved. Rachmael was no longer simply tolerated at Velvl's establishment. His arrival was eagerly awaited every night, and his day's production was soon snapped up at the standard price of eight kopecks, two for fifteen. Velvl stopped demanding rent since Rachmael had become his chief attraction. Life for Rachmael's little family changed, too. Although she disagreed with his new business venture, Sonya dutifully picked a few leaves for Rachmael every day while she tended her garden, taking care that no one observed her. The seeds she had planted in the woods were forgotten. Each night, long after dark, Rachmael furtively placed the leaves among the thatch on their roof to dry out. The new income began to affect their everyday lives. Besides the growing hoard of kopecks and an occasional gold coin that they kept in a crock buried in the wall behind the stove, their new prosperity became evident in shoes for the children, window glass in the front room, and two kilos of goose down to restuff their old quilt. Rachmael even began talking about buying a horse.

And then the shortage set in. A mere nine plants, even of the most vigorously growing weed, could not keep up with the demand for Rachmael's improved product. And because of over-harvesting, only three flowered as the growing season progressed. Rachmael could visualize his newly acquired prosperity going up in smoke. He tried cutting back the amounts he worked into each cigar, but his customers soon noticed the difference. To their complaints he replied that he had gotten a "weaker batch" of tobacco, and would be able to go back to his old formula "soon." Even though he lowered his price, there were no longer any eager buyers. One night, he returned home to Sonya empty-handed. He put his unsold tray of cigars on the table and slumped into a chair. "Tea," he said, "make me a cup of tea, *pajalsta*. I need it."

Sonya ran to him and put her arms about his shoulders. "What is it? What happened?"

"It's over, it's all over. I'm running out of merchandise. I . . . I tried to cut back, but they noticed right away. The plants are almost stripped bare, and only three look like they'll seed. I'm out of business, too soon. Much too soon." He turned, put his head on her shoulder and sobbed. "I've failed you and the *kinder.*"

She kissed his brow and stroked his hair. "Sh, sh, my only love. How have you failed? You've done the best you can for us."

"I wanted to get us out of here, to England or America. Look at this. This is no life!" His eyes swept around the room, taking in its whitewashed walls and their few possessions. "This is no life," he repeated, cradling his head on his arms on the table-top. "I accepted it because I *had* to, until I saw a chance to hope for better. There isn't enough money," he moaned. "I need another year!" His fists pounded the table. "I can't go back to the way we were."

She stepped back and regarded him sharply. "Is *that* what this is all about? Getting us out of here? Why didn't you say so? Maybe I can help you."

He raised his head. "How? I can't even sell the one-kopeck stinkers any more. Everybody is used to the real stuff."

"I know where there are three more plants. I planted them myself."

"Where? Why?" He sat upright, open mouthed, eyebrows raised.

Her voice was as if from one in a trance. "Don't ask me why. I didn't even remember until just now. When I planted your seeds, I kept three out and put them down in the woods. I don't know why. Something made me do it. . . ."

The devil's work, for sure. "Forget about why, my pet." He jumped up and embraced her. "It's too dark to look for them now. We'll check on your plants in the morning." *And deal with the devil when we have to.*

MBA, CPA, *writes about consumer economics and current affairs in a monthly column in the Greenbriar Voice, and in letters in the Longboat Observer and Sarasota Herald Tribune. An agent is peddling two novels and The Cigar Maker. He is president of the Sarasota Literary Society.*

LESTER AGELOFF

REPORT FROM THE FRONT

by Lester Ageloff

ATTENTION, INVESTORS! A VAST, untapped market awaits in Central Europe. Put in the simplest terms, their ladies like to let it all hang out. Our own society creates engineering miracles. America's superior anti-gravity devices support our women far better than their trans-Atlantic cousins. Yankee ingenuity to the forefront.

No such space-age falsities for those Germans, Austrians, and Hungarians. The current European style is loosely-fitting or over-sized sweaters and blouses. The visual effect of an approaching Mittel-European female resembles two kittens fighting under a blanket—or in some cases, cats. This tends to fascinate the male eye and may contribute to their high rate of urban auto accidents. *Watch the road, Wolfgang.* Continental feminine freedom knows no age limits. Ladies of every vintage promenade on the *strasse* displaying a variety of muscle-tones. A bra-using minority consists mainly of unfortunates to whom nature has been so parsimonious that they opt to disguise a planar landscape behind a false façade. (Note: this conjecture may require further research.)

Opportunities await the clever entrepreneur who could alter urban European scenery with a persuasive advertising campaign. One can imagine a TV as campaign: "Elevate your outlook;" "Stand out in a crowd;" "Give yourself a lift;" "It's what's up front that counts." Perhaps even a singing commercial: "Keep your sunny side up."

However, potential investors should be aware of the substantial risks involved. In developing this business, American engineering and marketing would threaten the most popular middle-European art form. Germanic womanhood may oppose a policy of containment, opting to cleave to their old habits and not relinquish their freedom of movement for any false front.

Your correspondent will continue to scrutinize this market closely to keep abreast of significant developments.

THE SEER

by Lester Ageloff

OTHER PRISONERS EYED JOSEPH curiously as he was thrust into their cage. Feigning nonchalance, he squatted with his back to the wall, spreading a greasy pack of cards on the ground.

After Reuben helped him escape from their other brothers, he had run away to find work on a distant plantation. Three days later, the boss' wife cornered him in the barn and tried to get into his pants. To be caught with a white woman was sure death. He pushed her away and ran. She followed, yelling, "Rape!"

The judge was sceptical, because Mrs. Potipher had a reputation in the parish. He gave Joseph sixty days for vagrancy until things cooled off.

"What you doin', black boy?" asked a menacing inmate.

"I tells fortunes," he replied.

The huge form kneeled beside him. "Yeah? Tell mine."

Joseph's reply was as much wish as prediction. "In three days, you's gone."

"Gone? How gone?"

Joseph drew his finger across his throat and assumed his fiercest expression. The hulk staggered back, shaken.

Other inmates crowded around. "Tell mine." "Tell mine."
Joseph drew on his instincts, freeing less-menacing ones, condemning the others. His guesses turned out sixty percent accurate.
He soon was regarded with awe.

The warden visited the cell. "Where's that nigra that tells fortunes?" All eyes indicated Joseph. "Come with me, boy." Outside, the warden asked, "Wanna join a carnival? Only, you dassn't come back." Startled, Joseph nodded wordlessly.

As Joseph boarded a battered truck, the warden pocketed fifty dollars. He laughed. "I got a feelin' that black con-man's gonna go far."

❦

YOU CAN'T GET TO HEAVEN WITH DIRTY FEET

by Ronald L. Anthony

H ER FRIZZY BLACK HAIR was unkempt and crawling with colonies of nits and lice. Her crooked teeth were badly decayed and her tiny ears were crinkled and crushed—most likely a genetic deformity after generations of tribal inbreeding. Ringworms had made silvery, circular encrustations on both of her cheeks, and her distended belly confirmed either malnutrition or a heavy worm infestation—probably a combination of both. She was suffering from what I labeled "PCOYSATULS," Persistent Clot of Yellow Snot above the Upper Lip Syndrome. The upper lip was a fashionable landing strip for hungry gnats and voracious flies. Except for a flimsy grass skirt wrapped around her scrawny waist and a string of discolored boar's teeth hanging from her neck, she was naked. But as was customary among the tribe, a generous coating of rancid pig fat shielded the exposed parts of her body from the cool mountain air. The smell was sickening—a blend of cat piss and sauerkraut. But her eyes, her big brown eyes encircled with the ocherous mud from the river, were beautiful. The moment she looked up at me, my heart was abducted. She was probably about ten years old and her name was Yikamugwe Kalakamabin.

164

Yika, as I soon came to know her, belonged to a primitive tribe that lived in a small valley in the interior of Irian Jaya, Indonesian New Guinea. When I first entered her village, I knew immediately that God had created this unspoiled place on a very special day for a very special people. The surrounding mountains were topped with glistening snow and the fertile valley was carpeted with the greenest leaves of the sweetest sweet potatoes, *boening*, that you could ever hope to taste. As the sun rose each morning, a heavenly rainbow appeared atop the limestone cliffs. A frothy river flowed through the arch and, after sending a spray several hundred feet into the sky, it began its final cascade to the valley floor. It only seemed right that He reserved this valley for the kindest, most considerate, sincere and caring individuals on earth, the Nduga Tribe. But then something extraordinary happened. God forgot about them.

During the centuries following His absence, Yika's ancestors came to embrace the ways of the Devil. Gods took the form of grotesque fetishes, and treachery and deceit were the most praiseworthy attributes in a tribesman. Warriors strove to establish feigned friendships with their enemies and, after fattening them up on wild boar meat and *boening*, they would put an arrow through their gullible enemy's heart and then feast upon the roasted human organs. Cannibalism and brutal wars between neighboring tribes were important cultural traditions that had to be preserved.

But by the early 1950's, God had seen enough and He returned. The first Christian missionaries found their way into the hidden valley, and the teachings of the Bible began. A church was built, schoolrooms were constructed and a medical clinic was established. Bows and arrows and religious idols were piled high and burned in glorious bonfires. There was much cause for celebration as love and honor displaced deceit and treachery.

I arrived in the valley about forty years later, not to spread the word of the Lord, but to stop the spread of malaria. On a beautiful Sunday morning, when the tribe's people were busy having their souls cleansed in church, I walked down to the river to cleanse my body. It was there on the river bank I saw her. Yika was sitting on a small rock, humming the catchy tune, "Do Lord, Oh Do Lord, Oh Do Remember Me," and she was splashing the cold water over her feet. She didn't hear me come up behind her.

I greeted her with the customary, "*Jepmum* . . . ."

Startled, she jumped up from her perch and said, "*Jepmum*, Doctor."

Staring at this pitiful little creature, I fought to hold back my tears. I couldn't help but wonder why God had now forgotten about this pathetic little girl.

Yika's future looked grim. In a few more years her family would trade her to a sinewy tribesman for a dozen piglets, six chickens and one or two bags of *boening*. Nine months later, she would be giving birth to her first baby. The delivery would be primitive, next to an open fire on the dirt floor of the family hut and, without help from a nurse or doctor, there was a good possibility that the baby would die. If so, Yika would bury it in a shallow grave down by the river, and she would be expected to mourn her loss for at least a few days. But before the end of a week, she would relent to her father's demands and offer her milk-filled breasts to the newborn piglets of a favorite family sow. Then Yika would go on to have another baby and another and another, every year until one or two of them did survive, and the misery and suffering of the tribe was preserved.

But God's messengers would tell us that they have given Yika something that her ancestors did not have—hope. She had hope of going to some wonderful place called The Kingdom of Heaven, a special place where her soul would be saved, and she would enjoy an everlasting life in peace and joy. But Yika knew that she had to be a good Christian to get into The Kingdom of Heaven. She had to work hard and, above all, she had to obey her parents. She had to learn to read the Bible. Yika had to be a good person and a good wife and a

loving mother. She had to go to church every Sunday—and sometimes on Wednesdays. It wasn't important that Yika would never
wear a fancy pink dress with a lace collar, and she would never own
a pair of shoes—not even a two-dollar pair of rubber sandals. She
would never go to a birthday party to play pin the tail on the
donkey, or to eat ice cream and cake. Yika would never shampoo her
hair or brush her teeth. But if she wanted to go to this place called
The Kingdom of Heaven, she must have faith and live every day by
the ways of the Lord. After all, he put her on this earth for a purpose
and she was His child.

Concerned that she might lose the blessings of both God and
the missionaries, I asked Yika why she was not in church with her
family. Wouldn't she be in trouble? God would be angry.

Flapping her long black eyelashes, she looked up at me and said,
"My mother told me that I couldn't go into the church because
my feet were dirty. Can't you see? I came down to the river to wash
my feet."

"You can't go to church with dirty feet?" I asked.

"No, you cannot," Yika said. As she started back up the path
leading towards the church, she stopped for a minute and turned
around. With a reprimanding glance down at my muddy rubber
sandals, she shook her index finger at me and said, "And don't you
know, Doctor, you can't get into heaven with dirty feet either."

After Yika was out of sight, I sat down on her rock and dipped
my tired feet into the cold water. I found myself humming, "Do
Lord, Oh Do Lord, Oh Do Remember Me." Looking up at the
morning sun in the heavenly blue sky, I wondered if Yika's law was
ever enforced. If it was, then heaven must be a pretty empty place.
But just to be sure, I scrubbed my feet and toes until they were
angelically clean.

THE HARRIED HOUSEWIFE GOES TO COLLEGE

by Pennee Atkinson

LAST WEEK I WENT to the community college in Ft. Myers to sign up for an English course. Since I was a college graduate and had been through the registration process many times, I drove to the school and walked confidently into the Palm Square Building where registrations were going on. I assumed that this would be particularly easy after they found out I already had a college degree. I was kind of a VIP, I thought. I got myself on a line, standing tall and just waiting to tell the registrar that I already had a college degree, and I was only looking to have some fun with this course I was about to take.

Soon, I was standing in front of this teenage-looking girl who was telling me that I had to fill out an admissions form before I could sign up for a class. What did they mean—"fill out an admissions form?" I was a college graduate! I should not have to fill out a silly admissions form. But, I decided not to press the issue, filled out the form and stood back in line.

Next, I was standing in front of a new teenage girl who had the nerve to tell me I didn't fill in all the parts of the form. "Well, of course I didn't fill every part of the form," I said. "What do you need all this information for? I am a college graduate! Why do you need to know where I went to high school? Okay, okay, I'll fill in the empty spaces."

Next, I was standing in front of my third teenage authority figure and he was telling me I couldn't take an English course without taking a preliminary course, or taking a test to see if I was qualified to take the English course. "But I am a college graduate!" I said, wide-eyed and aghast. "Then you'll have to show proof of your degree—a transcript or a copy of your diploma will do," he said with—I swear—a smirk on his face. "But that was sixteen years ago. I don't know where those things are now!" "You can have your college mail you a copy of your transcript," he said again with—I swear—a smirk on his face. "But school starts Monday and today is Friday." I said, becoming more agitated as each word came out of his "smirky" little mouth. My eyes stared at him. My palms sweated. My jaw jutted out. I was old enough to be this ratty kid's mother. I was being bossed around by a child!

"Well, then," said the snotty little brat that was probably living at home with his parents who had just bought him a new car. "You'll just have to take the proficiency test to see where we can place you." I wanted to grab him by his grubby little shirt collar and pull each and every tooth out of his pimply little head. But, instead, I said with bulging eyes and clenched jaw, "Where do I take it?"

Now we are at war, I was thinking as I moved deliberately and defiantly towards the testing center. Kind of like John Travolta in *Saturday Night Fever,* moving my shoulders to some beat that was pounding in my already-filled-with-128-credit-hours head. "This measly community college is gonna hear from me!"

"Where do I take the proficiency test?" I inquired loudly to the new and more arrogant looking teenager at the testing center.

A drop of spittle flew from my hardened mouth onto the formica counter that separated us. I let it sit there as in mock defiance of the entire college and its ridiculous protocol. My eyes stared into hers with a glassy determination. *Just give me one good look at this test. Just give me one good look,* I thought. "You'll have to wait your turn," she said, and turned to talk to the boy who was standing in front of the line I had just mistakenly broken into. "Oh, excuse me," I said, and turned military style on one heel and marched to the end of the line.

There I was, sitting at a computer, hopping from screen to screen reading instructions for this test. A strange anxiety started to settle in. *I must do well on this test,* I thought, *or every little pimply faced teenage squirt whom I faced today will laugh with abandon at the shoe sticking out of my mouth.* Thankfully, the person administering the test was a woman who was about my age. I was certain my score would be posted on the cafeteria wall for all to see, anyway.

Finally, the first question came up on the computer. It was a reading comprehension question. I studied it as if my entire life depended on finding the right answer. Every question thereafter I did the same. My brow furrowed and my eyes stared at the screen, afraid to blink or I would miss something. I was sure that I was at a disadvantage taking this test on a computer. I was used to interacting with my tests—feeling the test paper beneath my hands, holding my #2 pencil, brushing eraser debris from my lap. This computer was hindering my creative thought process, I was sure.

The test had no time limit. That was a relief. I noticed only slightly that some students had come and gone while I was there, determined to prove that I really did not need to be.

Finally, all the English questions were over and an algebra test popped up on the screen. I took this as a sign that my nightmare had finally ended. But when I told the woman I was finished, she told me I was not. I had to take the algebra test, too. *But I am only taking a writing course and that is only for fun, and I am already a college graduate, and this test is one big colossal mistake,* I thought.

"OK," I said in a wide-eyed stupor, feeling kind of like a Stepford wife. I was trapped in another dimension, alone with my fear of being found out that I had forgotten everything I had learned in the last forty years.

I sat down again. I was now experiencing fear in its finest and wildest form. I had not seen things like this: $(2X + 6Y)\ 3Y - 6X) = W$, in the past several hundred years. I didn't know they still existed. I thought that kind of stuff was abandoned with the onset of the electronic revolution. I thought that was why God made calculators.

I am going to die here, I thought. *Tomorrow they will find me dead with my eyes still open. I will not fall over because every muscle, every joint and tendon I own is stiff already. I will be buried with a mouse in my hand, sitting in a metal chair. And all those smirky, pimply-faced teenage brats who conspired this thing will come to my funeral and laugh and point their fingers at my poor dead body.*

OK, Pennee, get ahold of yourself, I commanded my tired brain. *I can and I will do this. I am a strong and capable woman. . . . I want my mommy!*

Time went by; pages and pages of scrap paper at my feet. I finally finished the last question. I walked out of the testing room.

I noticed that the sun had set. Everyone was gone except the woman who gave me the test. She had a look of relief and pity on her face. She invited me to come into her office. Because the test was done on the computer, the results were already in. I was given permission to take the English course. But if I ever wanted to take a math course, I would have to pass a remedial course first. I didn't care. At this point, if she told me I had to take kindergarten over again, I wouldn't have cared. All I knew was that I was alive and I had survived.

"Are you parked in parking lot B?" she asked with a genuine look of concern on her face. "Yes, I think so," I replied. We walked out together, in silence. No words needed to be said. She understood.

MAMIE'S TOMORROW

by Pat Bailey

*Y*OU'VE WON THIS ONE, *you mighty devil, you and your damnable friend, the wind. You've ripped out part of my soul, and you roll contentedly as if nothing's happened.* Mamie's thoughts scream in her head as she stands, arms akimbo, glaring at the sparkling ocean. "Look at what you've done! Don't you give a damn?" she suddenly rages aloud at the surf, shaking her clenched fists high above her head.

Tears salt her cheeks even as fragments of a favorite show tune from THE UNSINKABLE MOLLY BROWN begin to tinkle in her head. "Damn right, Molly! I ain't down yet!" She skips a step or two in time to the notes in her head. Small in stature she looks minuscule against sea and sky, standing alone in rolled up pants and her husband's old baggy sweat shirt, her gray hair tucked under her floppy straw hat.

Mamie closes her stinging eyes. "Thank you, God, I left when the evacuation order came. I almost didn't. Tom and I had battened down and weathered hurricanes before." She shakes her head and grins a twisted grin as she thinks about her final futile gesture before leaving—she had locked the door. She had had no idea the only way back to the island this morning would be by launch. The causeway is out. Remaining remnants of the road down the island are buried under sand.

She braces herself and swings around resolutely to face the devastation on shore. The magnificent primary dune she loved is gone, flattened to the smoothness of a road bed. All traces of her spacious wooden deck that had crowned the dune have been washed out to sea. So, too, the steps that had led down to the beach. Her little bit of heaven, the aging weathered cedar shake cottage nestled into the top of the second dune, is gone.

Only the ragged tops of rent pilings poking above the sand mark its site; the dune, resculpted into strange, unfamiliar forms of sand.

Mamie slips and slides as she clambers up the loosened, soft sand. From the top of the dune she spots part of her roof, blown three dunes away. Looking across the island she sees the corridor of complete destruction between the ocean and the sound. She frowns as she notes cottages on either side of the path damaged in varying degrees, but still standing. "That's it!" she exults. "It wasn't the hurricane. It was a tornado spawned by the hurricane." Her belief in the structure of her house reaffirmed, she feels vindicated. Looking skyward, she smiles and whispers, "Your house didn't fail, Tom. It was helpless."

"Why did the tornado choose that exact path?" Fleetingly, the thought, "Why ME?" crosses her mind. "Why not?" she shrugs." No favorites here."

She sand surfs down the other side of the strange new dune formation and begins to poke at random in the freshly rearranged, soggy sand. She spots a lamp base, but where is the shade? She pulls a soaked batik skirt out of the sand, wondering wryly, "Where is the closet where it hung?" There, half buried, is a bent, warped bamboo chair from the great room.

"Hello, sweet old friend." She digs it out with her hands.

Laboriously, she drags it up the back side of the dune and carefully positions it at the top. "Whew! I'm not as young as I used to be." Out of breath, she sits at the oblique angle necessary not to fall out of her newly found beat up treasure. "My throne," she chuckles. "Not too comfortable, but mine."

Once settled, Mamie gazes long and intently at the scene. She begins to feel her relationship to her surroundings resurging. "I BELONG HERE," she pronounces in CAPITALS.

Once, she and Tom had nurtured the storm ravaged dunes by stringing sand fences and planting sea oats and vines, layer by layer, as the dunes grew. They had protected and encouraged the twisted scrub that grew contorted in the face of the constant winds off the Atlantic. They were there when there wasn't another cottage in sight. They had warred with trespassers who thoughtlessly trampled the growth, pulling down the sand on the dunes and bending down the fences as they sought access to the beach. Mamie giggles as she remembers Tom's horrified reaction the day he came home and found her, rifle in hand, in a stand off with a group who refused to listen to her warnings. He thought her flair for the dramatic got a little out of hand that day.

"I've still got it in me. I can help these dunes recreate themselves. The wind, my angry foe last night, will be my ally. Once, Tom and I built a house. I can build another. Do I want it just like the other one?" She pauses a few seconds. "No. Hell, no." Picking up a shard of house timber she begins drawing in the sand. A new house plan begins to emerge. "I've changed. My life has changed. Change the house to fit. The kids'll still love to vacation here. If they don't— tough. It's my house." Yeah, the juices are beginning to flow.

"Wonder who'll scream the louder, me or the insurance agent? Wind damage first or water damage first? Who'll pay? God, what a fight this will be."

"When can I start building? When will the causeway be rebuilt?

Awfully expensive to haul materials in by boat. But, I want to get going." Now, she's pacing. "Whoops, better start walking back to the sound. The sun's dropping. Last boat to the mainland's leaving at 5:30." She bows to her throne, "You just sit right here, honey. You're my symbol that I'm here to stay. Nothing much here to salvage. It can wait until later. Mostly buried, anyway. Scavengers don't waste much time digging."

Mamie turns slowly in a circle, looking again at the sea, the sand, the sound, the sky. Today, so different to the eye. But, as always, nourishment to the soul. She blows a kiss, spreads her arms, embracing tomorrow.

ETERNALLY YOUNG

by Pat Bailey

WORLD WAR II. YOUR DRAFT NOTICE arrived. You accepted. You reported for duty.

One by one, Aunt Josie and Uncle Harry's three sons received their notices. The boys responded without question, even with excitement. Their parents "accepted." They mourned inwardly, but held the stiff upper lip. The times demanded stiff upper lips. One by one, they dutifully hung the three blue stars in the front window.

James Lyon, the oldest son, was known by both names, a common practice in the south for boys and girls. His small east Carolina home community smiled upon him with pride—a junior at N.C. State, an engineering major, engaged to his hometown childhood sweetheart. He was tall and muscular, with wavy dark brown hair and dark brown eyes that always seemed to be laughing. Oh, how he enjoyed teasing me, his young cousin.

Although he and Sara Marie, his fiancee, desperately wanted to marry before he left for service, they bowed to her family's wishes that they wait. Young girls of proper southern families listened to their parents in 1942.

James Lyon trained as a radio operator. He was assigned to bombers in the European theater. We didn't know exactly where. Bombers' names, like "Flying Fortress" and "Liberator," made my spine tingle, but gave my ten year old mind assurance that James Lyon would be safe. The names sounded solid, safe, impenetrable. I thought about Uncle Harry holding me spellbound with stories of unbelievable combat conditions he had survived in Europe in WWI. He'd had no Fortress or Liberator to protect him, and he came home.

The day of the second Ploesti oil field raid, a disastrous low-level bombing mission, James Lyon was not scheduled to fly. His plane was being repaired, having received extensive damage in a previous raid. One of the radio operators scheduled to fly was ill. James Lyon volunteered. One hundred and sixty-three bombers reached Ploesti. One hundred and nine returned. His plane was not solid, not safe, not impenetrable. Taking heavy enemy fire it exploded in midair. No survivors, no recoverable remains.

Aunt Josie called my family long distance. She sounded excited as she recounted the dream she had had the night before. James Lyon was home, standing in the bathroom shaving while she leaned against the doorjamb talking with him. The dream had been so vivid that she dared to hope it might mean he was coming home.

The official telegram read—"regret to inform you." The date of her dream and the date of his death were the same.

A memorial service. No grave. In the front window, a gold star replaced a blue one. My world was shaken. As an only child, close to my cousins, I had lost a "brother."

Everett, the second son, was a student at UNC when he was drafted. In my child's mind he was movie idol handsome, blonde, lean, and lithe. It was whispered that the hearts of many young women palpitated when in his presence. He became a Navy pilot. My, oh my, so glamorous in his dress whites.

What happened? Who knew for sure? A midair collision over San Diego Bay.

Both planes burst into flames. Official investigation concluded that the sun had blinded the approaching pilot. Everett had attempted evasive action, but had been unable to avoid the crash. Only a glove, his name stenciled on it, was found floating on the water's surface. No survivors, no recoverable remains.

Once again, Aunt Josie had a vivid dream. Everett was home, sitting in the kitchen talking with her, relishing a thick slice of his favorite chocolate cake, telling her, as he always did, that she made the best chocolate cake in the world. The next morning she called us. The dream had made her nervous.

Once again, the telegram read—"regret to inform you". Once again, the date of Aunt Josie's dream and the date of death coincided.

A memorial service. No grave. A second gold star replaced a blue. I was devastated. I couldn't reconcile what I knew with what should have been.

Robert Perry, the third son, another double named son of the south, was assigned to ground forces in the Pacific. He was an intense, mild mannered young man, just out of high school. He smiled a slow wide smile that always made me smile back just as broadly.

After the deaths of his two brothers, he became eligible for reassignment to the States, should his parents request it. He felt he should stay on assignment, but Aunt Josie and Uncle Harry signed the papers.

On a calm, sunny morning the plane returning him lifted off from Saipan. The takeoff was smooth. The plane cleared the island, climbed out over the Pacific, and leveled off for the flight home. Suddenly, explosion, fire, crash. Verdict: mechanical failure. No survivors, no recoverable remains.

Aunt Josie was visiting my family at the time. She awakened my parents in the middle of the night, tearfully, hysterically, begging my father to take her home immediately. She had to be with Uncle Harry. She knew a telegram was coming. She had dreamed Robert Perry was home, working in the rose garden with his father—a passion they shared—while she sat in the gazebo talking with them. It was too vivid, too familiar.

For the third time, a telegram she could recite by heart, terrible word by terrible word.

For the third time, a memorial service, no grave to be dug. Aunt Josie and Uncle Harry blamed themselves for their son's death. They never forgave themselves. I was eleven. I raged. I couldn't forgive the war.

In the window, three gold stars, empty tribute to the senseless deaths of three young men. In the cemetery, three memorial markers, mute testimony to three unfulfilled lives.

Aunt Josie and Uncle Harry used the proceeds from their sons' GI insurance to install a carillon in their church. It became a lasting tribute to their sons who would leave no living legacies.

Today, those bells still peal daily at noon, on Sunday mornings, and on special occasions. Recently, I've been privileged to hear their beautiful sounds again and to remember the young men I'd known as a child—James Lyon, Everett, Robert Perry.

I've visited their memorials and the graves of their parents. I no longer feel fury or disbelief, just residual grief.

Visiting with succeeding generations of relatives I asked if they knew how those bells came to peal. They had vague, sketchy impressions about happenings in World War II. To the young, those young men were unknown, fading images in old photos and entries in the family Bible we found in an attic. No one knew where any news clippings were. No one visited the cemetery. I told them the story.

One kid remarked, "So, they were cremated."

I wanted to hit him! "We don't know whether they were cremated or burned to death," I snapped. "There's a hell of a difference."

"Either way, they're history," he shrugged.

For a moment I was a child again, raging against something I couldn't understand and couldn't control.

Coincidences? Divine plan? Was God so cruel? Or, was he beneficent? Useless, unanswerable questions. Without question, one had to marvel at the uncanny bonds that had existed between mother and sons.

Suddenly, shock! Am I that old? Am I one of the last old enough to remember and appreciate the unbearable grief of those parents and the impact on those close to them? How can they not be known? Are they just history? Yes, but for me they will always be three strong, beautiful young men, my "brothers." Eternally young.

FRANKIE PLUTO AND THE SWEET MYSTERY OF LIFE

by Alan Berg

I HAD KNOWN MILCHMAN for a short time. He was struggling, as we all were then. The man was a gem, but very rough. His speech was Brooklyn, his writing barely expressive, and his spelling non-existent. Still, he was ethical and in his own way, compassionate. That's how we got involved in the maturity rite of Frankie Pluto.

At about eighteen, Frankie worked for Milch as a helper. He was learning the trade and showed promise as a mechanic. His boyhood and background was Pleasant Avenue Italian, although his hair was light and his eyes blue.

"Hey Frankie, how come a New York Wop Sicilian has light hair and blue eyes?"

"My old man told me that Sicily belonged to all kinds of people. So I guess some of them had light hair and blue eyes."

"C'mon Frankie, some Hun worked his looks in there along the way."

"What do I know? Who cares?"

Then he'd relax into a grin that seemed to show more teeth than Nature wanted anyone to have. Since his disposition was laid back

182

and his ears just a little long, he suggested a resemblance to the public's favorite cartoon pooch. And Frankie Pluto he became.

Frankie had a big problem. For an Italian kid to be eighteen and not to have known a girl the way he should have known her was to be ridiculed by his community. Even the Italian mamas gave him the fish-eye. "What'sa matter, Frankie, your papa no tell you about girls? Hey Frankie, how you gonna make her happy some day when you don't even know how to start?"

He didn't know how to answer. He didn't know how to tell them, "Loan me your daughter Clara, loan me your Lina, give me your Angelina for a little while. I heard they got a lot of practice and are anxious to teach." So he just took it in his good-natured way, feeling more miserable every day.

By the time it came out in the shop and Milch knew it, his couple of guys knew it, and even I knew, just calling on him to sell supplies, Pluto was a whipped kid. His body pressured him without mercy. His late teen-age society wouldn't let up on him. He was unable to get a girl to give him a push into manhood.

We realized that something had to be done. Milch and I could afford to be caring and sympathetic. Our young marriages were solid. Our emotional and physical needs were cared for. So, on to save the kid. But how to arrange it, and with whom? I was in the shop one afternoon when Milch blurts out, "Why not just get him a local broad? They wouldn't charge him and it would be a novelty to break in a white kid."

"Milch, are you nuts? They're dirty and they could have a disease. . . . We could get trouble from the neighborhood."

"Nah, why? How could the neighborhood not feel for a kid who can't scratch his itch? And I got a pill. I give it to Frankie before and he's covered—no clap, no syph. Besides, we ain't getting him a wife, just his first *shtup*. So he knows what to do with it and where it goes."

While we were kicking this around, I caught a look at Frankie.

It's obvious that black wasn't necessarily beautiful to him. When Milch mentioned pill so that he couldn't catch anything, Pluto's face was down to the floor. But need was overcoming prejudice. And then we asked, "How about it, Frankie? Should we fix it up?"

"You gotta. I gotta get started."

The bigger the city, the more small-town its enclaves. Just as Pleasant Avenue knew of Frankie's dreadful problem, so Milch's section of One-twenty-fifth Street knew of our intended solution. All, it seemed, had a comment. Local businessmen, the beat cops, the junkies, the residents—they all had an opinion on what we proposed. Nathaniel Double X, the local militant, told us that it would be fine justice. The idea of a blue-eyed white devil facing his indoctrination to life's great mystery at the whim of a black sister filled him with hope that the devil might, with Allah's help, contract a serious disease.

"Thanks, Double X, but he'll have penicillin first."

"Then Allah will find another way to punish him. . . . I say do this, do it."

"Appreciate your input, Double X."

The store-front lawyers came by. They were brothers, and a pole apart on most everything. "This is a disgrace," said Teddy Schwartz, "to hold a white kid up to ridicule by the black people."

"But Teddy, his own people are ragging him something awful right now."

"Of course'" said Irv Schwartz. "A woman is a woman. In Frankie's condition, anything goes."

"Thanks, boys. Sure appreciate your interest."

Richy McLarin said he talked it over with some of the boys at the precinct. "I was surprised. Some were for it, some against. But when I asked who had experience with the local girls, nobody would own up. And I know some of them would screw any broad in the area who would hold still."

"Well, thank the boys for their interest. We'll let them know how it turns out."

"No need. We'll know it all."

While we theorists were debating, it remained for Roosevelt Jackson to put the situation into cold perspective. Roosevelt worked with Frankie and had two common-law wives as well as a couple of girl friends. "If'n you don't help that poor boy, he's gonna hurt hisself beatin' on it. Lemme ask Miss Lucinda Williams if she'll loan herself to Frankie. She ain't no pro, but she sure can do what people is made for."

It seemed that she would do it. Roosevelt brought her by the shop to get the protagonists introduced. So here's Pluto, light, white and Italian, giving his shy and toothy grin to a young woman who looked every inch the Central African belle—protruding behind, small belly, erect carriage. Now there remained only where and when.

The "where" was easy. Milch's shop had a basement with a light. We could put a table down there and find a pillow and blanket for cushioning. The "when" was not so easy. Unless we kept it real hush, the neighborhood would want to buy tickets, and we couldn't have a mob scene.

We kept it so hush the locals knew almost before the promoters knew. On the morning, a small crowd had gathered before Milch opened the shop. When Frankie showed up, there was a small smattering of polite applause, as you'd give a challenger stepping into the ring. Right after, Roosevelt Jackson brought Miss Lucinda Williams to the shop. She was the hometown favorite. The crowd roared approval.

"Do him good, Lucinda honey."

"Show him who really into this thing, darlin'."

"Make him see stars, baby."

Milch stood there presenting the pill with as much pride as any best man offering up the ring. We all went outside and waited. It didn't take long. Miss Lucinda came out of the shop. She was laughing. Frankie came out grinning even more teeth than the too many he had grinned before.

"O.K., Frankie," said Milch. "Now that you know this job has benefits, let's get back to work."

Born and raised in New York City. Went to school and college there. I was in business there forty years, and had some funny and sad experiences. That's what I write about.

ALAN BERG

A GIRL'S BEST FRIEND

by Nadja Bernitt

ARLY AFTERNOON SUNLIGHT BEAMED into the Van Leuten's Victorian parlor, a powerful light that warmed Mimi Van Leuten's wrinkled left hand and glanced off her hefty diamond. Mimi took it as a sign and shifted her gaze across the room, first to her handsomely square son with his unfortunate vacant stare, then to his gum-chewing fiancée.

"Come here, Veronica." Mimi patted the chair next to her own with one hand, while her other hand stroked her cat's marmalade fur. Once the young woman had settled her pudgy bottom into the chair, Mimi boldly flashed her five carat solitaire. "My husband, James, rest his soul, walked on his knees the night he gave me this ring."

Veronica arched a thin-plucked eyebrow, hovering over the brilliant rock.

Mimi leaned closer. "When I die, this is yours."

Veronica nearly swallowed her gum, but managed to recover her cool. "Hey, is it true what they say, Diamonds are a girl's best friend?"

"Aren't you the clever one, Veronica. Do you know the movie?"

Peripheral vision caught Mimi's son's discomfort. His mouth twisted first in one direction, then the other, as he struggled for something to say. Finally, Leonardo offered, "Mother watches old movies."

Everyone knew this, certainly Veronica. "I can't get into black and white," she said, "unless it's Lenny in his Tuxedo."

Mimi relished the innuendo but winced at the mutilation of her son's name. Maintaining her placid demeanor, she confided, "All I want is my Leonardo settled and happy before I. . . " Her sentence dangled, and she lowered her eyes for effect.

"Don't talk about dying, Mrs. Van Leuten. You're gonna live forever." Veronica's gum-chewing slowed, and she eyed her betrothed. "Won't she, Lenny?"

Like a stop-action flash, Mimi pictured stocky, square Veronica dancing on her grave, then blinked it away. "Pour me another tea, darling, would you? And tell me your honeymoon plans."

Veronica's smile widened, exposing piano-white teeth. She poured the tea, then returned to Leonardo's side. From her purse, she pulled a crisp printed sheet, offering it to Mimi. "Here's the itinerary. Damn well took me a week to put it together. But, then, my modem is sooo slow." Veronica winked at him, as if he understood.

Holding her hand in his own square paw, he said, "I love the way you take charge."

"James, too, loved a woman who knew her mind." Mimi sighed. "Having a man is everything, Veronica. Life loses all meaning without one." This time her eyes lowered with true passion. James Cagney, the cat, leapt to the floor, swishing his orange tail as though sick of the swill-like patter.

More of it filled the afternoon with talk of the honeymoon cruise through the Greek Islands. Mimi drifted into memories of her own nuptials and Aegean trip, she and James running like mountain goats up serpentine hills, past windmills and whitewashed houses—James with his wild, dark hair. "Zorba," she had called him. Darling Leonardo, how like his father in appearance and manner, doting on his mother and now on Veronica as well.

The sun fell lower and Veronica coaxed Leonardo into taking her home. When the front door closed, Mimi rose, moving to the window for a view of the couple, strolling to Leonardo's BMW, a metallic patch of blue. Veronica held his gaze, beguiling him, Mimi supposed. It was so easy to do. Leonardo pointed to the broad expanse of lawn sweeping down to the water. Recently, he had talked about expanding Wuthering Tides, as they called the estate. Mimi, as always, guided her son, encouraging him to build west away from her private garden. She enthusiastically embraced his creativity; after all, she had projects of her own.

Mimi settled herself in the media room, listening to the house creak with quiet. It always did on the nights the servants were off. The deep walnut shelves shone from polishing, a task she supervised carefully, and though a large room, it offered a womb-like comfort. She sighed, snuggling back into her down-filled chair and darkened the room with her rheostat. She channel surfed on her theater-sized television, delighted to chance upon *Casablanca*. Lost in the drama, time flew, and soon Claude Raines and Humphrey Bogart strolled off into the mist arm-in-arm, the unlikely couple, claiming the start of a beautiful friendship. It captured her fancy and when it ended, she found a copy in her video library and watched it again. Repetition pleased Mimi, for she firmly believed practice makes perfect. Midway through the video, she heard Leonardo shuffling down the hall and switched off the set. She raised the lights and beckoned him to her.

Sitting across from her in the velvet plush winged-back chair, her son crossed his legs. "Why do you do that, Mother, promise your ring when you die?" He appeared truly troubled. "Veronica is worried. Anyway, you're healthy as a horse."

"I am. Are you disappointed, darling, secretly wishing to have

Wuthering Tides all to yourself?" Prior to James death, she had just those wishes and Leonardo was, after all, her son, too.

"Mother, how could you? I... I adore you." He moved to her side, bent down on his knee, "But as long as you've brought it up, living here is not going to work. Veronica wants a place of her own. Her parents don't have much, you know. . ."

Not only did Mimi know, she encouraged Leonardo to seek young women from lesser backgrounds for several reasons. One, they lit up like neon at sight of the mansion. Two, they groveled at Leonardo's every halting word, kept him home and entertained. And three, they jumped at her ring like fish to bait.

Leonardo struggled to deal with the financial difficulties of living on his own, spouting financial catch phrases, "The bottom line is. . . consolidating debt. . . with my annuity and the ten acres Dad left me, maybe. . ."

Rearing children was no easy task. "We'll work it out, Leonardo."

"Leonardo? I hate this Leonardo business. My name is Leonard."

"Leonard, Lenny, it's all so ordinary. After all, names project destiny, dear." She searched her son's boyish face. "You love this Veronica, don't you?"

"With all my heart. I know this is hard for you, Mother, but I need someone."

Mimi squeezed his hand. "Your happiness means everything to me."

Pale eyes misting, Leonardo nodded. "After Rebecca, I thought my life was over."

Mimi recalled the greedy woman and her slobbery, oafish ways. "I know, darling, but you see, it wasn't. Just look at you now."

A resilient boy, Leonardo came close to beaming and excused himself, "I'm having a time, deciding what to take on our cruise." He kissed her cheek and left.

Mimi felt restless and wandered out into the grounds of their estate. Due to James' losses in the stock market, the original five hundred and twenty-nine acres had dwindled to seventeen. But iron-fisted Mimi had managed to save the reflecting pool, the stand of old pines, the formal memorial garden, and the smaller garden where she now strolled. Flowers reflected an eerie glow in the light from the golden moon. Mimi touched their soft leaves as she glanced about, admiring her handiwork, her fascinating landscaping achievements—projects which she planned to formally name one day.

The brook was last year's addition and included a collection of massive rocks, guiding a bubbling rush of water. How it sparkled on sunny days.

Mimi sighed and turned her gaze to her newest project, the lake. A simple plan, really, with its turquoise Fiberglas shell to reflect the bluest skies. Presently, soft earth stood in piles beside a deep boxy crevice around the pre-formed lake, waiting for fill. As instructed, the gardener had left the shovel and Mimi used it to test the soil. Ah, the good earth, the dank smells of early evening, a scent filled with expectation—yet a chill crept down her spine. She glanced over her shoulder, shivered, then proceeded to the memorial garden.

No longer golden, the moonlight slanted through the open branches of a live oak, casting silver rays on the crypt. Mimi settled on the stone bench across from the marble edifice and brooded over her late husband.

"Oh, James," she called out. "Words, wit, and movies may entertain me, but I'm mad that you died." Her eyes misted for a moment and she softened her tone. "I don't know what I would do without slow, devoted Leonardo. He is so like you, darling. And it will always be just the two of us here at Wuthering Tides."

She stood, smoothing her skirt and Veronica came to mind. Certainly, it was time to call. Mimi delved into her pocket for her cellular phone and speed dialed.

The young woman answered. "Yeah?"

Mimi gushed, "Veronica. All evening I've been thinking about your wedding. You see, dear, I noticed how you admired my ring and thought it would look lovely on your young smooth hands. Why wait? Won't you wear it as your engagement ring?"

Mimi heard Veronica's gum pop, a breathless pause, then, "Hell, yes. Sorry, Mrs. Van Leuten, but wow! I'll knock 'em dead."

"Yes, you will, dear."

"God, when can I have it?"

"What about tonight?"

The following week found Leonardo frantic—Veronica had vanished, leaving no trace. Melancholy flooded Leonardo's body like a virus, and Mimi consoled him. "The sun also rises," she encouraged, brewing teas from herbs grown in her flourishing garden. Still Leonardo's psyche slid into despair.

Mimi restructured the honeymoon trip as a mother-son sojourn. Her concern, like salve, soothed his tender spirit. Miraculously, Leonardo brightened, trekking up the Greek mountain side to Delphi. Mimi posed at the oracle's temple, predicting good times ahead. An impressionable child, he soon doted on her as before. They played hide and seek in the Minoan labyrinth on Crete, reveled in the sea and sun.

Upon their arrival home, he began work on Wuthering Tide's west wing. A month later, Holly Gibbons entered their lives, the junior partner in the architectural firm they employed. A bright working woman, blonde and Viking-strong, Holly stood apart from the previous women in her son's life. Leonardo hung around the project day after day and romance blossomed between him and Holly. Mimi encouraged the year-long affair, delighted to see him once again content, but her exuberance faded when Leonardo purchased a ring. What could she do?

Mimi bolstered her spirits and took control. She requested he announce the engagement in the breakfast alcove, viewing the grounds through leaded glass. "It's breakfast through Tiffanies," Mimi mused. "How apt." Prisms of colored light spotted the room and gaiety filled the air—another honeymoon afoot.

Leonardo assured, "We'll tour classical Greece."

Mimi nodded approvingly, as always, and tickled Cagney's neck. The vibration of his purr heightened the sizzle inside her. She said, "I like your name, Holly. It's so . . . so botanical."

Holly crossed her long legs, her icy blue eyes sharply focused. "Interesting you say that; I garden too. I find it both an agony and an ecstasy."

Charleton Heston flashed before Mimi's eyes and she viewed Holly in a different light, perhaps more clever than Veronica.

Holly sipped her tea, her pinkie finger pole-straight. "Leonardo approved my design for an arboretum. The footings are dug. Nothing else. Of course, we'd want your approval."

"An arboretum, how lovely." But Mimi shifted uneasily in her chair. Even Cagney tensed until the Titanic moment sailed by. "Every now and again, I do something whimsical in *my* garden." Cold steel edged the lilt in her voice. "Perhaps I'll do something with holly." Tilting her head, she imagined a botanical plaque: Holly Goes Lightly. It came as easily as the others had, Rebecca's Sunny Brook, and, of course, last year's Veronica's Lake. Mimi adjusted her diamond, subtly mentioning, "It falls from the weight."

Outspoken Holly didn't beat about the bush. "I covet your ring."

Despite Leonardo's slowness, Mimi noted his apprehension.

Morning sunlight creamed the room pale yellow as Mimi lifted her hand, creating still another set of prisms with her gem. Her familiar phrase popped out, "It's yours when I die."

A smile flickered across Holly's lips. She said, "Really?"

Holds a master's degree in creative writing from the State University of New York and has a passion for mysteries. Several of her short stories have won in competitions held by Writer's Digest *and* Mystery Writers of America. *Her current full-length mystery takes place in Sarasota.*

NADJA BERNITT

MANIC

(EXCERPT FROM THE NOVEL)

by Bill Carrigan

A COUPLE OF HOURS after meeting in the Blue Marlin Bar, we were strolling along the Tampa Bay waterfront toward our cars, about to go our separate ways. Two guys unknowingly headed for the same hell.

It was around nine and just getting dark. Despite a light breeze, the passersby were sweaty from the long June day. Some had paused at a chain-link fence to watch a freighter dock against the sunset, now a crimson streak. The relentless traffic had briefly ceased, arrested by a distant red light. Alcohol-happy and with nowhere to go, I was attracted by the freighter and started to cross the street.

Suddenly there was chaos. Sounds of rapid gunfire seemed to come from all directions. The only available shelter was a doorway. A second later I backed against the doorjamb, stretching to make myself as thin as possible.

People were yelling, screaming, running. Several threw themselves to the ground; others crouched behind parked cars. A few feet from me, a man spun around and sprawled on the sidewalk. A woman knelt at the curb clutching her head, watching her blood spatter the pavement.

A red Blazer passed and I saw a man shooting from the right front window. His face was obscured by a red bandanna and the stock of the submachine gun. The fire came in bursts, an almost random spray. Then I was thrown against the door by a violent blow to my shoulder. The beers I had drunk did nothing to dull the pain.

Sinking against the door, I saw the Blazer turn a corner in the path of an oncoming truck. Screeching brakes failed to avert the collision. Then, through mounting agony, I watched my barstool acquaintance run toward the stalled car. What was that crazy fool—? Now I saw him try to wrest the gun from the stunned killer. He was twisting the barrel to free the clip from the window frame. But the automatic weapon fired and he doubled up and fell. It was all played in slow motion under the headlights of the semi.

The Blazer backed up, wildly reversed direction, and sped away. There was another, distant burst of gunfire. In its wake the screams around me turned to groans, the frantic activity to stunned immobility. The wantonness of the drive-by shooting lent to the shock of injury and death.

I tried to rise but fell back against the door, swept by a wave of pain and nausea. Blackness shut down an image of my foolhardy companion, still on his feet, staggering as the truckers approached him. . .

He had introduced himself as Bruce Mann. Firefighter, paramedic. He had talked a lot about the rescue squad he headed and the ambulance they had just bought. It could have been the one that took us to the hospital; I can't say. I was later told I fainted from stress and loss of blood.

※　※　※

Three days after the shooting, Bruce and I shared a room near a nursing station and were able to trade impressions of the incident. We didn't talk much, though. Bullets at close range had torn up Bruce's liver, and a long incision had been made to stop internal bleeding. I was in a cast that encased my shoulders. We had been moved from Surgery to Med-Surg and were still connected to monitors and bottles. As our drugs wore off, pain came on big-time. In view of Bruce's stoicism, I had to quell my craven impulse to beg for analgesics.

The local TV channels aired the shooting repeatedly. Unfortunately, there were no pictures of Bruce's bold attempt to seize the weapon in case the killer revived. He smiled at my disappointment. If the act had been mine, I'm sure I would have bragged a little. Not Bruce Mann. He was one of those types who scale burning buildings to rescue stranded fat ladies, and plunge into frozen rivers after kids. He took his courage for granted. Act first and *don't* think about it later.

We were mentioned by name in an evening newscast. Our injuries, though, were overshadowed by the eight deaths. Among the victims was José Castillo, a popular state senator. To account for his presence on the waterfront at night, relatives said he was coming to visit. A newspaper editorial, however, said he may have been meeting with members of Tampa's growing colony of ex-Cubans, his principal supporters. His grieving widow praised him as a family man and a patriot.

Bruce had a sister who visited him daily, usually with their mother. They often included me in their conversation. The sister was taking care of Bruce's German shepherd, Hogan, named after a childhood hero. In a brief exchange, she told me their father, a policeman, had been killed in the line of duty. The mother, stolid, taciturn, didn't react to the sister's distress at the similarity of misfortunes.

Among Bruce's many visitors—relatives, friends, and even strangers who viewed him as a hero—were two firefighters and a woman they called George. By dress and conversation, I gathered that their lives revolved around motorcycles. The two men stood against a wall and George drew up a chair. Since I wasn't introduced, I didn't pay much attention until I heard one of the men ask Bruce, "Can you describe this cowboy with the happy trigger finger?"

"Not so you could spot him," Bruce replied. "But I'll sure know him if I ever see him again."

The other man said, "If we can find out who he is, we'll get him for you. I'll push his face into a bike wheel—spinning."

The woman said, "Shut up, you guys. I'm sure Bruce has had enough violence for a while." Though not unattractive, she was brawny and her features were coarse. I thought of other female Georges—George Sand, George Eliot—who had taken men's roles. "Let's talk about the celebration we're going to have when Bruce gets out of here." Looking across at me, she said, "And you're included."

I was a little surprised. Women seldom notice me. My occasional success must be due, I think, to the maternal instinct, which I had done nothing on this occasion to arouse.

As they were leaving, she asked Bruce if there was anything they could do.

"Yes," he said. "Keep your ears open and spread the word. Let me know if you hear anyone bragging about a drive-by shooting. Then I want to get a look at him, and I'll let you know if he's the one."

"We'll help you find him," said George, squeezing his hand. "Bikers stand by their friends." I was amused when she blew me a kiss on the way out.

Later Bruce said he was hardly a biker, but often drove an old Suzuki with Hogan in a sidecar. He had nothing to add about George except that she was "one tough gal."

During those first days, Bruce and I learned about each other. We were both in our mid-twenties and unattached. Both had dropped out of college. Bruce's reason was financial, mine personal. My father had persuaded me to study administration, and I just couldn't picture myself administering anything. Someday I may enroll again and take subjects I enjoy—say, journalism or film-making. Meanwhile, like Bruce, I was doing all right on what little I knew.

My father flew down from Washington, D.C., bringing me a box of chocolates (for the nurses) and a paperback novel. I recounted my experience, and he told me things he thought I should know about the office. He had to return the next day to his real estate practice. (Actually *our* practice, since I'm now a junior partner.) I was surprised and grateful that he had been able to give me that much of his time.

My father and I have lived together and grown closer since my parents' divorce. My younger sister, Jean, lives with our mother and stepfather. To my regret, Jean and I seem to be drifting apart through our divided loyalties. She did call once and we chatted briefly. With all this time on my hands, I planned to write her a long letter.

Another visitor was a detective from the Tampa police force. Ulysses S. Scott was big, black and angry. He hated senseless killings. And he had liked Castillo, whose mission in life was to spark a reinvasion of Cuba. This, said Scott, would be a boon to Florida if it got rid of some of the Cubans. He asked if I was up to answering a few questions. Since Bruce was asleep, he would interrogate him later.

He placed a small recorder at the foot of my bed. No, I didn't mind if he taped our conversation. With the tape running, he grunted a few words of introduction. Then he said to me, "I want to know exactly what you saw on the night of June six, O.K.?"

"O.K."

"First, your full name, please." The light jacket he wore over a

T-shirt bulged persuasively. I sensed that he would continue to be civil if I cooperated.

"Rodney Cooper Kent. Call me Rod."

"Residence?"

"Cabin John, Maryland. It's just outside the District. Until I got shot, I was staying at the Wild Palms Motel on Shore Boulevard. But my father may have checked me out. . ."

"And you're visiting our fair state because you like our summers."

"Yeah, right," I said. "No, I do real estate for my father, based in D.C. I'm trying to buy a certain house for an old retailer who wants to retire and go fishing."

"I could use a little of that myself. Where is this house?"

"On the Hillsborough, where it runs east to west."

"All right! Now, when did the shooting occur and what were you doing?"

"I'd say about nine. I had just left a bar with that guy there— Bruce Mann. We'd both had a few beers. Maybe that's why he did that crazy thing . . ."

"Crazy? Like what?"

I described the collision, Bruce's deed, and the rest, up to my collapse in the doorway. Scott asked what the motherfuckers were driving.

"A red Blazer with a Florida tag. Not new, but I couldn't say what year."

"Maybe rented. That might give me a place to start. Did you catch the license number, or any part of it?"

"No. It was too far away."

"Then I don't suppose you got a look at them?"

"No—but Bruce did. They were right in the lights of the truck when he went for the gun."

Scott looked thoughtful. "And you figure he did that to prevent further killing?"

"That's right. He says he would have grabbed the shooter—if he hadn't come to and plugged him."

Inspector Scott shook his head and, with a look at Bruce, asked, "How's he doing?" I thought I heard a note of genuine compassion.

"I don't know. He doesn't eat much and he sleeps a lot."

Scott turned off the recorder. "O.K., Kent. Thanks. I'll be back tonight with mug shots. This is one drive-by they're not getting away with."

And a senator's slaying, I thought, would spark action, even if Castillo did sound like a troublemaker. The crime, I saw as vandalism at its worst. Though soft on capital punishment, I was all for the state's best shot in this case: the chair. Also, I had a good impression of Inspector Scott. I would gladly cooperate to the best of my ability.

*   *   *

Admittedly, I had an ulterior motive. I would need help from the police in writing a magazine article I had in mind. I had already sold a few—two, to be honest about it. But I saw a door opening. I hoped to move gradually out of real estate as my writing paid off. That would inconvenience my father, whose small Georgetown agency, *Hill and Crowley, Realtors,* had been in the family since my grandfather's time. Still, I believed he'd be pleased if I could make it as a writer.

My idea for the article had occurred in the following way.

The day I arrived in Tampa, I drove out to the house. It came into full view from a shell driveway curving through Florida oak. It was small and old, but I could see why our Mr. Plotz liked it. The roof was tile, the exterior masonry, the interior largely cypress. There was a fireplace and a fairly new kitchen. Beyond the house itself, the attractions were a secluded cove, a dock, and mangrove along the opposite bank. I watched a roving pelican suddenly fold its wings and power-dive. The site was ideal for a fisherman in his golden years.

The only problem was Mrs. Whitfield. Though the house was vacant, the dear old lady, owner of several properties, was reluctant to part with it. Seems she had lived there with her first husband and was sentimentally attached. Our offer was generous, but she couldn't decide. While she thought it over, I returned to the site one evening to take pictures for our office album. She had lent me the key, which I saw as encouraging.

I parked my rented Honda Civic and shot six or seven views inside the house and out. No dogs barked, no nosy neighbors appeared from the houses dimly seen through trees and bamboo. Boats passed with no wake, as required by law. If Mr. Plotz wanted tranquillity, he had sure picked the right spot.

There was an old net hammock on the screened porch—just the place to drink a beer and enjoy the sunset. I gingerly deployed my lank frame among the fragile cords and popped a can. The cool beer, the shade of the porch and yard, an occasional breeze, made the heat bearable. Swinging gently, I gazed at the shimmering reflections on the wall and ceiling.

The owner's indecision was my excuse to linger in Florida. But I mustn't let our client slip off the hook. Should I contrive to have Mrs. Whitfield meet Mr. Plotz . . . ?

I was awakened from a nap by voices at the dock. It was still light enough to see men dropping from a cabin boat. Was it something they said or the vestige of a dream that told me they were smugglers, drug runners from Mexico or Central America? They had found a good place to land, one they may have used before. Would they enter the house? Holding my breath, I watched them pass, silent, purposeful.

I pictured their long run from Maracaibo, Veracruz or some other exotic port, the panels crammed with cocaine. They had dodged the

Coast Guard as they crossed the Gulf and slipped into Tampa Bay. They were armed against highjackers . . .

Then I saw that they carried—fishing rods! The illusion crumbled. Presently they returned to the boat with women, and I heard the motor start. Soon all was quiet again. Only echoes of my rampant imagination.

But it was then that I thought of doing an article on the drug traffic: how drugs are smuggled into the country and how they spread. The epidemiology of the trade. First I would sketch a typical import—the arrival, the initial sale. Then, passage to the cities, distribution among pushers . . . Research in police stations would be a start. More specifically, I'd begin with Ulysses S. Scott and the Tampa scene.

LIGHT'S DECEPTION

by Nico' Delonn

MEAN IS REALLY THE only word to describe Willie Johnson. My grandmother Ruby always said that high yellow people were the *nastiest* people and Willie Johnson is living proof of that! She also said that she thinks somebody must have messed with him when he was little. That's the only way to account for such meanness in a person. Can't love. Doesn't know how to. He was crazy too, just like his mother. Her name was Jacquelyn. but everyone called her Dirty Red. She used to laugh all the time but that was only because she had been cursed on when she was a teenager. Grandmother Ruby and Dirty Red both grew up in Washington Park. The neighborhood of Washington Park was named after a man named Riley Washington.

Riley Washington was the first black to come to Washington Park and build a house. Others soon left the farm life in nearby Ellenton and arrived in Washington Park to do the same. Riley Washington encouraged this exodus and was very instrumental in helping the others to become established in their new community. As a result of the community's gratitude, the neighborhood was affectionately named in his honor. Grandma Ruby went on to tell me just how Dirty Red got herself marked for life. "When we were teenagers,

Dirty Red had a silly habit of laughing at old people. She poked fun at them over the smallest things. One day while in Mr. C's Grocery Store, Dirty Red was standing in line behind Miss Irene. Miss Irene was an old lady who sold Juleps, which were frozen juice cups, in our neighborhood. Everyone that knew her knew that she would have an occasional bout with arthritis where her joints would just freeze up. She would hurt so badly that she would not be able to move. When a bunch of us, including Dirty Red, would be hanging out, we would go to buy Juleps at Miss Irene's house. Because of her condition, she would instruct us to just put our coins in a silver tin cup and pick our own Juleps out of the freezer. She repeatedly warned us not to try to steal from her or she would curse us and mark us for life.

This would frighten all of us except Dirty Red. She would just burst out laughing, "Curse us wid what, old lady, who you think you is . . . a witch?" Nevertheless, Dirty Red never stole anything from Miss Irene. She may have been a clown, but she wasn't a crook.

While standing in line at the checkout counter, Miss Irene began to have problems with her hands. She was having a hard time handling the money from her purse and had dropped her purse and personals all over the counter. "My God, old lady! You holding up the line! Why don't you just take your behind down to the old folks' home and stay out of people's way!" Dirty Red began to laugh hysterically over Miss Irene's confusion. Bystanders shunned Dirty Red for disrespecting Miss Irene and began to help Miss Irene with her things. Miss Irene turned slowly towards Dirty Red, pointing her trembling finger. In a small voice she said to Dirty Red; "You gone learn someday not to use the Lord's name in vain and since you love to laugh so much, laughing is going to be your mark for the rest of your life!"

So why would a person like Willie choose to marry? Grandma Ruby said that people like Willie likes to find ways and means to hate. Marriage is just another strategy to achieve just that. But in Willie's guise, who would not want to marry him? He was a seemingly stable man, who had never been married before and did not have any children. He had worked for 15 years with the Singletary Railroad Company and owned his own home. In 1973 Palmetto, Florida, he was a reasonable catch.

My mother, Helene, was one who could not resist this type of stability. She was once again back at Grandma Ruby's house. I was two years old at that time and Mama was pregnant again with my sister, Olivia.

Being the oldest of ten children, Mama had been in a hurry to leave home the first time to escape the tremendous responsibility of co-mothering. So at the immature age of nineteen years old, she entrusted her love and her life to a man fifteen years older than she was.

Bobby Wilcox, my father, was from Gifford, Florida. Mama did not know anything about Gifford, but because it was out of town, she believed that it must have been a bigger world than her own.

Mama told me that my daddy was a beautiful man. He was tall, slim, and fair. He wore his hair in thick, curly locks. His eyes were deceptively swooning, which made him irresistible. So Mama had to have him and said that on the day they married, she felt a calm light that clothed her body and put her in a place where things seemed more beautiful and clearer. She was about to take on the world as a woman. She would have the storybook romance that she loved to read and write about.

At a small boarding house right off of 17th Street in Palmetto that my Mama had gotten for her and Bobby, she spent much of her time alone. Bobby spent most of his time running around with other women and gambling. Mama was two months pregnant and had to go on welfare. When she would see Bobby in public, she would argue with him and threaten to leave him if he did not come home. This would always result in Mama being publicly humiliated and beaten; however, Bobby would eventually come home.

Bobby had become a disappointing and trifling man. He absolutely detested belonging to someone else. He completely dismissed the responsibility of it all. Bobby's all night to week long sexual rendezvous, his public humiliations, and beatings of my mama continued to go on until she finally realized that when she argued with him and he would beat her, he beat her *because* she would not leave. Full of shame and run down, Mama went back home to Grandma Ruby and Bobby left Palmetto and took up with a white woman down in Ft. Lauderdale. I don't remember him and Mama never saw him again.

When my mama met Willie she was seven months pregnant by my daddy with Olivia. Mama and Willie married soon after Olivia was born. So I guess he felt like he was *her* real daddy just because he was there from almost the very beginning. I had heard stories about when Olivia was born, Willie played the proud father by going out to the hospital taking pictures and making a big fuss over Olivia. At times, I felt sad and maybe a little jealous because there were no stories told about me. As Olivia and I got older, I frequently and secretly reminded her that Willie was not our real daddy.

We had been living for about five years in Willie's house that was across the bridge over into East Bradenton. On the street that we lived on, there were many children to play with. They all had a mama and a daddy living with them. Despite our situation, I was happy to fit in, at least on that level.

The house that we lived in never felt like my home. I remember that the air in the house appeared to have a thickness about it. It was void of the brightness that seemed to light up the homes of the people I had seen on television. The walls of the house had a faint gray color. The carpet was brown and matted. There was no comfort in the tan plaid furniture that we sat on. It was as if it detested its own existence in the house.

I used to plead with Mama for us all to go back to Grandma Ruby's house but she would always tell me to hush and stay in a child's place. That would always make me mad because I knew that she wasn't happy living in the house with Willie either. How could she be? He was drunk all the time and he beat her. Although I felt bad for Mama, I felt ashamed because all of the neighbors knew about it.

During one of the beatings, Olivia and I were outside playing. When grown-ups walked past our house, they would just turn and look the other way. The children in the street would point their fingers and giggle. Olivia and I would stop in the middle of our game playing and just wait. I remember waiting and hoping to become invisible, praying that the air around me would just squeeze me out of existence.

On Saturday mornings, I dreaded the ritual of Mama taking the braids out of Olivia's and my hair. After she shampooed our hair, she would go about the business of cleaning the house and assigning us specific chores. Between the laundry, cooking, and cleaning, our hair would have dried into tangled and matted knots before mama was able to get back to it. Olivia and I had to take turns lying across mama's lap and agonize while she pulled a Goody comb with as much gentleness as possible through our hair.

On this particular Saturday morning, while I laid across my mama's lap, I could feel her eyes looking down, not at my hair, but in avoidance of the fear that seemed to fill every corner of the house. That fear made me hate Willie. I remember the sullenness in my mother's mood. I felt her crying soul. For my sister and me, there were no bedtime stories or kisses. It was fear's job to nurture and protect while love stood silently by.

On the night before, Willie had come home late. I remembered that it was close to midnight because my mama had been waiting up for him. I don't think that she was concerned about his safety, but afraid for hers. She was bracing herself for the inevitable routine.

When Willie came home sloppy drunk, he wanted Mama to get up and clean the living room because it wasn't clean enough! She pleaded with him to keep his voice down because we were asleep, but we never were. He yelled back, " I don't give a damn, bitch! You just clean this filthy house up, you sorry mutha-fucka!" Once again she pleaded. From our bedroom, we heard a slap, cry, and crash all at the same time! My sister and I held each other tight, screaming for our mama. "Please, Willie, please!" Mama cried and cried. . . and cried, but what went on in that living room seemed to go on forever. He beat her until he got tired and until we all cried ourselves to sleep.

While I was lying across my mama's lap, she sat quietly, mechanically going through the motions. When Willie finally woke up, he tried to engage Mama in a little small talk but she would not look up at him. I guess that she was ashamed of the bruises on her face. Willie would never stick around the house long on his days off, so around 2:00 in the afternoon, he was off to wherever and who cares.

I fantasized about being big enough so that I could kill Willie! I just couldn't stand his nappy-headed, drunk self! Anyway, my mama barely spoke a word that day. We tried to pretend that we didn't notice the bruises on her face.

By midnight, Willie still hadn't arrived home. I got up to use the restroom and about that time I saw my mama in the kitchen, pacing back and forth with a butcher's knife in her hand. I heard what sounded like crazy talk to me. "What am I going to do about my babies?" I was really confused as to what she was talking about.

What *was* she going to do with us? She kept on mumbling. As I walked out of the bathroom, further down the hallway, I saw her hand bleeding as she was hitting the blade of the knife in her hand. "I'm so tired. I just don't know what to do! Lord help me! I don't know what to do!" "Mama," I called out softly. But at that moment Willie walked into the house. I stepped back into the doorway of the bathroom so that I couldn't be seen.

Willie was barely able to stand up. In his stupor, he knocked over what-nots as he tried to use them to balance himself. Mama at this time was standing in the kitchen, tall, erect, and hand filled with blood. As Willie fell to the floor, she walked over to him. Willie looked confused as he looked up into Mama's face. "Helene, Helene, what the hell is wrong with you? Help me up!" But she just looked at him and kept walking closer and closer to him. "What the h___!" Willie screamed in surprised confusion. He was able to pull himself up and attempted to raise his hand to strike at Mama. Mama grabbed his hand and, with her blood-filled one, she held the butcher knife to his throat and said, "Do what you want because I mean to kill you tonight!" Willie looked more than startled, more than frightened. He was trembling so that he was not able to keep his stance. It was as if the ground beneath him would not be still. Willie struggled to break free of mama's grip. The more he struggled, the weaker he seemed to become. Mama looked taller and stronger to me.

In her madness, she pressed the knife closely to Willie's throat. He pleaded for mercy. She began to cry, "Lord, what am I going to do?" Sweat began to run down Willie's face as he pleaded for his life.

I tried to call out to Mama but the words would not come. Blood began to run down Willie's neck. I became frightened. I did not want him to die by my mother's hand. When I opened my mouth, I thought that I had made a sound, but it was like that of a faint cry of the dead calling out to the living who cannot hear them. So I braced myself, determined to break my own silence, determined to be heard and bring my mama back!

My heart was racing fast. The sweat of my body weighed my gown down until it stuck to my skin. I took a deep breath, crippled by my own doubt, but no turning back now! I opened my mouth and pushed my voice through all of my fears and inhibitions. I opened up so that my soul could cry out and rebuke the spirit of evil delusions—so that its unresponsive consciousness could be awakened. The house with its cynical self decided to defy gravity with 180-degree turns from left to right, but I was indelible! With all that was within me and from the force that beckoned behind me, I cried out, "MAMAAA!" And the house stood still!

Mama looked over at me. She was trembling and her eyes were filled with tears. When she released her grip from Willie, the knife fell slowly from her hand. Her eyes searched me with wondrous confusion. "What am I going to do?"

I looked at Willie lying there on the floor gasping and bleeding, but not bad enough. He was able to make his way to the door.

Twelve and one-half months had gone by and Willie had not returned home. Mama had gotten a job at the Tropicana Orange Factory on Ninth Street east in Bradenton. It was the first time that I remembered mama working. We were all very proud of her. Every now and then, she would take us to her workplace and show us off to her co-workers. Before we left, we would always get a free bottle of orange juice. Sometimes when we would just drive by Tropicana with the car windows down, we could smell the oranges being made into delicious juice. I didn't care much to eat oranges, but the smell from the factory was very compelling. The oranges had a smell of sweet yellow cake.

Although mama loved her job, she told us that handling the oranges was a wicked task. The acid from the oranges would cause abrasions in her hand; therefore she had to wear gloves all of the time, even at home.

Things were going all right for us. I even washed dishes and cleaned up around the house to help keep things moving along.

Although we had very little money and bills were frequently paid late, Mama would somehow be able to treat us to McDonald's every Friday night. That was our designated family night when we would just talk, make one another laugh, and love one another. Finally, no more tears!

One night, as I lay in my bed, I was thanking God for my family no longer being afraid. I began to remember the song frequently sang by Grandma Ruby that God "took me out of darkness into the marvelous light!" I smiled with understanding.

On that same night, I noticed under my door that there was a light on in the house. "Mama needs to keep her light bill down," I thought. I opened the door and walked down the hallway because the light appeared to be coming from the kitchen. I slowed down as I heard some type of beating noise. As I walked a little closer, I heard some mumbling noises. I moved closer and closer to the noise. "Mama," I whispered. There was no response that I could understand. As I walked to the end of the hallway, I turned my head into the direction that the noise was coming from. As I stood there, looking into the kitchen, my body became numb. I felt my mouth freeze open and my skin was beginning to leave me. I looked upon my mother. Her mouth was white and her eyes were gray. She did not notice me. She was looking straight through the living room towards the door. "Ma," I spoke softly. There was no response. The mumbling became clear. My eyes became focused on the beating noise. I looked down and saw Mama's bleeding hand, the butcher knife up and down and up. . ."Ma," I spoke out again. Her soul had been dismissed by irrational thoughts. She stood there listlessly. Her mind and spirit had been tragically transformed.

I focused on her mumbling until it became clear to me that, as she was looking towards the front door, she was asking a question, searching for an answer.

Despite the twelve and one-half months of apparent peace, tranquillity, and light that had once been darkness, she felt that she had been deceived. Whatever lay beyond the door, into the darkness, left her dubious that she had found the answer that she had asked herself almost two years ago, "What am I going to do about my babies? LORD WHAT AM I GOING TO DO?!"

※

Education: B.A. in Interdisciplinary Social Sciences; M.Ed. in Curriculum and Instruction.

Profession: Educator, Manatee County Schools, Florida; Freelance writer; and contributing writer to Tempo News Magazine.

She is 28 years old and resides in Bradenton, Florida with her husband, Troy, and five year old daughter, Tyra.

NICO' DELONN

LATE FOR SERVICE

by Lorene Erickson

DAISY WAS IN THE hospital with fluid in her lungs the Christmas her husband, Creepin' Jesulus, died.

"I'm not havin' no funeral for him, Grace Pauline," Daisy said. "Ain't nobody to go to it, ain't no church to have it in, ain't no preacher to tell lies over him, anyways. I'm havin' him cremated, and if that son of his or the rest of them damn Catholics says one word, I'll give 'em hell." She picked at a loose thread where she'd stitched 'jollups' across the enormous front of her chartreuse nightgown.

"He only came to visit his daddy in the home twice. Said he couldn't take it. Doll, it broke my heart. That Polack wife of his never came even once. I'm too old for such foolishness," she said. "You know, Doll, I wanted to adopt you. I wanted you to be my real daughter, 'cause I never had one. I tell everybody you're my daughter-in-law. I don't tell 'em you're my ex-daughter-in law. None of their damn business."

When Daisy asked Grace Pauline to take her to church on Christmas Sunday a year later, Grace Pauline couldn't say no.

"I want to hear Baptist sing," Daisy said. "If he hadn't looked out for me after Creepin' Jesulus died and I was so sick, I'd have had to go to the home."

Baptist was Reverend Blount's son. Reverend Blount was pastor at the New Hope Fundamental Baptist Church. Baptist looked after Daisy, shopped for her groceries every week, prayed with her, even though she wasn't a member of his church, wasn't even Baptist.

"You can do your missionary work on me 'cause I'm a fallen-away Catholic," she told him, "and you're my hunk."

* * *

Grace Pauline drove to Daisy's four-room house in Detroit. Daisy was in her La-Z-Boy in the frog room, watching TV. She had covered her 330 pounds in red pants and a hot pink sweatshirt flocked with red and green frogs wearing Santa hats.

"Like it, Doll?" she asked. "Lord, let me have bright colors."

Daisy collected frogs. Shelves and shelves of them—stuffed, inflated, crocheted, carved, and plastic. Frogs that lit up; frogs that croaked; wind-up, battery-powered, and squeeze-bulb frogs that leaped. She had turned the one with genitals over on its back so that its scarlet penis pointed up like a Christmas candle.

"Turn off that damned machine, will you, Doll?" she said, and Grace Pauline followed the trail of tubing to the oxygen generator and flipped the green switch. "Hand me that package over there." She pointed toward a pile on the table. "These're for you."

Grace Pauline picked up a red paper plate piled with crocheted tree ornaments—a snowman with a green felt hat, red yarn scarf and yellow sequin eyes, a Santa, a stocking, and a wreath, all decorated with pearls, sequins, and beads.

"I couldn't do no bakin' this year, no pe-can pies, nor no fudge. My legs and my lungs is just too bad, but my eyes is still good, and

I can live it up with my cro-shayin'. These're your Christmas jollups. And Peanut Brittle; my dirty old cousin from Georgia sent us his nuts again. They're in the fridge." She wiped her face with a bandana.

"Well, the shack looks pretty good, don't it?" she said.

Three artificial trees crowded the tiny room, swags of tinsel and bells crisscrossed the windows, and two ceramic trees blinked their glass candles from opposite ends of the frog shelves.

"Texas from across the street put up the trimmin's for me this year. She's a sweet thing, but her boyfriend's no good. Got mean eyes and a foul mouth." The frog pinned to the top of the La-Z-Boy 'rrrrrped' as Daisy leaned forward and turned off the TV.

"I got a bad call this mornin', Doll. I knew it was comin'. My brother in Lu'seana died. I prayed he would. You know, Alzheimer's, same as Creepin' Jesulus. Twelve years. My old man was the worst for only a year." She steadied the end of her cane on the floor between her swollen ankles. "I didn't mean nothin' callin' my old man 'Creepin' Jesulus.' She pulled herself up out of her chair. "It's a bad neighborhood, don't take your purse."

✳ ✳ ✳

"Well, I'm here," Daisy called to the three ushers at the church door. "I told you I'd come, and here I am. Sorry we're late, but my legs is no good."

"Praise the Lord you're here, Mrs. Becker," they said.

"This here's my daughter-in-law. Now, c'mere, one a' you hunks. Let me lean on you while I get up these steps. I need to sit at the back, case I got to leave in a hurry. Get short a' breath, ya know. I don't want to disturb nobody."

Three glass-paneled doors and a series of windows separated the lobby from the nave. Grace Pauline could see the kindergarten choir through a window.

Daisy nudged Grace Pauline. "Them in the long dresses is Baptist's kids," she said.

One of the ushers led Daisy and Grace Pauline down the side aisle past the empty pews, halfway to the front and three rows behind the last occupied pew. Backed by a steady beat from a taped automatic rhythm section, the eight kindergarteners in a ragged row on a bare platform were dragging through "Jingle Bells."

"Get us a program, will you, Doll?" Daisy asked. "I want to know when Baptist's going to sing."

Grace Pauline took two programs from the usher and edged into the pew first so Daisy could sit near the aisle. Three third-graders read a skit about finding Baby Jesus in the manger. Then, the junior high group, anchored by a thick-bodied girl in a lavender skirt and blouse, and a thin black boy in dark pants, white shirt, and bow tie, sang three songs and stayed in tune and in unison.

As the children and their teachers took their bows, Daisy said, "Doll, there's no tree nor no decorations. Where's the Christmas jollups?"

Grace Pauline shook her head.

Pastor Blount dimmed the lights. The vocal strains of "O Come All Ye Faithful" came from the back of the church. The New Hope Singers, five men and six women, each holding a lighted candle and a song book, sang the first verse at the opened doors between the lobby and the nave.

Daisy pointed. "There's Baptist. Ain't he a hunk?"

The New Hope Singers, led by Baptist, marched down the center aisle, singing the second verse.

"Four of them girls is Baptist's sisters," Daisy said.

A tall man in a sport coat, dark pants, and shirt open at the neck followed the last singer down to the front row and stopped. As the New Hope Singers lined up on the platform, he turned and walked back up the aisle, past the congregation, past the empty pews, and out into the lobby through the center door. The pastor turned up the dimmer switch to medium light, and the Singers blew out their candles. Pastor Blount adjusted the tape recorder and the sound system. The tall man in the sport coat came down the side aisle and took a seat in the pew in front of Daisy and Grace Pauline. During "Good News," the tall man began to sing. His voice carried over the New Hope Singers, up over the prerecorded automated music. When the singers paused to get ready for "Sing Praise," the tall man stood.

"It's His birthday. What should we give him for a present? Our hearts, our minds, and our souls." He sat down.

"He's had a belt or two this mornin'," Daisy announced.

When Pastor Blount's daughter, Beth, sang her solo lines, "Sing praise to the king of kings, sing his praises," the tall man stood and added, "Jesus is Lord, Jesus is Lord." People began to shift and stir.

"The congregation went when the neighborhood turned bad. Baptist says nobody's here no more," Daisy said.

Baptist stepped down from the platform and took his place at a podium at the side of the church near Daisy and Grace Pauline. He adjusted the microphone and recited: "While Joseph and Mary were in Bethlehem, Mary gave birth to her firstborn, a son. She wrapped him in a cloth and placed him in a manger. There were shepherds living out in the fields nearby, keeping watch over their flocks at night."

"I think Baptist's on tape," Daisy said. "I don't see his mouth moving."

"They were terrified. But the angel said to them, 'Do not be afraid. I bring you good news of great joy that will be for all the people. Today in the town of David a savior has been born to you. He is Christ the Lord.'"

The tall man stood again. He tipped his head back on his neck and gazed at the vaulted wood ceiling. He stretched his arms out from his sides, his hands turned palms up. "We all can use the word a' God, even the worst sinner can use the word a' God. Amen."

"What's that fool doin'?" Daisy asked.

The congregation shifted again. They looked at the tall man standing with his arms out and his head back, and they looked up to see what was there.

"He's not drunk, Daisy, he's just confused," Grace Pauline whispered.

Pastor Blount's daughter, Denise, began "O Holy Night" a capella.

"That's my favorite song," Daisy said. "Baptist says none of his sisters never got married. They all still livin' at home. This one's got big boobs. You'd think she'd have a scootie-balootie hangin' around." Daisy dug in her pockets. "Did you lock my house, Doll? Do you have my key?"

The tall man stood and faced Daisy. "Jesus died for our sins," he said. "Knock. Knock on His door. His is the Kingdom of God." He walked up the aisle to the back of the church.

"Well, I s'pose it's only Christian to let him be here," Daisy said.

Grace Pauline turned and watched him go out the doors, across the lobby behind the windows, into the church again, and down the far aisle. He was singing, but Grace Pauline couldn't hear the words.

"Why don't they let Baptist sing a solo?" Daisy asked. "I came to hear Baptist."

The New Hope Singers swung into "Let all the earth be glad and celebrate the coming. . ."

The tall man walked through an empty pew and stood near the middle in the center aisle. When the New Hope Singers finished, the tall man faced the congregation.

"The wages of sin is the word of God," the tall man said.

Pastor Blount turned toward the congregation and stared down the aisle. He pointed to Baptist at the side aisle, then pointed to the tall man. Grace Pauline watched Baptist scoot in a half-crouch down the side aisle and gesture to the three ushers who came down the center aisle behind the man. Baptist crossed through an empty pew and faced him. Together, they led him into the lobby. Pastor Blount cued the New Hope Singers to move into position. Kim Blount, gaunt in her red sateen dress, stepped to the microphone, ready for her solo. Her voice was clear and true. "God's own son came reaching," and the New Hope Singers joined with "And with these eyes I saw Him, with these hands I touched Him."

Grace Pauline turned around. Through the lobby windows, she could see the tall man pace to the far end and back, followed by Baptist and the three ushers. She could see the tall man raise his hands, could see his mouth move, could almost hear him. Then they cornered him. His back was to the wall. Baptist and the ushers faced him in a half circle. The tall man looked full of spirit.

"Do you have tic-tacs?" Daisy asked. I didn't bring no tic-tacs."

Pastor Blount moved to the microphone. As he adjusted the height, the feedback reverberated.

"When Handel wrote "The Messiah," he said, "it was presented to the king. When they got to the Hallelujah Chorus, the king stood up. Asked why he stood, he said . . ." Here, Pastor Blount referred to a note he was holding. "'In such presence that God has been glorified I could do nothing but stand.' It has been our tradition since then that when we get to the Hallelujah Chorus we stand, and we're doing that number now, so I ask that you all rise in honor to God."

Daisy waved from her seat to Baptist as he hurried down the side aisle to join the New Hope Singers on the platform

"I ain't gonna stand, hon," she called. She tapped one of the returning ushers. "Tell Baptist I can't stand. He'll know why," she said.

At the last hallelujah, Grace Pauline looked for the tall man. The lobby was empty. Pastor Blount moved to the microphone.

"You can sit down," he said. "Now, the first time that Jesus came to this earth," he said, "He came and was born in a manger. I don't know what that does to you, but it touches me so deeply when I realize that God himself came as a baby." His voice trembled. "Not only did He do that, but grew up as a creature, like you and me. And then, He let the creature that He made, man, crucify him, dying for our sins. That's all done, and it will never again have to be done because He died once and for all. But you know what?" He paused. "He's coming back. But the next time be comes, it's not going to be as a baby. That's what this song is about."

Ruth Blount sang the solo parts.

The pastor turned off the tape recorder and turned up the church lights as the New Hope Singers filed off the platform and down to their seats in the side pews. The audience clapped. Daisy wiped her eyes.

"Well, now, after that fine concert and all that good singing, I know you want to get home to your Christmas dinners, but I hope you'll give your preacher a few minutes to recognize our guests here this morning. Let's see who you are," said Pastor Blount.

He shielded his eyes from the glare of the lights.

"Now, we tried really hard to bring some new folks here this morning to enjoy our fine New Hope Singers. They practiced lots of hours just to sing for you. So, now, we'd like to recognize anybody who brought enough family or friends today to fill a pew." From below the platform an usher held up his hands to the pastor. "Well, I guess a full pew might be about seven people. Yes, seven could qualify. Anyone here with a pew of seven?" Several hands waved. "Well, now, here we have, who? . . . the Washingtons . . . and they brought. . ." He leaned forward. "Who did you bring? They brought Grandpa Washington and their two little nieces, Charilyn and Prinzetta, to hear our Christmas concert this morning. Thank you, thank you. Now I just want us to say a special welcome to Mrs. Daisy Becker who is able to be with us in our church this morning for the first time. We're so glad she's here." He looked across the nave. "Where is she?"

"Here I am." Daisy waved.

"We've prayed for you, Mrs. Becker, to be able to come to church. Our prayers are answered."

The congregation turned to nod and smile at Daisy. A woman slid out from her seat, came down the aisle, and hugged Daisy's shoulder.

"Oh, Sweet Jesus," she said, "We're so glad you're here. Praise the Lord."

"I read my Bible ever mornin'," Daisy said.

"Now, will all our visitors please raise their hands," Pastor Blount said. "We have a gift for each and every visitor here this morning. Ushers, will you please get the boxes. Friends," he continued, "we have for you a framed Bible verse." He held up a glass-covered inscription printed in calligraphy. "We think it's pretty handsome. Brother Ronald did the frames for us so's you could just hang it right up in your living room or kitchen. And we'd like you to fill out one of our little blue cards, too, askin' you to join. I just know some of you here for the first time today may have a special need. On this blue card there's a place to check if you're one of those people. We can help you bring Jesus into your heart."

Each usher moved down an aisle with a box of framed verses and blue cards. Daisy raised her hand.

"I'll get me one for my frog room, Doll," she said.

She took 'for God so loved the world, that He gave his only begotten Son, so that whosoever believeth in Him should not perish, but have everlasting life.'

"Here, Doll, fill out this card for me," Daisy said.

"What special need do you have?" Grace Pauline asked.

"I don't. Just give 'em my name and address. That's enough," Daisy said.

"I wonder if the tall man got a card," Grace Pauline said.

Pastor Blount was still talking. "Now, I have a question for all you folks. What is Christmas for?"

"I'm tired," Daisy said. "Let's go."

In the lobby, Baptist, now dressed in a Santa Claus suit, waited for his father's signal to march down the center aisle with a pillowcase full of boxes of candy.

"Before you go givin' out the jollops, Baptist, help me down the steps here so's I can go home." Daisy leaned heavily on Baptist's arm. Grace Pauline carried the framed verse.

"What happened to that man who kept coming in and going out?" Grace Pauline asked.

"We had to ask him to leave. We couldn't let him spoil the program for all the folks who came today. My father and my sisters worked so hard." Baptist shook his head. "We'll pray for him"

"I sure did enjoy the music, Baptist, but I come to hear you sing a solo," Daisy said.

"I'll stop by on Tuesday, Mrs. Becker, and I'll bring you a tape of today's service," Baptist said.

"Don't you never tell my son I was here," Daisy said.

In the car on the way back, Daisy asked, "Do you know this one, Doll?"

'Here's to life, and ain't it grand!
I just divorced my old man.
I had to laugh at the judge's decision.
He awarded him the kids,
And they ain't even his'n.'

"I'll tell that one to Baptist next time he comes," Daisy said.

Received a Creative Artist Award from the Michigan Council for the Arts for her short stories. She and her husband, Robert, co-write plays. Her one-act play, A Curious Adventure in St. Petersburg is included in the Eldridge Plays and Musicals Catalog. Her book of poems, Bread Upon the Waters, Michigan State University Press, is forthcoming in spring 2001.

LORENE ERICKSON

THE ADVENTURES OF JOHN MIDO

by Brian Fuller

(12 years of age)

CHAPTER I   *The Discovery*

EJECTEDLY, THE SCIENTIFIC INVENTOR slumped in his padded leather chair, off in one corner of his laboratory. Tattered sketches and wood pieces lay scattered around the floor. Already John Mido began to cough from the dust clinging to the chair legs.

In the center of the room was a vehicle that looked somewhat like a model-T car except it had no roof. The thermonuclear generator that he had installed so meticulously on its underside hummed quietly as it powered down. "Dang," the renowned inventor John Mido said to himself. "Why can't it work?" Then, for the fifth time that day, the tired inventor struggled up from his armchair to once again inspect the machine he had been working on for years, and to which he had devoted so many hours.

He carefully examined the high-powered engine, but found absolutely nothing wrong. "This time machine should be working," he said angrily. "The formula should be right!" He banged his fist

225

against the engine in frustration. Suddenly, the engine sprang into life with a noisy rush of power. Looking into the front seat, he saw that on the display panel all the lights were on and even the time transfer switch was glowing, ready to channel the energy needed for time travel. The very excited inventor began jumping up and down and dancing around the room, not caring that downstairs the house-maid was extremely puzzled at why the ceiling was shaking.

CHAPTER 2   *The Start of a Journey*

Shirts and pants nearly flew from all directions as the very excit-ed inventor began to pack for an adventure. Toothbrushes, tooth-paste bottles and a few other items also found their way into a tight-ly-packed leather suitcase. After packing, the doctor rushed back up the carpeted stairs to his laboratory.

The time machine John had so carefully made was still humming noisily, ready for time travel. He climbed into the time machine with reverence, for he knew this would be the most important discovery of all time. Slowly, he entered the year he would like to visit. "Year 20,000 B.C.," John said. "Visiting the past should be interesting!" After entering the destination in the display panel, John Mido slowly pushed the time travel button.

Suddenly, a blinding, bright blue light began to glow around the vehicle and, as if in a dream, he sat in the machine as it lifted off the ground!!! The time machine flew upwards through the laboratory ceiling as if the ceiling wasn't there. The vehicle's velocity increased steadily, and soon the Earth was left behind. The sun of our solar system grew in size as the time machine approached it, but strangely, John felt no heat at all. Soon, he had passed the sun's outer layer, and now the light was so blindingly bright that John could see nothing. His eyes began to mist over, and suddenly he and his time machine appeared in a very different, strange world.

CHAPTER 3 *The Crowning*

Three men were standing before the inventor with their mouths hanging open in surprise. They were obviously primitives, due to their unkempt and bushy hair, and their fig leaf coverings. Two clubs and other assorted items were strewn about their feet, apparently dropped in surprise.

The closest one to John fell to his knees and said a command to the two men next to him. They both then fell to their knees as well. John began to feel awkward since he had not come prepared for three men to fall down on their knees before him. Quickly, all three men stood up and the one nearest to John began to try to communicate through a series of movements and noises. Seeing that John could not understand him, he simply pointed toward a village in the distance. John quickly pulled his time machine behind a boulder and then followed the three men to the entrance of the village.

The obvious leader of the three strangers ran ahead down the straight lane in the center of the village. On each side of the dirt road there were many huts made of dirt and straw. At the end of the lane there was a larger, more decorated hut that seemed to be the Chief's hut. This is the hut to which the strange man seemed to be going. Soon, he entered and disappeared for about ten minutes. Then he and another very decorated primitive came out of the hut conversing between one another. The new, decorated primitive seemed to be the chief. Presently, the Chief looked down the lane and, after seeing John, he too kneeled before him. As he fell, though, he gonged a bell that was near his side.

Great cries came from huts around the village, and all the villagers who were inside the many huts began running toward the central square in the middle of the village. One of the villagers grabbed the startled and puzzled time traveler by the hand and yanked him along in the rush. Once they had all assembled at the central square, the Chief began a long story of which the first half seemed to be about how the three scouts found the very puzzled inventor. The second half of the story, however, John could not comprehend. If he could have understood it, it would have gone like this:

"As you know, our legends tell of one who will suddenly appear out of nowhere and lead our people to prosperity. The legend also says that this man will wear strange clothes and will not speak our language, but that he will speak the language of the gods. This man has all these things true about him. He must be crowned as the king of our people. All in favor, raise your hands!!!"

John watched the gathering as everyone's hands shot up in the air. The Chief called out a loud command and another primitive came forward holding a wooden box. The crowd parted, allowing the box-bearer to get to John. With much reverence, the box bearer opened the box, revealing a crown! This crown was made of wood and was inlaid with many precious stones, and feathers were set in it. John suddenly realized that the tribe wanted to make him king! He then tried to do the thing we would probably do in his awkward situation: he tried to escape! He tried to break through the crowd, but they held firm against his onslaught. He didn't want to be a king! He had come to the past to explore, not to be stuck in a palace hut all day and night!!! The crowd had held firm against John's attempts to escape, and soon the man with the crown was near at hand, and John Mido was forced to be seated on an old wooden chair. The man with the crown took the crown with reverence and put it down upon John's head. The crowd applauded. John grimaced. Now he was a king!!!

CHAPTER 4 *The Plan*

John hated being king! With each passing hour he learned to hate having to rule the tribe of primitives even more. He soon learned after his first hour of being king that the tribe had no fires at all! No one in the entire tribe besides John even knew what fire was! John hated having to show them how to do everything. He had to show them how to cook their food and how to irrigate the land. Most of all, though, he hated not being able to learn their language! Due to the fact that he spoke English and they spoke their tribal language, he could never understand what they were saying. For all these reasons, John made a plan.

John's only chance of escape was the plan that he had designed. The plan was very simple and clever enough not to leave a trail. One night, approximately one month after John had unwillingly become king, he put his plan into action.

He slowly and quietly put on his old clothes (for he had been forced to wear the tribal clothes when he was king) and hopped out of the window of his hut. He silently stole past the village guards and crept out of the village gate. He was nearing the boulder behind which his time machine was hidden when he rammed right into a village patrol! John dodged past them as they tried to attack him with their clubs. He ran as fast as he could to the spot where he had concealed the time machine. Luckily, the time machine was still there, safe and sound. "So much for a quiet escape," John thought to himself as he hopped into the front seat of his time machine. The sound of pursuit got louder as John turned the machine on and entered the time coordinates. Just as the patrol came near enough to hit John with their clubs, John pressed the time transfer button on the time machine.

CHAPTER 5   *John Returns Home*

The village patrol seemed to be frozen still as statues as John's time machine took off from the boulder-covered ground. On this trip through time, John closed his eyes, for he did not want to experience the blazing sun's light as he did last time. All John Mido knew was that about thirty seconds later, he landed with a bump in his laboratory, all safe and sound. "Maybe the world is not ready for time travel yet," John thought. "At least I got home alive, though." John was really home. He was finally home.

❧

Hi! I am in the 7th grade, and I wrote "The Adventures of John Mido" as an end-of-the-year story when I was in 6th grade. I enjoy rollerblading and video games, and I play the trombone. Thank you for reading!

BRIAN FULLER

THE HOUSE ON LIME KILN ROAD

by Claudia Vennell Fuller

THE DOOR WAS AJAR. So it wasn't like breaking and entering. We had watched the little house for years and never seen any signs of life. As early June campers on bird watching car trips, we had seen this deserted and very neglected property on our crack-of-dawn jaunts. When we were observing green-throated warblers, veerys, chestnut-sided warblers (and once, a huge turtle laying eggs), we sometimes thought about the name of the road and wondered about the lime kiln.

Our nature walks often included all kinds of facts like all about lime kilns, but the house wasn't near shipping piers and the swamps nearby couldn't be lime pits. What was that little house (not a farm) there for? It had a small barn out back and a garage, on the road, which was almost completely overgrown, but we had peeked in to see two old rusting cars. We couldn't tell much without sawing our way in, but one was a little pickup, like a Model A.

Every June our leader took us around to the good birding spots and every year, the house looked a little more run down.

Gradually—no mailbox, no driveway marks, no walk path. We went about our annual activities and wondered about "The House." We asked our leader what he knew about it. He said he had never seen anyone there—which wasn't what he knew about it, but we didn't realize that. About the fifth June, we decided to "go see." We thought of looking in the windows; we wondered where to park the car. The decision to investigate took a lot of nerve. We bolstered each other with all kinds of excuses. When we saw that the door was ajar, it seemed a sign that it was OK to enter.

It was dead quiet. No refrigerator running, no lawn mowers, traffic, electric clocks—nothing. I could hear my ear noises louder than ever, and, when a big fly lazily crossed the room, it sounded like a bee. The curtains that we had seen hanging out of the broken window were faded and tattered. The linoleum was worn in floorboard patterns. The kitchen table was old, but not broken. In fact, there were little papers that looked like they had been left a couple of weeks ago! Why hadn't they yellowed?

We went on into the small dining room, living room, and bedroom. There was bedroom furniture (from the '30s?) and on the bed (no bedding) was a ruffled dress. On the dresser in a cardboard photographer's frame, we saw a wedding picture. If that was from the fifties, surely it was a daughter of the people who used to live here. Then a close examination of the dress on the bed revealed that it was the wedding dress in the picture. Why had this picture and dress been left like this? Was the daughter in the picture (if it was the daughter) gone forever? Was the owner of the house lost, estranged, dead?

As we were talking about possible scenarios, I started picking up the little papers and putting them with the others in the kitchen. As a further invasion of the mystery person's privacy (and I don't know why this seemed the worst), I decided to read the notes. Maybe I'd find an address, I rationalized.

Oh, no. The person who had written these notes was trying by writing to straighten out certain things in his/her own mind. Over and over and over—the same words, figures, subtractions, additions, and a few names. "Gert – 10,000." "Roy – 6,000." "What happened to 4,891?" "20,000 missing." Then household figures. "Tax 211." "Electric 9.20." "Call J." Lots of "Call J." Could "J" be the girl in the picture?

It was about the same year the word *Alzheimer's* started to be used instead of *senile*. The notations showed a mind in trouble—but then what? Why was the furniture left in the kitchen and bedroom, but not in the living room and dining room? There was a TV antenna, half off the roof, so somebody watched "The Ed Sullivan Show," "I Love Lucy," "Howdy Doody."

We left the little house and wondered how it would fare through another winter. The following June, it looked even worse. We went in, of course, and somebody had built a fire in the middle of the living room floor. They had broken a kitchen chair and tried to burn it. The raggedy curtains were still hanging. Some food cartons were scattered. Wasp nests on the ceiling. Goodbye, little house.

One more year went by. This time our bird tour didn't take us on Lime Kiln Road. They said there wasn't room to turn around on that narrow, swampy road. So, of course, one afternoon we had to check on the cottage. The little barn had had a fire! We walked around the remains and saw writings on the door frames and front wall that said "Death to whoever did this." Uh oh! There must be relatives alive. It's a good thing they don't know the rest. If they think burning the barn is bad (it could have been lightning), think of what they'd think of keeping a wedding photo, a wedding dress, many little papers, a pink and green glass ceiling light fixture, a crock, and an old match holder. I happen to know where these things are, and one of these days perhaps they will be returned to the house on Lime Kiln Road.

Grew up in the Midwest, taught school, raised three daughters, enjoyed sports and camping, wrote many plays, special lyrics and some truly awful doggerel. Since moving to Florida, she has taken up traveling. Recently married, her life now includes new friends, new family and a sailboat.

CLAUDIA VENNELL FULLER

TRIBUTE TO A GHOST

by Ted R. Garrison

IT'S ALL PART OF another world now. I often wonder about it on nights like these, when it's bitter cold and the moon is high and full above my house. I'm not absolutely certain as to how it all began, there are those little lapses of memory that distort so easily. But left alone on quiet nights like these, much of it comes back to me and I am out there again in the cold of a long ago night.

From my bedroom window I look out on what is my garden in the summer, now billowy with snow in little mounds of moonlit whiteness. In summer, it is warm and filled with the mint-like fragrance of things growing, while beyond it lay the fields and orchards, green and cool in summer breezes, filled with the hum of insects, patterns in leaves and shade upon the ground. Now all is still and cold and snow glistens. How very much like the place where my strange friendship began.

Perhaps you remember those ancient times and that ancient war called World War II. I say ancient because it now seems like it happened in another age and to different people. Whenever I mention that war to my kids, that strange look appears on their faces again. After all, one of them drives a German car, and the other does real well in science but poorly in history and is a nut on the work of Werner von Braun. "Why did we fight them?" they ask.

It had been a long way from the beaches of Normandy to the spot where we'd finally bogged down. We'd been pushing the Germans back to their Fatherland all along the line. The little villages and big towns would pour out to welcome us in languages we did not understand. There was a feeling of relief, tears of happiness on the faces of strangers, old wine long hidden brought out to wash away the long nights of fear and hunger. Then, suddenly, it got rough. It was in Belgium. You may remember it, the Battle of the Bulge. It had been a clever plan by the Nazi hierarchy to dress German troops in our G.I. uniforms and then send them through our lines. Our lines started to crumble as those men, briefed in American slang and mannerisms, began accomplishing what they'd started out to do—break down our forces and kill as many of us as they could. The last of them were being rounded up when I got word from Colonel Holt to get over to G.H.Q. on the double. The jeep ride was cold, windy, and the two M.P.s who checked my identification were surly in appearance and manner. There were those questions we'd used to trap the Germans with: "Who won the Pennant in '44? Where'd you get your basic? Yeah? What state's it in?" Satisfied at last, they apologized. They didn't have to. I knew what they'd been through, what still might lie ahead for them. They took me to Colonel Holt's tent. It seemed colder in there than outside. The mud and turmoil of combat was in there, the feeling of the closeness of death, the weariness of nights without sleep. On a makeshift table of small boards spread across the tops of empty gasoline drums were the maps of war; a regular army man, drawn from retirement, was seated at that table, shoulders slumped. Only the neatly trimmed grey mustache and buttons still polished on rumpled clothing reminded me of the West Point man I knew him to be. About him, about the tent, was the smell of dampness and clothes worn too long, the sharp smell of burning distillate from the wick in the lantern.

"Stand at ease, Captain Wheeler," he said. "This area on the map—you're familiar with it, are you not?"

"Yes, sir. . ." I paused. There were places on that map I was not familiar with. "I know some of it, sir. I did some scouting before the Krauts pushed us back."

"We're in trouble, Captain. I hope you can remember what you saw. The Germans have us stopped here. Our forces are starting to move very slowly, but we've got to get through here if we're going to make any headway at all." He brought his finger down hard on a place on the map that showed three small hills—two in front, one behind—in a kind of wobbly triangle.

"What success have you had so far, sir?"

"We sent a small patrol in there the other day. None came back. As you can see on the map, there's a road that weaves around through those hills. That road is a vital link. It connects with points beyond it that we'll need if we're going to end this war anytime soon. We'll need it for men and supplies. A lot of lives depend on it. The Germans know that. They may try to blow it up while we're on it. We've kept them pretty busy lately, so they haven't had time, Or . . ."

"Or what, Colonel?" As I asked the question, I noticed the lines of dread grow deeper on his face, the sudden huskiness of his voice.

"Or they're waiting for something to happen before they do. They're not a bunch to quit without a struggle. It's all so unreal, some way."

"And you want me to find out what that something is. Is that it, sir?"

He nodded slowly. "That's it, Captain. Take a patrol of ten men. Leave in an hour. I needn't tell you how to do it, you've done things like this before; that's why I've chosen you. I don't want any snafus if they can be avoided. Too much is at stake here. We're counting on you, Captain. Good luck."

We saluted and I left, but, before I dropped the flap on the tent,

I looked back and saw him going back over the maps on the table in the yellow-white light from the lantern. How tight can you stretch a chain before it breaks? I felt that strain myself as I joined the noise of the trucks and men shouting outside. Each step that I took grew heavier as I walked back to the jeep. You know you're part of something big when the top brass talks to you that way. But all of a sudden I had that sinking feeling. The war had become very personal to me.

I had no trouble picking the men I wanted. They were all as tough as they come, hardened even more over the events of the last few weeks. We took the usual steps. Removed rings or anything that would cause a reflection. Emptied our pockets of all loose change, keys, or anything that would rattle. On nights like that when it was still and cold, you could hear each little twig snap beneath your feet for a long way. That finished, we blacked our faces and put on dark clothing and started out.

We hiked most of the way in that cold clear night with a bright full moon shining over our heads. The snow was six inches to a foot deep all over and we could see in all directions. Ahead of us was a small rising, one of the hills Colonel Holt had shown me on the map. We were in enemy territory now. I gave the signal. From here on in it would be tough going.

Keeping low, taking advantage of whatever cover we could find in shadows, stalking, crawling flat on our stomachs, anything that would keep us from being seen. I could not remember this place from my previous wanderings, but it looked like the kind of a place that could easily spark off a lot of those *regret to inform you* telegrams to the folks back home. It was a natural place for an ambush with little cover for those on foot as we were. They were out there someplace. But *where?*

Halfway up the side of the first hill I turned the column over to the sergeant. They were told to hold up there until I came back. If I came back! Then I went on alone. At the top of the first rising were two large boulders about the size of wash tubs, two feet apart. I started to ease my head up from behind one of them when I felt it. A man's hand on my shoulder, a strong hand pulling me down hard, the grip so cold I could feel it even through my thick coat. I've never felt anything like it before in my life. My whole body went numb under it.

"You wanna get shot?" The voice was strange, remote. I turned quickly.

"I thought I told you to stay with the other . . ." This wasn't one of my men! Instantly I went for my side arm.

"Take it easy, Captain. You can't hurt me. Nobody can now. If I wanted to get you out of the way, all I'd have to've done is to let you stick your head around that rock like you were fixin' to do. There's a Kraut machine gun nest on top of that hill over there. They're watching this place pretty hard."

I was laying on my back now looking up at the face of the man who was kneeling over me. But something was wrong. There was no face under the rim of his helmet. Only blackness. Nor could I see the steam cloud of breath when he turned his head in the bright moonlight. It was the way the light was hitting him, I thought, that his helmet was shading his face from the strong rays of the full moon. I was helpless now. Maybe this guy was a Kraut. I thought of the way we'd been taught to catch the Germans that had slipped through our lines. To ask them questions about America and Americans.

"Who's Babe Ruth?" I waited for his answer and eased my hand tighter around the handle of my sidearm.

He told me. Even part of Babe's history. Then with a drone of irritation in his voice, he went through the other questions and their answers. It was kinda weird listening to him as he wandered on in a monosyllabic tone. I tried to fix the accent but I couldn't. There was not the rush there of the city dweller, or the plain folks talk one hears in the country where they live in simple ways. Just the kind of timeless speech that seemed to know the outcome of everything that was about to happen as though he were reading it from some future almanac. . . My questions had annoyed him. "Look, Captain, I'm Sergeant Massey, I came here with. . . well, we'll skip that." Then he stood up!

"Get down, you idiot. They'll shoot you."

"They can't hurt me. They can't even see me. Only you can do that. Now, listen to me. That hill over there is five feet higher than it shows on the map. The Krauts have a bunker there and a mine field up the side of it, and the road's got TNT under it from one end to the other. They can set it off from up there. They want to use that road themselves for as long as they can, but, if we start using it, they'll wait until it's heavy with men and convoys and then blow it up. The loss will be heavy for us and the Reich will have another victory to gloat over. It's a king-sized trap. But you can break it. Look down there at the bottom of this hill. See that ditch? There's a little water in it that's frozen over now. It's about the only thing the Krauts didn't get around to mining. Take your men up it, staying in the dry areas. It'll lead you within twenty feet or so of that machine gun nest and bunker. You'll know what to do then."

"How'd you know so much about this place?"

"I've had a lot of time to look it over. In a way I'll miss those men. I'll be here a long time after all of you are gone."

It was a long time afterwards before that last thing he had said to me sank in. I was so wrapped up in what had to be done I hardly thanked him. We found the ditch. After that everything went according to plan. The bunker went up like a fireworks factory. Demolition men removed the explosives and, before you knew it, trucks and equipment were rolling. All along the line things began to crumble. Colonel Holt was ecstatic about it. A wedge had been opened that would not be closed. But it wasn't until later, when I was talking to Brick Edwards about the man out there on the hillside, about Sergeant Massey who had given me the layout of the land that had made the whole thing a success, that I felt that cold again.

Lt. Brick Edwards was in charge of the squad that was there before us. He had sent out that first patrol into the hills. Brick was a tall man with wide shoulders. The thing that most people noticed about him, though, was his hair, the deep red color of his native Georgia clay, and a face so freckled it looked as though a grade school artist had practiced spatter painting on it. There was always a smile on that face that made you feel welcome like the big letters on doormats are supposed to do. Anytime you'd see Brick, day or night, he looked as though he was heading for a country hoedown with his best girl; but he wasn't smiling now. Around Brick, it gave you an eerie feeling. We both noticed it, that feeling of dread that comes with hot wax and flowers and people offering comfort. It was Brick who broke the long dread of silence.

"Are you sure you know what you're saying, Captain?"

The words came from somewhere deep inside of me. I heard them from a distance. The medium's own voice stilled, the unbelievers aghast, and I was the most unbelieving of all. "Sergeant Massey. . . He. . ."

"Captain, that man was dead long before you headed out with that patrol. He led that first patrol into those hills that didn't come back. I talked to the squad that buried them all. I handled the papers and dog tags."

I never tell my wife or friends about Sergeant Massey anymore. They have a funny little way of looking at me and then at each other. One day I will go back to that place—where the hills form a wobbly triangle—to wander alone, preferably alone on a night like this. Go there, not to stay, as I would have had to do had I not listened to the ghost who saved my life.

After nearly a lifetime of working in the technical part of show business with many famous people, I turn now to story telling.

TED R. GARRISON

ONE THAT GOT AWAY

by Scott Helling

I T WAS AN ORDINARY Wednesday at work. I stopped and checked the mailbox as soon as I got home and was looking through the mail as I went into the house. "HI HONEY, I'M HOME!" I called out in the same goofy 1950's-TV-show way I always do when I get home these days.

Annie was just coming downstairs from the spare room she uses as an office. "How'd it go today, sweetie?" she asked as she gave me a kiss.

"Same ol'," I answered. "The Building Inspector caught the screwup I told you about the other day. The boss is pissed. He wants me to work some overtime this weekend to fix it."

"Yeah, that sounds like the same ol'," she replied. "The boss screws up and you have to work overtime to fix it. Still, we can use the time-and-a-half pay."

"Yeah," I said half-jokingly, "especially now that I have a wife and kid to worry about."

Annie was beaming as she gave me a hug and held me tightly for a long moment. She's not really my wife, but she loves it when I call her that. I only met her a few months ago through one of those internet personals sites. We sent a few E-mails back and forth and finally met for drinks. I've always believed in love at first sight, but never thought it would happen to me. We had a wonderful evening right up until it was time for her to go home. Then she dropped the bomb: she's still married, though separated from a drunk, abusive and tyrannical husband, *and* she has a nine-year-old daughter.

"There's still some coffee in the pot," Annie said as she pulled away. "Want me to warm it up?"

"You already warmed *me* up, you hottie," I joked. "Why not some coffee?"

Annie laughed as she headed into the kitchen. "Where's the lil' pun'kin?" I asked as I followed.

"Upstairs, doing her homework. Don't forget you said you'd drive her to soccer practice."

"Yeah, I know," I answered half-mindedly as I leaned against the kitchen counter next to the wastebasket and resumed going through the mail. I dropped two catalogs into the trash, but set aside the grocery store ads. I used to throw them away, but now I'm one of those "coupon people" as I used to disparagingly call them. I started looking over the electric bill but was interrupted. A freckle-faced, nine-year-old bundle of energy flew across the kitchen and slammed into me.

"Joey!" she squealed as she squeezed me tight. "You're taking me to soccer practice, right?"

"Of course!" I exclaimed, trying my best to match her enthusiasm. "And I wanna see you kick some major-league butt tonight! Okay?" Her head, still pressed against my chest, nodded hard. "You'd just better hurry up and finish your homework," I added, "if you want me to take you and your friends to the Dairy Queen afterward."

The nodding stopped and she let out a whiny little moan. "Awww. . . Okay. . . ."

I watched her run out of the kitchen toward the stairs, then looked back over at Annie. She was gazing at me in that weird way she does sometimes, smiling but almost crying at the same time. I smiled at her, then resumed looking through the mail. Annie said something right after that but I didn't really hear her. I was staring at the address card they send along with the bulk-rate junk mail.

I've seen a million of those cards over the years. On one side is an advertisement. On the other side, with your address, they have a picture of a missing child and the phone number of the National Center for Missing and Exploited Children. This particular kid caught my eye. My heart sank. She looked about six or seven and was very cute. Under the photo was a caption. "MISSING: HEATHER FENDLYNCH." Under that it said: "Last seen with: Rebecca Ann Fendlynch." Any idiot would know it was the girl's mother.

"Hey! I have good news!" Annie exclaimed. "When my boss called this morning he said that my appointments last week had the highest percentage of sales that any of his callers ever had! They're sending me a bonus!"

"That's great!" I responded. "Y'know, it's true what I always say: You *are* the best! In fact, I'd like to give you a bonus myself!"

Annie laughed but her smile slowly faded. She knew something was bothering me. She always does. I love that about her. "What's going on?" she asked as she walked over to me.

I showed her the junk mail address card. "It's a damn shame," I commented. "Just tragic that someone would abduct such a sweet kid away from a happy, loving home, isn't it?"

Annie looked at me. "Do you think anyone will recognize her? Call either these people or the police?"

I shook my head. "It's an old photo. Says so right there. And no one really looks at this junk mail stuff. It'd be different if her picture was on the side of a milk carton where people would be staring at it for twenty minutes while they munch their corn flakes. Besides . . ."

"How can they call her abducted?" Annie interrupted indignantly. "There must be thousands of kids who really *were* kidnapped and in danger. How the hell can they call her 'missing and exploited' when they know damn well she's with her mother?"

"The important thing is that she's safe," I insisted. "She's with her mom and I am quite sure that her mom is smart enough to know what's best for her child."

Annie slowly nodded. Then the phone rang. I answered, then gave the phone to Annie. It was her boss.

Annie said she'd call right back from her office, then hung up the phone. "Shit! I'm late calling in my afternoon appointments," she exclaimed as she hurried out of the room.

I poured a cup of coffee, then went through the rest of the mail. By the time I was done it was almost time to go. I took a long last look at the missing child on the address card, then tore up the card and threw it away. Heather Fendlynch won't be found. I'm sure of it. I finished my coffee, then went upstairs to change my clothes before I took her to soccer practice.

⁂

After moving to Sarasota in 1998, Scott wrote "The Big Trip," published in Eclipse Magazine. *A suspense thriller novel,* The Finder's Keeper, *was completed in late 1999. "One That Got Away" was his second attempt at short fiction.*

SCOTT HELLING

A PLACE CALLED YESTERDAY

by Maria B. Kirk

For the moment I felt that everything was in a shimmering motion; air, sea, and land holding me closely, almost smothering me. I sat motionless until the feeling passed, and then I knew this was the place. The sounds, smells, small rememberings from deep inside me tugged at my mind. I parked the car on the concrete road alongside the path through the tall grassy weeds along the marsh. The sign read "Private." A fence, warped by time, lay across the soggy path. The morning fog had lifted, and the sun fell heavily on the windless marsh. I soon began to swat mosquitoes from my sweating limbs and face. I remembered how merciless they were, especially in the grassy marsh. I stepped slowly and cautiously along the path leading to the two-story white dwelling on stilts. As I approached, I saw the wooden deck, beach chairs, and colorful umbrella facing the distant sea. I looked around and marveled at the other ten or so worn old homes on stilts whose only approach was by the small boats anchored to their decks.

I didn't notice when the man appeared on the upper deck, but, when I did see him looking down at me, I tread lightly on the

247

creaking boardwalk so that I could stand beneath him. "Hello," I called. "Is this part of what was the old bridge on to Rio Grande and into the Wildwoods?" A breeze from the sea in the distance had picked up by now, and except for the scowl on his heavily-lined sunburnt face staring down at me, I was feeling a bit more comfortable. The tall grass waved in the soft fish-smelling sea air, and I breathed in happiness. I hoped he wasn't going to spoil this for me.

Gruffly, he answered, as he gestured towards the path, "Go back to your car and take the road on to the concrete bridge, turn left, and you'll be on Rio Grande." He pointed to the monstrous bridge in our line of vision. "Don't you read signs?"

"Sir, why are you so surly? I know this is private, but I'm looking for something, and there's no one around I can speak with. If you live here, certainly you can answer a simple question and I'll be on my way." I stood looking up at him defiantly.

He growled back at me, "And what can you possibly be looking for in this deserted marsh land a few of us cling to?"

"I'm looking for yesterday," I replied simply.

Embarrassment overtook me as he jumped up and down roaring with laughter. He banged on the rail and leaned over so far I was afraid he'd fall over. I didn't see the humor in my question. Unless the man had come to this place only recently, he would otherwise appreciate what I was saying.

Finally, much composed and to my surprise, he asked, "And how long ago did you leave your yesterday here?" His scowl was gone and I knew he understood what I had asked.

And so I told him. "We've been living in Southern California for about twenty years and, while I visit Cape May Point often, I've simply not come by this way for many years. Even as it is now with the wooden bridge community gone, I can feel and smell the air filled with fish and rotted wood, and I remember the indescribable happiness we all felt when we came over that bridge to the island, passing the houses on stilts. We were city folk and this was quaint, another world, people tending their nets, cleaning boats, living in marsh water. There was no place to stop to say hello. It was merely a ride on a rickety wooden bridge to get to the shore. Seems it had to change before I got a chance to stop and say hello. I waited patiently for his answer.

"And now you've found yesterday. Things have changed. I don't really know what year the highway and the concrete bridge were put in. I came here later looking for a bit of contentment. I found it here. Just a few of us are left, trying to hold on to the only piece of marsh land not connected to the mainland. How long we can stay we don't know. We call it Grassy Sounds. It speaks to us and we live quietly listening to what it has to say." He paused and I thought he was finished. I wanted to say thank you, but then he went on, softly, "Do sit, listen and enjoy for as long as you feel the need." With that he quietly disappeared through the doorway.

I sat facing the sea, I don't know for how long. When I was saturated with peace and contentment, and before the sun went down, I left and took a bit of yesterday with me. I would not forget this place, ever.

※

A native Philadelphian, resides in southern California with her husband of fifty-seven years. "A Place Called Yesterday" is an expression of her love for the South Jersey shore where she enjoyed the summers of her younger life and raising a family. In addition to writing stories for their four children and six grandchildren, she participates in a weekly creative writing workshop at Mira Costa College in Oceanside, California.

MARIA B. KIRK

A LIFETIME OF CREDIT

by F. R. Lewis

S ITTING IN HIS CAR in the line at the toll booth, the boy's father slaps his palm against the steering wheel much as the boy slapped his palm against the keys of the piano while he, the boy, tried to learn— that is, to learn once more, to learn over—music for his audition, working, the boy said, until his arms ached, trying, the boy said, not to make the mistakes he had been making, any of them, again.

The boy and his father are driving to Boston, to the music school the boy picked after his first college, the one straight from high school, proved the wrong choice.

"I want to leave," the boy said in February. "I hate it here. If you pick me up this week, they'll give you back half the money."

"We're busy this week," the father said. "And the week after. We sent you to one of the best schools in the country," the father said. The boy was in the second semester of his second year. "Think about it. Call us back."

"I'll work," the boy said the next night. "I'll make money. I'll take a leave and go to music school this summer," the boy said. "If music is the life I'll stay. Otherwise I'll go back to this college."

"Why will the going back be different?"

"Because. . . then I'll know."

"I already know. The whole semester you'll spend all day in bed and all night with your friends. You'll drive my car, use my Mobil card. I won't have it," the father said. "Or you."

Instructions for his music school audition arrived at the boy's home in May.

"With all my experience, I'll rip it," the boy said. "I'll just re-learn something. Chopin or maybe Beethoven. I'll call Mary."

Mary, the teacher, taught the boy piano from the time he was four until he left for college, except for two months the boy's junior year when he claimed to have given up the piano forever.

The boy's hands, his teacher said. Not a pianist's expected hands. Playing the pieces the teacher selected showed not-quite-long-enough fingers of not-quite-large-enough hands flying over keys. The boy's hands looked like his father's hands.

"And I'll pick something new. Something rock, that I can sing with, too," the boy said. "There's this graduate. He's famous. I'll pick a song by him. I can do it."

The boy charged his new music on a credit card supplied by the bank that encouraged him to "start on the road to a lifetime of credit" and didn't require a second signature.

"Musicians," the boy told his father. "We deserve a lot of credit."

The father shrugged, made a noise in his throat. "Don't expect me to pay," he said.

On most days during the weeks between semesters, the boy did not leave his father's house for the clothing store where he worked until the mailman had delivered, calling the clothing store on days he was assigned morning hours to say he wasn't feeling great but could probably work the afternoon—if afternoon was all right, and if he felt better.

The letter arrived. The boy did not shred the letter, did not flush pieces of the letter down the toilet, did not hide the letter beneath potato peelings, carrot tops, pepper seeds, onion skins, corn cobs or leaves of wilted lettuce in the garbage, put it, the letter, in the center drawer of his desk, the drawer without a lock, the drawer where anyone who might have the curiosity to look could find it, the letter, designating him, the boy—a high-scorer in "Eco-theory" only—academic probationer.

The work, what the boy told his father was the real work, the re-learning of the piano piece, did not go as the boy had predicted. The piano seemed to fight the boy, the boy's fingers resisted flight. And his new, bought-on-the-credit-card music—that music, the boy said, needed transposing before he could sing along.

"No time," the boy said.

"Not that I couldn't do it," the boy said, much as he had said, "Not that I couldn't have been a pitcher," when he hadn't made Babe Ruth. For his Little League team, the boy had once pitched thirteen strikeouts in a row. "Besides, if I don't audition this summer, I can always audition in the fall."

Two nights before leaving for Boston with his father, the boy raced along the strip of road known as "center-of-the-universe," past shopping and eating and banking and gassing-up and sleeping, all on a road full of automobiles, glass, tiny pieces of rock. Pieces of rock set the front wheel of his fragile speed-bike trembling. Knuckles almost white, the boy clutched the front of the handlebar worked it to keep his body from flying into the path of the cars at his back, to propel his body onto curb and sidewalk. One knee was cut, an elbow scratched, the other knee scraped raw.

"We can't come to the phone. . .," said the father's voice on the answering machine. The boy called his friend in the nearby city who borrowed the family car, picked up the boy, drove him home. The boy painted his knees with iodine, clutched the hand of his friend. The boy's father came home.

"Couldn't you just have finished packing your room and gone to sleep?" the boy's father said. "Why are you always running around?"

In the morning, the bicycle store took the boy's bike wheel as an emergency. The boy's father bought the boy a new lock—the old lock had been sawed through to free his bike at the end of the spring term, the boy having lost his keys—and they tried on helmets and couldn't agree on one to buy.

Out the kitchen door early in the morning at the end of the three weeks between semesters, the boy handed plastic crates to his father.

"I can't remember if I even went through these things," the boy said, more or less to himself. "Probably not," the boy's father said, shoving crates into the rear of the station wagon.

"Wait," the boy said. "First we have to put the trunk in—and the keyboard and the amp."

"Put your shit anywhere you want," the father said. The father disappeared into the house.

After the station wagon back was filled, the boy decided he, too, had to sit in the back with his things. His legs should stretch out, he said. Because of his knees. And arranging the back to accommodate the boy meant rearranging the boy's things so that the boy's bicycle wouldn't fall on him, which meant time—and, finally, a line at the tollbooth.

"You can't even ride the damn bicycle after all that," the father says, yanking the ticket from the toll machine. "You should have left the damn bicycle at home."

"I won't not be able to ride the bike forever," the boy says.

"You never listen," the father says.

"What do you want me to listen to?"

"I tell you the right thing to do and you refuse to listen."

"Maybe it's not the right thing for me."

"See," the father says. "See."

They eat lunch at a Roy Rogers, sharing four pieces of chicken—the father eating the dark meat, the boy the white—a large order of fries, hamburger fixings from the hamburger fixings bar, and ginger ales. The Roy Rogers is clean despite the number of people, the father notes. They say to each other, the boy and his father, that they liked the Roy Rogers. The boy asks is Roy Rogers a real person.

"You never heard of Roy Rogers?" the father says. "You never heard of Dale? Or Trigger?"

A light rain is falling when they walk from the Roy Rogers to the car and the inside of the car steams up as soon as the boy and his father are inside and the doors closed. The father opens the windows.

"Everything back here's getting wet," the boy says.

"I have to clear the steam out of the car," the father says.

"When are you going to learn? You have to use the defroster. Opening the windows won't do it."

"How long have you been driving? Who is the one with the tickets? Who is the one with the accidents?"

"You're just lucky. You don't get caught."

"I was planning to take you out to dinner," the father says, "I was planning to unload your things and take you out to dinner, to a nice restaurant, Durgin Park or Locke-Ober's or for Indian. Whatever you wanted. But why should I?" the father says. "All you do is argue and all I do is forget you already know everything."

"Are you going to tell stories about where you went to school and worked and all that?" the boy says.

"Do you want me to?" the father says.

"Oh yes. I always enjoy that part."

They exit the Mass Pike in the neighborhood in which the father went to high school, but only where the high school had been is there to be pointed out.

"This was a slum," the father says as they drive on into a neighborhood of row houses.

"Not any more," the boy says.

"Not any more."

"Could've picked them up for a song," the father says. "Now probably couldn't touch one."

"Mrs. Flannery lived there," the father says, pointing to one of the row houses. "She was our landlady. My mother hated Mrs. Flannery."

"And why was that?"

"Mrs. Flannery expected to be paid."

The boy laughs.

"And that used to be Katz's drugstore, I think," the father says. "I worked there a couple of years. Twenty-five cents an hour and all the Trojans I could steal."

"Did you have a lot of girls?"

"None. Sold the condoms to guys who did have girls. For movie money."

"Westerns," the father says. "I loved the Westerns."

"Did you really try out for the Red Sox?" the boy says. "Did you try out in Fenway?"

"What do you mean did I try out in Fenway? Where else would I have tried out?"

"Sorry."

"I played sand lot ball—outfield—for years, high school and

college. The Sox had these tryouts one spring, for the hometown boys. When I got to Fenway, it looked like the last sand lot player was trying out."

"Were you good?"

"Pretty good."

"How come you didn't make it?"

"I wasn't good enough," the father says. "I just wasn't good enough."

Boston is so changed since they were there last, the boy and his father, that the father says he doesn't know for sure in which direction some streets run anymore or how to get to the street with the music college. The father says he has forgotten how Boston drivers drive, driving being not so aggressive in the suburb where he lives or in the city where he works. The father refuses to believe, he says, that the driver of the newish-looking truck standing at the intersection will continue to pull into the lane toward which the father's station wagon moves to close the opening, no matter how long he, the truck driver, has been waiting. Neither truck nor car gives way.

"You're crazy," the truck driver yells at the boy's father after truck and station wagon kiss. "You're some kind of real nut."

Careful to not crawl on his loosely-bandaged knee, the boy climbs out of the car. "Don't mouth off to my dad," the boy says, arms rigid at his sides, fingers splayed, not even brushing his hair out of his eyes. "You're the one who did it. It was your fault."

The father and the boy stand side-by-side, shoulders almost touching.

The boy cannot keep his bicycle in Boston. With the music college, that's the rule. No cars. No bicycles.

"So we dragged the damn bicycle for nothing?" the father says.

"That's okay, I can't ride it now, anyway," the boy says.

"Besides," the boy says, "you'll never guess what got left behind."

"Your condoms," the father says.

"No," the boy says, "not condoms."

The father shrugs.

"The front tire from my bike—the front wheel," the boy says. "When we re-packed the car, I left the front wheel in the garage."

"Jesus Christ," the father says, just as he said, "Jesus Christ," every time the phone rang for the boy during the break between semesters.

When the caller was one of the boy's male friends, the father said where the boy went even when the boy said telling wasn't wanted. The father carefully wrote down messages left by the boy's male friends, left the messages where the boy couldn't miss them.

The calling voice very often did not belong to a male friend, however. Then, "No, he's not," the boy's father said to Heather or Jill or Amanda or Beth.

"I don't know," the boy's father said.

The boy's father did not ask for messages, said he had forgotten.

"Who are all these names?" the father said. "Don't you have Janice in Boston? Don't you ever get enough?"

The boy's room is in a building old enough to be the original music school. The room is tiny beyond even the tiny indicated in the contract. An almost floor-to-ceiling window opens onto an airshaft. In the window screen there is a hole.

"Look," the boy says, "We have our own bathroom and shower."

"You could fit that closet in a corner of your closet at the house," the boy's father says. "And here you have a roommate."

In the room when the boy and his father arrive, the roommate says music school is his summer vacation. "I won't have much to hang," he says. "I travel light."

The boy begins to pile polo shirts and button-downs in dresser drawers.

"That's not the way to put your shirts," the boy's father says.

"I know how I want them," the boy says.

"Well, you are wrong."

The boy continues piling.

"You are really stupid," the boy's father says. "Someone who doesn't know enough to follow sound advice is not good for much of anything."

The boy turns away, opens another drawer, begins to load his underwear into the dresser.

"Why don't you hang the button-downs over the slacks?" the roommate says. "That'll save a lot of drawer space."

"Thanks," the boy says. "Good idea."

With the roommate, who waits for his keyboard and clothing to arrive from the airport, the boy's father stands outside the music-school building, next to his car, while upstairs the boy finishes loading his closet and his dresser drawers.

"How old are you?" the boy's father says.

"Twenty-four," the roommate says. The boy is nineteen.

"What do you do?"

"Software engineer. California."

"And you came all the way here?"

"I've always liked to do music."

The boy's father shows the roommate the pieces of parking light cover and painted-to-look-like-metal trim that the pick-up truck driver had knocked off the car just an hour previous and asks what the roommate does for a living.

"His brother is in computers, too. You'll be a good influence," the father says, much as he said when the boy was four or five that playing with the neighbor-boy—the one whose mother did not tend to his teeth and whose father on weekends until the weather got too cold screamed four-letter words into the neighborhood—would "broaden the boy's outlook."

The father and the roommate have nearly identical haircuts: trim, business-manly. Of the students going in and out the music school's doors, the girls have short spiky hair, the boys long sausage curls—like Shirley Temple had—or pony tails. The boy came home from his hated college, his hair in sausage curls, some gathered and banded to rise in a tuft from just above his forehead: a pony tail.

"Think of me as your son Pebbles," the boy said to his father.

"Pebbles?" the boy's father said.

In the smallness and remoteness of the hated college, his hair had made him look, the boy said, musical.

"Cut your hair and I'll give you a job," the man who was the father's friend told the boy. The father's friend parted his hair just above his right ear, then combed the long side hairs over what the boy called a "top-level recession."

Not interested in the fact that, as his father reminded him, the man owned a second store, in Boston, not too far from the music school, where he, the boy, could have earned enough to pay his credit card bills, the boy said, "I just can't cut it."

The boy appears with the empty trunk for his father to drive back home, along with the bicycle. Another boy helps carry the trunk, protecting the scab hardened on the boy's knee.

"Well," the father says, extending his hand to the boy, "I don't want to get caught in rush-hour traffic. Good-bye," the father says. "Good luck."

In the rear-view mirror, the boy's father sees the boy standing where he has been left, on the curb in front of the music-college dormitory, watching the station wagon pull away, his hands at his sides, fingers curved into fists. The boy's father drives through Boston and through Brookline, buys gas. If there has been a sign pointing to the Mass Pike, the boy's father misses that sign, driving through Brighton and Waltham before there is a sign that he sees.

After an hour or so on the highway, the boy's father stops at a Roy Rogers. He buys a small order of chicken, all dark meat, and coffee in the smallest-sized cup. The boy's father doesn't eat the drumstick, only sips the coffee.

"A wasted day," the boy's father says, slapping his palm against the steering wheel. The boy's father switches on the radio, roams the dial through stations of rock and oldies to find Beethoven or Mozart, works tongue and lips until his lips are moist, ready to whistle in tune.

She writes stories and essays in the wee hours of the morning at home in NYC, or wintering in Sarasota. She also teaches writing via the internet.

F. R. LEWIS

SITTING PRETTY

by John McCafferty

Y OU CAN TRAVEL THE world but you won't find many places more pleasant than your porch.

Some people have fancy names for porches—verandas, terraces, and loggias come to mind. They're all kin to the porch and can't do anything a porch can't do. To perch on a porch is to sit on the 50-yard line as the game of life goes by.

As a kid living in a Philadelphia row house, I only knew front porches, though today people put porches on the side or back of dwellings as well. Charleston, S. C. has lovely second-story porches which many people call piazzas.

Porches are great for greeting neighbors and for morning coffee and evening wine. You can sit on a porch, in your pajamas or nightgown, with beard stubble or hair curlers, and enjoy the birth of a new day. At twilight, a porch becomes a sanctuary for reflection and purging your mind. Some porch lovers say a sip of chardonnay with Brahms nearby enhances the pleasure. So does the sight of a robin or blue jay, but porches aren't fond of pigeons.

Furnish your porch right and you'll enjoy it even when nature scorches the lawn or sends rain tumbling down the roof and spouting. If your porch is screened, you can thumb your nose at skeeters, wasps and gnats, to say nothing of skunks, squirrels and toads, though an occasional ant may find entry. Porches aren't perfect.

In my youth, the front porch of our Philadelphia row house didn't have screening. It was an open porch with a knee-high railing between our porch and the open porches of our neighbors. In many row house neighborhoods, you can sit on your porch and shout your opinion down a long row of porches until your message reaches its target six houses away. Verbal sparring with the neighbors from one porch to another is good for your vocal chords if you plan to become an opera singer or hog caller.

The porch I grew up with was my introduction to national and world affairs. Sitting on their porches after supper, my parents and neighbors discussed issues large and small every summer night. Because the porches were close together you often heard four or five opinions expressed at once. Everyone seemed to have immediate solutions to problems that plagued our nation. What puzzled me as a boy was why our politicians couldn't come up with these same common-sense solutions. It still does.

For some folks, porches are secret hideouts. Not even the CIA knows you're there, though I wouldn't bet against Sara Snoop across the street who knows everything about everybody and sees and hears through hedges, fences, brick walls, and manholes. If you're going to have a porch, beware of the Snoop family. Most neighborhoods have one.

Over time, your porch will archive memories of friends entertained, books read and ideas hatched there. I can't think of a better place to display your amaryllis and sweet william. If it's fantasy you want, hop aboard a porch rocking chair and watch those excess pounds disappear from your mind, if not your waistline. Actually, it's hard to lose weight when it's so easy to cook a mouth-watering T-bone on a porch grille.

Not all porch memories are pleasant. I was mowing the lawn once when the earth suddenly started spinning. Feeling dizzy and out of breath, I staggered to a porch chaise lounge. If you're having a heart attack, a porch is as good a place as any, I guess, to await the Grim Reaper. However, my wife thought otherwise and called a doctor and paramedics who put me on a stretcher, then into an ambulance and whisked me to a nearby hospital. I eventually needed a heart operation which they did in the hospital because they can't do surgery on a porch. Porches do have limits.

We enjoy our 12th floor porch overlooking the Atlantic in Ocean City, Md., and have spent many hours there hypnotized by the waves, serving hors d'oeuvres and flammables to friends, and scouting dolphins and bronzed bodies below. At dawn, our porch is perfect for watching the sun peek over the horizon. At midnight, it's ideal for counting stars, dreaming dreams, and embracing moonbeams. But don't try sky watching in January or February. Ocean City's porches aren't much fun then.

Florida is a good place to enjoy a porch in winter. In Venice, where our porch overlooks a lake and golf course, we're far enough away so that we can only imagine, not really hear, what the golfers say when they slice a ball into the water. I'm not sure but I don't think it's, "Aw, shucks."

So, there you have it. Bon voyage if you're off to Disney, Fiji or Paris or wherever a crowded plane, train or bus takes you. The best things in life aren't just free, they're often closer than you think. One is a porch—a soul mate for vicarious pleasure. Incidentally, my porch, as I'm about to demonstrate, is also a great place for a nap.

CLOCKS

by N. J. McKeever

T HIS IS A POEM about clocks; tall clocks, small clocks, all clocks.

An anniversary clock whose pendulum is like dancers floating back and forth while timing the passing seconds of the passing day.

A grandfather clock which stands tall and proud, like a patriarch, displaying its moon-etched face while heralding the parade of hours with a deep, melodious gong.

A coo-coo clock, that noisy alpine critter, whose loud tick tock is at times overwhelmed by the perky little bird bursting through its tiny door to count yet another hour.

An alarm clock that waits silently all night, poised like a stalking cat, so it can leap into your dreams and drag you back to reality at an appointed time.

A wristwatch, the smallest of clocks, but mighty, like a
symphony conductor, which when heeded will get you
through the day in an orderly fashion.

This is a poem about clocks; tall clocks, small clocks, all clocks.

THE PREACHER'S WIFE

by N. J. McKeever

MARTHA JAMES WAS A typical minister's wife. She worked hard serving on fund raising committees, teaching Sunday School and leading Bible study classes. She diligently worked with the church's youth groups. Nothing was too much if it helped her adored husband, Robert.

The young reverend had been assigned to this quiet central Iowa parish in late winter and had eagerly thrown himself into his new ministry.

Martha was pleased with the change. She had been glad to leave the Nebraska church. They'd never appreciated her there. No matter how hard she'd worked her committees never met their goals, her bible stories were always mixed up and, for some reason, she had never gained the young peoples' confidence. She suspected they laughed at her behind her back.

More importantly they had left behind, what was to Martha, a serious threat to her marriage. The Nebraska deacon's nineteen year old daughter had all too willingly volunteered whenever Reverend Robert asked for assistance. Martha, well aware of her own dowdy appearance, felt she was no match for that tall, willowy beauty.

Not that she didn't try. Once she had used an auburn rinse on her mousy hair but the brassy result had caused a stir in the Senior Woman's class, and each time she lost ten pounds she'd gained back fifteen. Grateful for this fresh start in Iowa, Martha was sure things would be different this time.

Robert, too, was happy for the move. His devotion to his work, his mission, blinded him to Martha's unspoken needs. He thrived on the added responsibility and challenge of the new church and was unaware of Martha's problems.

The parsonage at the new church was beginning to look like home. Martha had been unpacking boxes and moving things around for a week. As she was arranging books in her grandmother's solid cherry bookcase, the doorbell rang. Since their arrival there had been a steady flow of church ladies offering assistance and delivering aromatic gifts of freshly baked goods, most still warm from the oven.

Martha opened the door to a short, plump, middle-aged woman dressed in neat, matching casual clothes.

"Good morning, Martha dear. I hope I'm not intruding. May I come in?" Her voice was soft and pleasant.

"Yes, of course. Do. . . " Martha swung open the door.

"My, you have this old place looking quite nice! My name is Dana and I've been sent to help you. I should have been here sooner but my last assignment took longer than expected." Her easy smile contrasted with her sharp facial features and dark, piercing eyes.

"I'm just finishing up in the living room. I'll get us some tea and we can chat."

At first Martha felt uneasy. This woman had a strange, almost eerie air about her. She was warm and friendly, but her eyes remained as dark and cold as deep mountain pools at dusk.

"Are you a member of the Parish?" Martha asked politely.

"I'm new here myself, but I'll be a member as long as I'm needed."

"You mentioned having been sent. What did you mean?"

"Oh yes, Dear. I work for a benevolent organization that helps people get what they deserve. They've taken an interest in you and feel you could use some assistance. I'll be here to advise and counsel you for as long as you need me." Dana's quiet, melodious voice had a calming, almost hypnotic effect on Martha. What a comfort it would be to have someone she could confide in and trust.

As the weeks passed, Martha settled into her new routine. To her dismay, she was as inept at her duties here as she had been in Nebraska. This time, however, she had Dana. Each time failure seemed inevitable, Dana would quietly intervene and, before long, Martha gained the reputation of being a steady and efficient manager.

Robert's office was in the church, next to the social hall. He spent a great deal of time there working on his sermons and dealing with the needs of the church.

Dana kept the parsonage from being lonely. She spent a lot of time there with Martha, filling her in on the latest gossip about the parishioners. As time passed, she seemed to focus in on one in particular, the Widow Martin.

Alice Martin was a pretty, sweet and lonely young woman. Devoting her free time to the church gave her comfort. She particularly enjoyed working with the young people, and they enjoyed being with her. Martha had never been able to bond with teenagers, and their acceptance of Alice caused her a great deal of distress.

Robert began to rely on Alice to lead the youth and plan their activities. They had roller skating parties—Martha stayed home and baked cakes. They went on picnics—Martha stayed home and made pies. They went to the movies—Martha stayed home and made fudge.

Each time Martha stayed home preparing snacks for the group, Dana was there and she never missed an opportunity to impress upon Martha the danger of her situation.

"You know, Dear, when I was at Walgreen's yesterday, I saw the Widow Martin coming out of Robert's office at the church. She was all smiles, almost giddish. What are they up to now?"

Martha's back stiffened and her breathing quickened.

"Robert seemed to be in an extremely good mood, too. Are they planning something special?"

Martha turned to take the cupcakes from the oven. Her throat tightened. She could barely breathe.

As Dana watched, her dark eyes seemed to soften. There was a haunting, reddish glow deep within them. A hint of a smile crossed her face. "It just seems there must be some reason they're spending so much time together," she suggested.

Martha turned back to the table, her face flushed and dread in her eyes. "There's the outing at the bowling alley tomorrow night. . . ."

Dana reached over and patted her hand. "I think you should go along this time, Dear."

The next evening Martha went with the group. She was the only one who couldn't bowl at all. Try as she would, Martha's ball seemed to have a will of its own. A couple of the teenagers began to cheer when her ball went down the alley instead of the gutter. She was mortified.

When they got home, Robert tried his best to console her, but, by this time her humiliation had turned to anger. It was all his fault! His and Alice Martin's! Martha ran to the bedroom, locked the door and called Dana.

It was Halloween eve. Martha had spent the afternoon baking pumpkin cookies. The party for the youth group had been postponed until the next night, but she wanted to be ready early because she planned to attend. Her relationship with Robert was fast deteriorating, and she was determined to show him how important she was to him. They had barely spoken since the night at the bowling alley. She blamed him and took offense at his questions and offers of peace. He was completely bewildered and confused.

As Martha finished in the kitchen, she heard a car pull up outside. Glancing at the clock, she expected to see Robert come in for supper. Instead, it was Dana.

"Are you busy? I had to come by and let you know I'm leaving. I received notice this morning that I'm to be at my new assignment first thing tomorrow."

"No . . . No! You can't leave! Not now!" Martha was stricken.

"Yes, Dear, I must. Don't worry. You're going to be fine. Everything is going to turn out just as planned."

Martha was speechless. Her mind was numb and tears welled up in her eyes.

"There, there, Dear. I'm sure you will do quite well without me." Dana patted her cheek, swept out the door and was gone.

Martha hadn't regained her composure when Robert got home. *This is probably all his fault, too. He never liked Dana. He's done something to make her leave.* She turned on him as he entered the house, lashing accusations at him.

"Now look at what you've done! Why have you turned against me like this?" She had started to cry but the anger dried her tears.

"I don't know what you're talking about," Robert retorted. He had no idea what had come over his wife and, after her curious behavior lately, his own anger was aroused.

"You know perfectly well what I'm talking about. You made Dana leave!"

"That's absurd. Listen, Martha, get a hold on yourself. What's happened to you? I won't argue. When you come to your senses I'll be at the church."

Her whole world seemed to be falling apart, crumbling at her feet. She didn't know how to stop it. She rewashed the dishes, wiped down the cabinets, ran the sweeper. Nothing helped.

Wait . . . he didn't go to the church. I know he didn't. He's gone to her! Martha grabbed her coat and ran out the door. Robert had taken the car, but it was only a short walk to Alice's and she was there in no time. She raced up the steps, across the porch and pounded on the front door. Hearing it unlock and the latch open, Martha pushed her way through the half open door, past Alice and into the center of the room. She had worked herself into a frenzy.

"Where's Robert? Where's he hiding?" She looked around the neat, pleasant room.

"I don't know. What's wrong? Why are you here?" Alice was startled and confused.

You know exactly what's wrong," Martha hissed. "He left me tonight and I know he came here, you slut!"

Alice gasped. "He's not here. I haven't seen him since Sunday. He never comes here! What are you saying?"

Martha's eyes searched the room. No Robert! There was a fire burning softly in the stone fireplace on the far wall. *What a cozy nest for a lovers' rendezvous.* Her throbbing head felt like it would explode, her chest ached. A cold sweat drenched her forehead and hands. Blinded by rage, Martha lunged at Alice, grabbed her by the shoulders and began to shake. "Where is he, you witch? You whore! Where's he gone?" she screamed.

Her eyes wide with fear, Alice pleaded, "Let me go! I don't know where he is. He's not here."

Martha snarled, "Go ahead, you filthy bitch. I'll find him." She shoved Alice with all her might, sending her sprawling across the room. She heard Alice's skull crunch as it hit the slate hearth. Alice slumped to the floor like a rag doll. Her half open eyes, empty and unseeing, stared at Martha.

Martha's rage turned to fear as she realized what she'd done.

"No! . . . Oh Nooo. . ." she wailed. She started to go to Alice but couldn't face those haunting eyes. Instinctively she knew she couldn't help her. No one could!

Whirling about, she searched the room for something, anything that might help. A cordless phone lay on the end table. Picking it up, Martha dialed 911.

She stood rooted, gaping at Alice's crumpled form. *Oh God! What have I done? I need help! They'll be here any minute! . . . Wait . . . Dana can help!* The cordless phone was still clutched in her hand. She punched in the familiar number but after one ring a stranger's voice said, "We are sorry but the number you have dialed is no longer in service. . . ."

It's true. She's gone! The phone slipped from her hand. Martha was completely alone. She heard sirens in the distance. In despair, she sank to her knees, covered her face with her hands and began to sob.

PLANE 23

by Holly E. Morgan

T HE OLD MAN SLUMPED on the park bench in the shade of a spreading maple tree, staring into space.

"Charlie, you OK?" asked the old-timer who shuffled up to join him, tossing a peanut shell at some squirrels before popping the nuts into his mouth. "Might as well give the whole dang thing to them," he complained. "Can't chew 'em anymore anyway. You OK?," he repeated.

"Been trying to remember a dream I had last night. Woke up real excited, like something important was about to happen. It's right on the tip of my mind, but I can't grab hold of it. He glanced at his friend. "Did I buy a newspaper yesterday, Ralph? Maybe it was something I read."

Ralph thought about it, but Charlie wasn't waiting for an answer. "No, I know it was a dream. I woke up feeling like I wanted to shout the good news to the whole world."

"I think that's the name of that church book my landlady's always waving around. 'Good News' something or other. I forget. She's always talking about Jesus this and Jesus that. Like he's still alive. Ralph snorted in disgust.

"Holy cow, Ralph, that's it! That's it!" He straightened up, laughing triumphantly and slapping his knee. "Not just Jesus, for Christ's sake, but everybody. The whole world. We're never going to die!"

Ralph looked at Charlie as if he were crazy. "Charlie, I'm too old to live forever." He sighed, shaking his head.

Charlie's eyes glazed over again. "I'm starting to remember it now. I fell asleep last night after reading the same paragraph three times in the mystery I'd been reading. That book wasn't what it was cracked up to be.

"The next thing I remember is this light in my eyes. Must've forgotten to turn my lamp off. You know how things from the real world end up in dreams. Anyway, I was standing in line at an airport, waiting for a boarding pass. Don't know where I was going. The sign up ahead said Plane 23. Not Flight 23, but Plane 23. Never heard it put like that before.

"People ahead of me would get their passes, then walk over to one of those metal detector arches you have to go through, y'know? The light that came on when they walked through was so bright that I couldn't see beyond it. The people just looked like they disappeared.

"Well, I told the guy behind the counter my name and he gave me a green pass. I didn't seem to have any luggage. Then I walked up to that security check. The lady attendant smiled and told me to walk through slowly. I had to almost shut my eyes at that blinding light.

"It was the weirdest feeling, walking through that thing! At first I felt like I was floating, then like I wasn't wearing any clothes. No, that wasn't really it. More like I didn't have anything *binding* on me. I felt free!"

Ralph threw another peanut shell to the squirrels, and Charlie tapped his knee to get his attention.

"Then, when I got to the other side of this thing—and it seemed more like a long tunnel than an archway, once I was in it—I wasn't in an airport anymore. I was in a huge garden, kind of like those manicured ones you see in pictures of France or someplace, y'know?"

Ralph shook his head doubtfully.

"I think the travelogue at the library last week was about France. You didn't actually go, did you? All those old farts sitting there with nothing better to do. Hmmph!"

Charlie waved a hand in dismissal.

"Anyway, I saw a guy, a gardener, I guess, trimming a hedge. You probably won't believe this, but he didn't have any clippers! He just passed his arm over the hedge where he wanted it cut, and that was *it*." Charlie's arm swept through the air to demonstrate. "There weren't any branches or leaves laying on the ground afterward, either.

They were just gone. I never saw anything like it in my life!"

Ralph leaned forward on his elbows, chewing his peanuts, and just shook his head.

"You never will either, Charlie. What an imagination!" Charlie went on as if Ralph hadn't said a word.

"I bet I stood there watching him do that whole hedge. He saw me, too, and waved and smiled at me. I don't know what kind of trick he had, but he was good!"

"Then—get this, now—then I noticed that the path I was standing on was made out of big cobblestones that looked like gold. I swear, they looked like real 24-carat gold bricks! And I was barefoot. I forgot to tell you that. I had on the same clothes that I'd had on in the airport, but my shoes and socks were gone. They felt good, those cobblestones. Not cold like regular stone. Kind of tingly.

"Anyway, I decided I'd better look around and see where I'd gotten to. The pathways were full of people. A lot of them were walking two or three together and talking. And there were what looked like classes going on here and there right on the grass, where people in long robes were standing up talking to little clusters of people sitting on the ground around them.

"I saw people of all ages and sizes and colors, and, well, it looked like we were in a movie studio. There were cowboys, Indians, Romans in togas, a lot of soldiers, aborigines, Eskimos, and I don't know what all. And, y'know, the Eskimo seemed just as comfortable in his fur parka as the aborigine did in his jockstrap. I couldn't figure it out. It wasn't cold and it wasn't hot. The sun wasn't out, but it was really bright. The air smelled—well—fresh, I guess. Don't know, it's been so long since I smelled good air.

"I sort of remember asking myself where the hell I was, and the next thing I knew this gorgeous blond with the most beautiful blue eyes I've ever seen put her arm through mine and started walking with me.

"'Welcome to the twenty-third plane,' she said. It reminded me of the Twenty-third Psalm. She laughed like she was reading my mind, but maybe she'd heard the comparison before. She said, 'It's OK. This certainly isn't the valley of the shadow of death. More like the green pastures.'

"I sure *felt* like I'd died and gone to heaven. Where else would all these different people exist all at the same time, I thought.

"Well, she really *must* have been reading my mind, because she said, 'The twenty-third plane isn't a destination, it's a way of getting there. Where did you want to go?'

"I said I guessed I'd go to Peoria to visit my granddaughter, if it was free."

"I thought your granddaughter moved to California."

"Yeah, but I guess I forgot. Anyway, listen to the rest. She laughed and said 'Oh no, I think I'd better explain. We are *between* Heaven and earth. These people you see are on their way from one lifetime to the next.'

"Sure I'd heard of reincarnation, but I never believed in any of that garbage. Who'd want to come back here again? Now, maybe I wouldn't mind coming back as a cat or a bird, or something like that. Something easy. Anyway, I said to her, 'Whadya mean? You can't tell me that all these people just died. That Roman over there must have been here for a thousand years.'

"She patted my arm and said, 'You'll understand better after I assign you to one of the classes, but time doesn't really exist as you know it.' Boy, she was getting too deep for *me*."

Charlie paused and gulped a quick breath.

"And then it occurred to me that these people had *died*. That kind of made me nervous. I said to her, 'Well, what am *I* doing here? *I'm* not dead.' She smiled—boy, she had a beautiful smile—and said, 'No, you're not. You're dreaming.' 'Whew,' I said. Then I winked at her. Ralph, I *winked* at this gorgeous lady, and she just smiled some more!"

Ralph just shook his head, chewing his peanuts.

"Anyway, she drew me over to a big *map*, I guess you'd call it, carved into a granite floor, and we sat down on some spongy stools—kinda looked like gigantic mushrooms, to tell you the truth. And then this chart got three-dimensional and a voice started to explain it. Like when you push a button at Disneyworld or a museum or somewhere and they tell you about the display or the pictures on the screen. Ever been there?"

"Where?"

"Never mind. This picture—it was more than a picture, it was like—well, *being* there."

"Where?"

"Damned if I know. Everywhere. The whole world. All the places and all the times in the history books. Even in outer space. Everywhere."

Charlie paused to get it straight in his mind, then continued.

"First he explained—this voice in the machine, if that's what it was—that time isn't real. Not the way we think it is, running from century to century. He showed me Earth with layers of, well, *time,* over it. And through it, and passing through each other. Overlapping and underlapping and looking like ten different movies being shown at once on the same screen. Yeah, like different movies on the same screen. Don't ask me who's running the projectors!

"There was an arrow on this map, or globe, pointing out 'You are here.' Only it was pointing to this flat disc, a *plane,* I guess, that was moving around and making stops like an elevator—or a tram—at different places, and some people got off and some got on. When it stopped, it kind of blended into a disc next to it, then speeded up and separated again. See what I mean?"

"No, but it's the best dang dream I've heard in a long time. My wife used to tell me weird dreams. Not that weird, but weird enough. I remember the time she. . ."

"I'm not finished, Ralph. Listen. This is important. When you die, you don't go to Heaven, you go to the twenty-third plane!"

He was excited, and breathing hard, oblivious to joggers and squirrels and kids riding their bikes past him. He gripped his friend's arm.

"Don't you see, Ralph? We don't die, we just go on to someplace else."

"It was just a *dream,* Charlie. Take it easy. Your ticker isn't too good, don't forget. Let's relax and go get an ice cream." Ralph started to get up. Charlie held on and pulled at him.

"But I can prove it, Ralph. I can prove it. Listen. I saw myself in other lives. It was like a movie reel going fast. Let's see—I remember drowning on a whaling expedition; cooking something greasy in an Indian camp—I was a squaw; standing on one leg holding a spear when I was an aborigine in Australia; and I was a knight and knew King Arthur, what do you think of that?! Oh, there's a lot more, Ralph. It's just incredible."

"You said it, Charlie. In-credible! That's just what it is. Charlie, it was a dream. I gotta admit, I don't know how you dreamed that one up, but it was just a dream. After all, you're sitting right here with me in Central Park. See the squirrels, the kids, the trees?"

Charlie's eyes clouded with tears. Through his agitation he insisted again, "Ralph, this is important! Why, there are probably people from those other times walking through us right now."

Ralph shook his head. "I once saw a ghost in a movie walk right through a wall. That's OK if you believe in ghosts. I don't, myself."

Charlie pushed himself up and started down the path, waving his arm as if to hush Ralph.

"Where you goin'?"

"Over to the *Times* office. *Somebody's* got to listen to this. It's important. They'll probably do a feature story on me. *I've* got news. How many other people do you suppose have been to the twenty-third plane and back?"

Ralph rose reluctantly to follow him. "Charlie, nobody's ever even *heard* of the twenty-third plane. You're off your rocker. They'll kick you out."

A bicycle bell tinkled a warning, and a young woman rode by, her blond hair streaming out behind her.

"Beautiful day, isn't it?" she said as she passed, smiling.

Ralph noticed what looked like astonishment on Charlie's face, and then his old friend clutched his chest and fell to the ground.

"My God, Charlie, you gonna let a girl affect you like that at your age?" he said as he rushed over and stooped down.

"That's her!" Charlie gasped.

"Who?"

"The gorgeous blond with the beautiful blue eyes."

"Sure, and I'm an Eskimo."

Ralph held Charlie's hand as the ambulance rushed to the hospital, but his old friend was out of it. As they wheeled him down the corridor on a stretcher, Ralph watched from the nurses' station. He thought he heard the orderly say, "Twenty-three" as he maneuvered the stretcher onto a service elevator.

Charlie heard it too, and smiled. The last thing he remembered was being on a table with blindingly bright lights around him, and then floating away, barefoot, without anything binding him.

A contributor to and editor of newsletters for many years. Her passion for exploring life's mysteries led to developing and teaching workshops in creative visualization and reaching one's Higher Self. Her personal experiences manifest in a book of closely-knit metaphysical short stories, as yet unpublished.

HOLLY MORGAN

HURRICANE WATCH

by H. Baxter Perkins

I sit rigid in the great chair watching the storm through the trembling
 window as the house pulsates to the rhythm of the deep-voiced wind,
and the weather stripping howls in noisy protest. The rain flows
 horizontal, unable to dance on the roof, while large drops slide
and drip on the chimney damper, tapping fathomless messages.
 Electricity flickers with tired, dimming eyes, and the
TV finally stares with a blank face. The refrigerator warms;
 the stove cools; dinner languishes unnoticed.

Trees are being stripped of summer clothing and bending over in
 naked embarrassment. Limbs have lost their grip and slipped
to earth. The hurricane rests as the eye debates which direction
 to take before the wind once more roars into action.
The surf continues relentlessly pounding, retreating and over-
 reaching again and again. Salt spray streaks the window. My
view becomes blurred. Finally darkness descends. I can no longer
 see the elements interacting. I can only hear

The Symphony of the Hurricane.

Born: Cambridge, Mass.
Graduated: Lasell Seminary, Newton, Mass.
    B.A. Boston University
    M.A. Boston University
In the 1950's had one short story and nine poems published in the same year.
Stopped writing until the mid-90's and won one first and one second in Florida
A.A.V.W. writing contest.
Now living in Sarasota, Florida.

H. BAXTER PERKINS

PRETEND

by Patricia Richards

Molly walks down the hill slowly, enjoying the sun. Drawn by the scent of warm hot cross buns she pushes open the screen door to Rafferty's Bakery, nods to the few patrons having a morning tea, and stands at the counter.

"Grand picture of yourself in the paper," an old woman calls.

Molly blushes.

"Your grandmother would be proud." The old man seated next to Molly holds out his copy of the *Irish Times*.

Molly glances at the picture and scans the article:

"The women of today must learn to confront truth. After years of subjugation—'hide your feelings, deny reality'—it is time to speak up, speak out, and state facts. No more hiding behind the screen of make believe," said the guest speaker, our own Molly Ryan, at Our Lady of Lourdes commencement exercises.

"Keep it." The old man waves off her offer to pay.

"Thank you, I'll take it to show Nora."

"Morning, Mary." She smiles at Nora's mother-in-law.

"Why, Molly, how nice to see you. I heard that you'd be coming back for the summer."

"Yes, for the whole summer."

"What can I get for you?"

"Four hot cross buns. I'm off to have tea with Nora."

Mary pauses, "I don't know if Nora would be wantin' a bun."

"Don't worry. If she can't eat two we'll put one away."

"It's just she's been doin' poorly, not holding things on her stomach of late."

"A bug?"

"No-o, it's the illness."

"You mean the cyst she had removed a while ago? She wrote about that. Surely, she must be recovered?"

"Aye yes, you see it is . . . ."

The stranger standing next to Molly leans forward. "Four scones, please."

Mary takes Molly's money and counts the change slowly.

"Have a good day, Mary." Molly leaves quickly, relieved to escape Mary's gloom:

Sure, now, mind that scratch or you'll be havin' your leg amputated, or, put your rubbers on, you'll be catchin' your death of cold. Molly smiles as she replays Nora's perfect imitations of Mary Rafferty. Behind her back they had secretly dubbed her "the mourner."

Molly continues down the hill to Main Street just as Gerry Rafferty is leaving the hardware store.

"Gerry," she calls.

He turns and greets her with arms outstretched. "Molly, Molly, it is grand to see you. Nora has talked of nothing else but your homecoming."

Molly laughs. "I can't wait to see her. In fact, I'm on my way there now. How is the Rafferty family?"

"Fine, fine. Nora's having a good day."

"Having a good day," Molly repeats softly, and starts to ask, "What does that mean?" But something in Gerry's face, the way he turns his head away, stops her.

Changing the subject quickly Gerry says, "It's a perfect day for mending walls before the sheep run away."

"Gerry," The hardware store clerk calls, "Your order is ready."

"You run along, Gerry. We'll have lots of time to reminisce about the good old days."

Molly slows her pace past the doctor's office and the hotel and then off to the right down the country road to Nora's house. Nora and Gerry had been the first to marry right out of school. Their cottage is always a welcome haven. Molly spends her school years teaching at the university in America but summers in Sheep Haven.

The marigolds at the door are all in bloom. It's the warmest June in Ireland for ten years. She taps on the door. Helen Gorman, Nora's mother, answers immediately.

"Why, hello, Mrs. Gorman, so nice to see you. Is Nora here?"

Looking over Helen's shoulder she is struck by the change in the room. Neat and tidy. Everything is in its place—starched curtains, rugs shampooed, dogs out of sight.

"She's been expecting you. Keeps saying that you'll come to see her first thing. I have her sitting up in bed."

Molly's face whitens, making her freckles prominent.

She follows Helen across the sitting room to the bedroom on the right. Nora is sitting up in bed, black hair brushed, cheeks rouged and powdered, and wearing a peach polyester bed jacket with matching bow.

Molly stares.

"Ah! God, it's good to see you, girl."

The words mobilize her, "And sure it's grand to see you," she responds, taking two steps across the room to hug Nora's thin shoulders.

"Here, sit down," Nora grins eagerly.

"So, how have you been?" Molly edges her chair closer to the bed.

"Fine, fine. Having a good day."

Molly bites her lip and tries to stabilize her facial expression.

"Sure, look at me in a bed jacket, it's something of a shock. Remember when we were kids we'd laugh at women who wore bed jackets and bows in their hair, and stayed in bed all the day?"

"We were young and foolish," Molly demurs.

"They do keep you warm when you sit up in bed for a long spell."

"I brought buns."

"Give them to Mam. I don't think I could keep them down. I tried one of Mam's dumplings last night—blueberry, just the way I like them. But it wouldn't stay."

"Sure, dumplings were meant for farm hands." Molly tries to laugh.

"You and Mam have them with your tea."

"Later."

Nora takes a breath, "Now tell me about America, your students, everything."

"It's different. So fast paced and noisy. The students care very little about Irish literature but . . ."

Molly babbles, all those years of teaching standing her in good stead. In a short time Nora moves restlessly from side to side.

"Do you want something?"

"No, no. Tell me about your flight."

"Good weather. Sat with a professor from Trinity and . . ."

Nora's eyes seek the vials on the dresser. Molly senses Helen Gorman hovering in the doorway.

"Well look, I have the whole summer, can't tell you all my stories in one morning."

Helen creeps through the door.

"I'll get your pill, Nora."

Nora's pale face draws in rapidly now.

Molly backs toward the door. "Suppose I come back later and stay for a little while? Mrs. Gorman, you could go the novena at St. Michael's and I could sit with Nora."

Nora nods, watching her mother's hands with the pill and water.

"Just give me a minute, Molly, I'll show you out."

Molly stands in the kitchen clenching her fists, staring at the statue of the Virgin, willing herself calm.

Helen walks her to the door.

"So good of you to come, Molly. Nora loves visitors, she looks good, doesn't she?" she says in a loud voice.

Molly wants to shout. *No! Look at her, she looks terrible. What are you saying?*

But instead she responds in a loud voice, "She looks great."

They step outside and shut the door.

Helen whispers, "She'll be better now. The pill will take effect in a couple of minutes. She'll get three or four good hours."

Molly studies her. "That's good."

Helen twists her apron.

"I do the best I can. Keep the house up, make sure the children do their homework, get the meals. . . . Gerry, God love him, isn't much good. Men never are. They just stay away."

"I'll come back later, give you time for church."

"Thank you. It would be nice to go to church. I won't stay long. She can't do without me."

Molly nods.

"I have to get back in now."

Molly turns down the path toward town.

Dr. Jim Nolan's van is in front of his laboratory. He won't be having visiting hours until after lunch. Molly taps on the side door, praying he'll be there.

"Come in," the old doctor calls.

Molly stumbles on the sill. Jim Nolan reaches out and steadies her. "Are you all right, child? Here, sit down, Molly. Been meaning to get that sill fixed for years. Disgrace for a doctor to have an uneven step like that." He takes the chair next to her.

"I've been to see Nora."

He nods. "I thought maybe you had."

"What happened to her?"

"Molly, I can't say. You'll have to talk to Gerry or her mother."

"I can't talk to them. They're running around treating her like a doll or a mental patient. She's dying and they're lying to her, pretending she's going to get better.

"She's dying," she repeats and looks to Jim Nolan for denial. He doesn't respond.

"It's cancer. The cyst was cancer." He looks at her steadily.

"Why are we wasting time? We could take her to Sloane Kettering in New York. It's world famous for cancer research. We could . . ."

He puts his big care-worn hand over hers. "Molly, Molly. There's no money for expensive trips to America. The Raffertys barely make ends meet."

"Money's no problem. I have money." She clutches her pocket-book. "I could pay her way."

"Molly, I know I'm only a small village doctor, but Nora's best left in her own bed with her husband and her children. I've consulted with everyone. Trust me."

"You can't give up—sit here in this stupid little village and think it's the world. There must be a way."

She starts to sob. He doesn't try to stop her. Time passes in cadence to the pendulum of the grandfather clock. Finally as she sniffles, he offers her a handkerchief and a snifter of brandy.

When she looks up to accept the glass, she realizes how Jim Nolan has aged in her year away. His face is gray and the circles under his eyes are very dark.

"I'm sorry for what I said, Dr. Jim."

"Don't worry about it. We all say things we don't mean when we're hurt. "

"Why don't they tell her the truth? She has the right to know."

"Perhaps they think it's too much for her. Maybe they can't face her illness. It's their choice, not ours."

"She's my best friend, as close as a sister to me. I could tell her, comfort her."

"Are you prepared to take everyone else away from her?"

"I don't know. I just don't know."

Yesterday she would have known. Truth was the only standard, unvarnished truth.

They sit in silence until the Angelus bell tolls.

"I'll go now, Jim. It's time for your office hours. You have a lot of other people to care for."

"Come in anytime. I'm always here"

She walks out into the sunlight, disoriented, and stands watching Father Donnelly weed the garden in front of St. Michael's.

"Hello, Molly."

"Afternoon, Father."

"Home visiting?"

"Yes, I've been to see Nora."

"I was there yesterday. Poor soul," he clucks, "and so young."

Molly closes her eyes and sways. "I think I'll just go into the church and say a prayer," she says, eager to escape his comforting.

She bends her knees onto the old wooden kneeling bench, relishing the coolness and the smells of wood polish and incense in the old church. She isn't always a faithful participant in America, but here, in the old country church of her childhood, she sinks into the comfort of a home and a father in heaven always waiting to listen to one's prayers.

"Please, God, don't let Nora die. She's so young, she has children.

We need her. Please, God, you can't let her die." Molly kneels there a long time.

Silence and later the hum of clippers breaks the stillness.

"A miracle, just a little miracle. We could take her to Lourdes. Yes, Lourdes."

She stands and walks to the front altar. Bows her head, lights a candle to the Sacred Heart, drops coins into the metal box, and leaves by the side door.

Nora, the feisty one, would believe in a miracle. Nora had believed that Molly's essay could win the scholarship to the big college in America. Nora had believed Molly could pass Latin. Nora had believed. . . .

Nora will beg to go to Lourdes.

She looks at the sky. Its time to return to Nora's.

Helen is standing in the doorway to Nora's room waiting for her with her sweater on and her rosary beads in hand.

They watch the sleeping figure.

"She weighs only eighty-six pounds. No more than a child."

Molly swallows and watches Nora's shallow breathing.

"God forgive me. I gave her an extra pill."

"It was necessary." Tears trickle down Molly's cheeks.

"Asked me today if I thought she has TB. She said, 'You know, Mam, I don't seem to be getting well.' And who could tell her? And then she said, 'Maybe we could go to the sea later in the summer.'"

Molly turns away. Helen closes the door and follows.

"Now I won't be long. I left the tea steeping and the buns on the plate. It's kind of you to stay."

Molly sips the tea, pushes the buns away, not sure she can swallow. *There will be no Lourdes for Nora.*

She retrieves *The Irish Times* from her bag and spreads it on the table.

Sister Maureen O'Hara's words flash back in her mind:

"Fine words, Molly, well spoken. Truth may be very in vogue at the university. But one doesn't know truth until it's tested."

Molly had smiled and mocked Sister O'Hara's words by ignoring them, shaking hands with the next person to her left without deigning to comment.

Well, the testin' had come, and quickly. She tastes only bitterness, not the tea.

"Molly, are you there?" Nora calls, drawing Molly out of her reverie.

"Yes, right here. I'm coming."

She puts her cup on the drain board and pushes open the bedroom door.

"Would you like a drink, some tea?" She smiles much the way Helen had smiled. "My, don't you look rested after your nap." She plumps Nora's pillow.

Really, it was quite easy to fall into one's part, to lie and pretend. *God help me.*

AFTER DARK

by Ann Robinson

She crept out of the house
Toward a row of swollen bags
Lining the curb for
Tomorrow's truck;
Squatting in the moonlight
She kept trying to bend
Arthritic fingers
Around the twisted knots
Her children had tied;
Frustrated
She rose and stabbed a hanger
At the plastic mounds
Over and over
Until their contents lay
on the ground
And then she could stuff
Both pockets
With small pieces of her life
The children had trashed. . .

A member of the Dramatists Guild; has won many national poetry awards. Currently preparing two holiday children's books, Tom Turkey *and* Sandy Claus *for e-book publication.*

ANN ROBINSON

PABLO. A STORY

by Jane Roehrs

W HOSE EYES DID HE have? Did he have her father's honest hazel eyes—or were those green eyes with the dark centers, so beautiful and full of mystery, more like her ex-husband's? Only lately had Carmen begun to consider reincarnation as a real possibility, in a user-friendly world where, according to Oriental religion, people who had messed up their lives—and the lives of others—could come back in some other form for soul purification.

Her father, who had died some years ago, might like to come back to retell some of those humorous old stories which were his standby, but her ex-husband Keith, whose death by auto was still a recent happening, had more need of spiritual rebirth. Had his soul been sent back for improvement in the body of a cat this time because he had not made enough progress with his soul on the first try?

Keith had been a charming bounder who used people freely and made a quick getaway if possible when the going got rough. It amused her to think that he might be reduced to being this four-legged creature in a kind of animal he had never even liked. He had always been a dog person, a dog being the kind of creature noted for undying devotion, which he always exacted of those around him.

Looking at Pablo, and thinking of Keith, was upsetting—she gave an involuntary shiver.

When a little paw touched her face, it was hard not to think that the gesture was loving and gentle as well as based on curiosity or design. But after all, with Keith it had been a love match, too—at first.

And when Pablo looked at her soulfully, with those big eyes, she couldn't help feeling a warm response to this little lost charmer that needed somebody so badly. So here she was, feeling loving and giving. And then he moved quickly—too quickly—and she felt pain as he scratched her neck. She was immediately on guard. "Get down," she said harshly, and he jumped down from her lap.

This was a rather strange animal, mostly fearful of people. He had all-over gray tabby markings except for white paws and white bib and collar. The way he came to her was unusual., as though preordained.

She had been feeding a stray that she gave the witchy name of *Bruga,* because it was overall black and had arrived on Halloween. It wouldn't go away. Then a gray and white mother with her small kitten began stopping by for food, too. She fed the extra animals for several days, and then, after the gray mom's good breakfast on the patio one morning, she headed in the afternoon toward the dripping faucet in the side yard, but on the way, keeled over, dead. Whether she was poisoned or had leukemia or some other disease, Carmen never found out. She was more concerned about the little survivor.

Who would take care of him if she didn't? She let him sleep on her screened porch that night, so he would not miss his mother too much, and larger creatures would not attack him. Someone had been kind to him before and bought him a flea collar, and he seemed less afraid of people than Bruga. Pablo purred appreciatively that first night as she babied him and gave him a saucer of milk, as well as the usual cat food.

It was natural for her to think at first of her father in connection with this motherless creature. Her father's mother had died when he was born. It had affected his personality.

He had been raised by a stern grandmother and had become somewhat standoffish, which was not always the case with Pablo. The kitten seemed to take it for granted that Carmen, at least, liked him and wanted to do for him.

He had a jaunty way of sitting on his haunches with his pretty white vest showing. His ears were always standing straight up, one completely triangular, the other notched where, no doubt, he was bested in a fight with another animal. He was feisty, as Bruga soon found out.

He was also affectionate when it suited his purpose—which was very like Keith.. She was surprised the first couple of times when the kitten bounded up onto her—even while she was standing up—in an effort to get her to sit so he could get in her lap. He purred tremendously in appreciation when she stroked him and then, after a time, with a show of indifference, he would bound off to sit in the most comfortable spot in the house, the corner of the living room sofa.

Pablo and Bruga both became house cats during a spell of cold weather when she felt sorry for them and let them come inside during the day.

Actually, her whole life changed because her first activity of the morning was no longer to turn on the computer and see if she had E-mail to answer, but to feed the cats and get them outside if the day was nice. "The sun's shining, go out and play," she heard herself saying, just as she used to do with the children when she was married to Keith.

Another reminder of those earlier days: the cats, Bruga and Pablo, were constantly fighting, just as the children used to. Keith had a daughter, Melanie, from a previous marriage—a girl of a rather unpleasant disposition who resented Carl, her child with Keith. Now away at school, Carl had learned to take care of himself. He had become a member of the college boxing team, and Melanie was now married and living in Miami.

It seemed these cats were just as much rivals of each other as the children had been. So here was the green-eyed monster again that had contributed to the unraveling of her marriage. Keith had been insanely jealous not only of the children and the amount of time she spent with them, but of the time she spent with anybody but him.

Pablo was quite possessive too. Each morning he would come up to the table for scraps when she was having breakfast, and, seeing Bruga standing guard nearby, would aggressively rush toward her. Each would stake out territories and the other would be challenged not to enter it. Then one would threaten the other to back down in a line of march. Pablo was frequently chasing Bruga and snapping at her tail. Bruga liked to fight, too, and often started the hostilities, using her sharp claws to attack and defend herself well. She was a good climber, and, if Pablo was too much of a nuisance, she sought the roof for a quiet snooze.

Carmen fed them in separate bowls, but, as soon as one started to eat, the other one was there, too, to try to get food from the same bowl. Only when they went outdoors to play and could get well away from each other did she get any peace.

One day when her sister, Maria, came visiting, she commented on the personalities of the cats. "You know, there is something about that little gray kitten that reminds me of Keith," she said. "You'd better be careful of him!" "And the way they fight—it's real sibling rivalry!"

Maria had never liked Keith. She had warned Carmen before her marriage that he had a terrible temper and a streak of mean. Her attitude was based on the remarks of a woman she'd known who said she had dated Keith at one time. Carmen still got jittery now thinking about how things turned out with Keith.

"I'd watch that Pablo," Maria said as she left. "First he'll be wandering off, then he'll be back like thunder—"

"Like little Pablo," Carmen said, laughing at the venom in her sister's voice being directed at such a small animal.

Strangely, what she said seemed to be prophetic. After she left to go north again—Maria stayed only during the winter months in Florida—Carmen began noticing that Pablo disappeared for longer and longer periods at a time, and even when she called the cats for supper, he did not return some evenings. He was not just being a natural male cat either—Carmen had taken the cats to a good vet and had them "fixed."

One evening, on a hunch, she went over to the apartment house next door to see if she could find the missing Pablo—and there he was, having a hearty supper in front of an apartment entrance. When she went up to him, they were joined by a youngish athletic looking man with clear blue eyes and blond hair, graying slightly at the temples. He was wearing tan slacks and a sports shirt, and carried an open sports magazine.

"So you are the other owner of my kitten!" he said.

"Your kitten? Why you must be the one who bought Pablo the flea collar before his mother died," Carmen said.

He was indeed the one, and from that time on, she and Scott became—not rivals over Pablo, but friends. Scott traveled as a computer consultant and was gone for extended periods, but when he came back from his next trip, she invited him over and cooked a dinner in appreciation of his kindness to Pablo. It was also partly to show Scott who really "owned" Pablo.

And Pablo began to display his possessiveness as soon as Scott came in. He let Scott know he was special to Carmen by trying to jump in her lap when she sat down, and, being foiled at that, by taking a station near her chair.

His rivalry with Bruga continued to concern her, and one night, the fighting of the two became so intense she had to intervene, receiving a deep scratch on her right arm as she finally separated them. She wondered then if this might be a warning of worse things to come, but tried to brush away her anxiety.

She didn't know if she imagined it, but Pablo seemed to be less friendly toward Scott every time he came by. She had never felt herself good at seeing into the future, but somehow she sensed something sinister was about to happen. For one thing, Scott was developing romantic notions—he had had a marriage that went bad too—and now he was hinting that he and Carmen could become special to each other.

"Oh, we're just friends," she would respond coquettishly, nodding her head with its black hair until her gold circlet earrings jangled. "We're all friends here together."

"Carmen, I don't think Pablo would let you have a relationship with anybody else," said Scott. He said it lightly but she knew he meant it. "He's really a jealous cat!"

She was surprised to discover she really missed Scott during the times he was away and looked forward to his return. When he invited her to dinner and they left to go out, Pablo would look at them with those baleful green eyes when she put him on the porch with Bruga.

Soon, she thought, it would be warm enough to let the cats sleep outside again. Meanwhile, as cold snaps continued and the cats were so used to sleeping on the porch, she put off trying to change them.

Her relationship with Scott was reaching a critical point. He had written her several times during a trip to Chicago, and he wanted her to quit side-stepping his romantic suggestions. She must give him a decision on which way their relationship would go, he wrote. I can't stand this halfway business."

She took a long walk the day he was due back, trying to sort out her feelings about him, and realized as she got dressed for dinner that she was still undecided and felt stressed out. As she brushed her dark hair and coiled it atop her head—she had not a single white hair, she was happy to note—she thought about the fire he kindled in her soul. Her eyes sparkled as she applied eyebrow pencil and lipstick expertly, and attached the beads and dangling earrings that set off her Spanish-type beauty. She swished her colorful skirt playfully— she had discovered Scott liked her to wear feminine clothes—as she went to the sofa to wait for him to come.

She smiled as she thought of Scott, who, she was sure, could make this a real night of enchantment. She would cooperate by continuing to hide one small secret—the fact that she was older than he. He must never find out!

She had fed Pablo and Bruga, but they were still underfoot when Scott came for their date. Scott's blue eyes were flashing, and he was enthusiastic about his trip—he had had a job offer in Chicago which would advance his career, but would require a move to the Windy City.

"I'll take it if you'll go with me, Carmen!" he said, reaching for her hand as they sat on the sofa to have a glass of wine before dinner. "I miss you on these trips. I want us to be together!"

"As more than friends?" she asked, as he put his strong arms around her and kissed her with a depth of feeling. As they stood up to go, she realized her heart was beating wildly. But just then she felt seven pounds of cat like a projectile against her. Pablo was throwing himself at her just as he did at times when he wanted her to sit down and hold him in her lap. She was so surprised, she stepped back and the spell of the romantic moment was broken.

"Maybe we could take Pablo with us," Scott said, with a laugh. "But I don't know—it looks like he's real competition."

Was Scott a jealous type too? That was something she needed to know.

Over dinner at a restaurant overlooking the gulf, she told Scott about the way her marriage broke up, how Keith had changed from a loving and caring husband and father, to a jealous tyrant. The climax came when he followed her to a restaurant one day where she had met a childhood friend with whom she had had a platonic relationship. She had told Keith about the luncheon date and that no romance was involved with the family friend. But he refused to accept it and created a big scene in the restaurant. Later he bought a gun, and she feared for the safety of both the children and herself. As soon as the children went away to school, she left him.

Scott's break-up had been less volatile but just as final, with no children involved.

"I have to give them an answer about the job on Monday, Carmen," Scott said finally. "I think we both need a second chance. Say you'll go with me!"

"Would we marry?" she asked, hesitantly, feeling insecure about the casualness of relationships in modern age lifestyles. The religious upbringing of her childhood still had a hold on her although it had lessened through the years.

"If things go that way," he answered. "Say you'll go!"

She wondered if he would be the kind who would never commit.

"But I have so many things to think about," she said. "There's the house, and what Carl's reaction would be. My son is important to me, too. She promised to give him an answer on Saturday.

"Decide things my way," he said, giving her his charming smile before he kissed her goodnight.

She had trouble going to sleep as she thought about Scott and the happiness their future together might hold. But she wished she knew more about him. He had said little about his past.

After talking to Carl, she decided she could hold onto her house for awhile—to give her son, as well as herself, a sense of security until a more permanent decision was made. She would miss the cats—Pablo especially. If she had to give them up, perhaps she could advertise and find good homes for them.

When she heard the doorbell ring in mid-afternoon Saturday, she knew it was Scott, unable to wait until their date to hear her decision. She felt like a teenager again as she heard the bell and got up to head for the door. *So this is the way to have an aerobic heartbeat without taking aerobics!* she thought.

She could hardly wait to tell him that she wanted to go away with him, that she was ready for some adventure in her life—whatever the future might hold! She almost danced as she ran to the door.

That was when the accident happened. Pablo was right in her way, and as he stopped her, wrapped himself around her ankles. She pitched forward and heard a snap as she fell with her left leg buckled under her. Scott heard her cry of pain and rushed through the unlocked door. "Are you all right?" he shouted as he tried to lift her to her feet. But she couldn't stand.

"Pablo," she said, simply, in explanation.

"We'd better get you to the emergency room," said Scott.

So that's why she stayed in her own home with a cast on her left leg, and Scott left for Chicago, alone.

He called but things were never the same afterward. Soon, she found out, he was meeting attractive women in the workplace, and had found again one particular one he knew from earlier days. As she hobbled around, she felt she'd be unable to compete. Maria who came to stay with her while her leg was healing, tried to boost her morale. "Where is your spirit, Sis? We come from people with fire who fight for what they want."

"I know, but in our family we fight too much."

"Perhaps your cats aren't the only jealous ones around here, and maybe you're a scaredy cat!" Maria laughed as she said it, but Carmen looked solemn, her eyes downcast. "Why don't you go to

Chicago to see Scott? I know you could compete with any of those women he's met! What's the matter? Don't be so sad!"

"I could be remembering *abuela* Carmen, our feisty grandma. Remember, she stood with the knife in her hand when the police came, while her beloved lay dead on the floor!"

"But *abuela* would have forgiven her," said Maria. "He knew he was unfaithful, and she had brought him happiness and children he loved as well as the sharp knife. . ."

"But I am her namesake. Maybe I am just like her. Maybe I go to jail too—"

After Maria left, Carmen sat wondering more than ever if Keith was somewhere in the nether world having a big laugh at her confusion. Pablo, his earthly counterpart, seemed quite content that Scott had gone away.

Served on the staffs of daily newspapers and trade magazines in the Carolinas, Florida and New York. She conducted the syndicates page on Editor and Publisher in NYC, and was reporter/arts writer for the Charlotte (N.C.) News. *Widely published as free lancer, she has completed a first novel.*

JANE ROEHRS

ROSA IN THE SUNSHINE

(EXCERPT FROM THE NOVEL *A GOOD FIST*)

by Barbara E. Rowe

JOHN HITCHED A RIDE on a freight heading north. In Mountain Home, a small circus heading west added its cars to the train. During the hook-up procedure, John wandered back to watch and find out who the boss was. He liked the boss and was sure Mr. Sanford liked him. John asked if there were any jobs available.

"See Andy," Mr. Sanford had said. "He'll tell you if there's a place." So here he was back with the elephants again. At least he knew the work and whenever he was idle, the boss sent him to help Andy, the head rigger, with the rings and swing bars for the acrobats and flyers. There was one girl about his own age John liked to watch. One day he asked Andy who she was.

"Oh, you mean Rosa? All her family are aerialists. She's a quiet little thing. One hell-uv-an acrobat and she's getting to be a pretty good flyer, too. That Carlo, he's real tough with his kids. Got them practicing all the time. It shows, though. They're top act in the Circus. If Carlo wants something, Carlo's gonna get it. Don't you forget it. He's starting to put Rosa up in the top, flying."

Andy eyed John and chuckled. "If you got eyes for that little Rosa, forget it. Carlo treats her special. Don't allow none of the men in the circus near her—not even to talk to her."

John learned that Rosa and her mother always came to the ring very early in the morning to practice. So, in spite of the advice from Andy, John took fifty cents from his pay and bought a little green elephant on a silky cord to give her as a present. He went to the ring as often, and as early, as he could after his own morning chores were done, hoping to talk to her. One morning his patience was rewarded. Rosa and her mother were there checking their apparatus. This was his chance! He gathered all the nerve he could muster.

"Hi!" He said. "My name's John. Andy and me'll be working here this morning." Rosa smiled and nodded, but did not speak. Her mother watched the exchange.

"She no talka to you. You talka to me."

John nodded. "Yes, Ma'am. I only work here sometimes. Mostly I work with the elephants. If you want them swings any special way, I'll do 'em for you best I know how." Rosa and her mother both nodded. Rosa pointed toward a swing bar dangling askew and motioned John to let it down.

"You sure look pretty up there, spinnin' around. I think I'd be kinda' scared up so high." Rosa shook her head and gave a casual wave of her hand, indicating she didn't think he would. He reset the bar, she nodded and they stood smiling at each other.

"I got something I'd like you to have," he said. "Sort of a good luck charm. It's an elephant, see? I take care of the elephants. You ride 'em in the parade. It's from me and the elephants to you. The lady where I bought it said elephants mean good luck. I hope they do. I hope you like it." She looked at the gift he had placed in her hand and, turning to her mother, held it out for her to see. Her mother nodded. Turning back to John, Rosa placed the cord around her neck, touching the little elephant at her throat, and smiled a brilliant smile of appreciation. John's heart twirled and leaped like one of the acrobats.

Rosa turned again to her mother, hands pressed together in an imploring gesture, then pressed a finger to her lips. Her mother responded again with a nod.

I wonder how's come they don't talk none? Maybe she don't speak English.

Every morning after that, early, when no one was around, he would go down to the ring hoping to meet her. On those mornings, they'd walk around the ring swinging a rope, testing a knot, her mother always close behind. He talked and Rosa listened.

He was sure he hadn't talked so much in his entire life. By the time the circus reached Jefferson City he had just about told her his whole life story. She, however, had not spoken a word.

Setting up very early that first morning in Jefferson City, Rosa came out to the ring alone. Overjoyed at having her all to himself, John asked her, "Rosa, don't your pa like you to have any friends? Andy said he don't want you talkin' to nobody."

Quickly she put her hand over his mouth, turning a little to look over her shoulder and put a finger to her lips. "You mean he don't know you're coming out here to see me? It's a secret? Then that means you want to meet me and you don't care if he don't like it." She nodded and smiled, then covered her face with her hands.

John could hardly keep from shouting, from grabbing her around the waist and swinging her round and round. He grinned from ear to ear. "Well, I sure won't tell nobody. But you know you ain't said one single word to me, ever? I wish you'd say my name, out loud."

She looked up with sad, melting, brown eyes, and shook her head. She put one hand to her throat, tapped it, then, touching her fingers to her mouth, made several small outward gestures and shook her head, no. She watched John's face all the while.

"I don't know what. . ." Then he understood. "You mean you

can't talk? You don't have any voice, or something?" Rosa nodded, watching his face.

In the gray dawn she looked so forlorn and vulnerable all he wanted to do was comfort her. He put his arms around her and just held her for a long time. Then, right there in the middle of the bigtop ring, he kissed her and didn't care who saw. Her mouth was so soft, her body so slim; she fit perfectly into his arms. He didn't want to just walk and talk any more, he wanted to hold her like this and kiss her forever.

The circus stopped in Springfield, Lebanon, Jefferson City and Columbia and, finally, in Kansas City for their last shows before moving south to winter quarters. On the long ride west from Columbia, he and Rosa did not see one another at all. He rode back with the other animal tenders. He couldn't stop thinking of her; of her silence. He wondered if she was thinking of him.

That first day the elephants worked raising the tents and John worked wherever Mr. Sanford wanted him—circling the animal cages, securing ropes, running at the boss's commands. He had no time to even think about Rosa.

In the grand parade she sat on a gold tasseled cushion atop one of his elephants, waving to the crowds. When she saw him, she smiled and blew him a kiss. She looked just like the poster he'd seen in Little Rock. Black hair shining, feathers dancing, all a-glitter in her spangles and red satin.

Long before dawn the next morning he was in the ring waiting, hoping she would be there. When he saw her at last, he ran to meet her.

"Come with me where my elephants are. Nobody'll bother us there and the elephants won't tell your pa." She tipped her head back laughing her silent laugh, shook a finger at him, tapped her head and shook it from side to side. John guessed at her signs. "I ain't thinkin'? . . . no. . . I can't remember? . . . What?" She pointed to her necklace and tapped her head again. "An elephant can't remember? . . . Oh," he smiled, "an elephant never forgets." She nodded, clapping. "And an elephant never talks, neither," John said, laughing at their game.

Together they filled the animals' water-troughs and pitched clean hay in the compound. "For a little girl you sure got alot a' muscles," he said, as he watched her heave a fork full of hay. She nodded, flexed her biceps, pointed above her and twirled her hand round and round. "You need muscles to fly?" She nodded, and pitched another fork of hay.

When John's chores were done, they climbed to the top of the bales of hay and watched the dawn break. He reached forward to touch the curve of her breast silhouetted against the sunrise.

"I bet you sure are pretty in your birthday suit." She looked down, touching her clothes, a frown on her face. "No, not your dress. Your skin. Like the day you was born." He grinned. "That's your birthday suit. I only seen one woman bare naked in my whole life. But that was my cousin and she was crazy . . . dancin' around with her nightgown over her head, so maybe that don't count. But I sure looked, anyway. I thought for a long time I was goin' to hell for lookin'," he grinned. "I never told nobody that before." Rosa gestured that she would never tell, and grinned.

She pointed to the sun, swung her arm in a wide arc, then pointed to herself.

"You're gonna do something tomorrow?" he asked. She shook her head no, then pointed to his eyes. "Oh," he nodded, "I'll see you tomorrow at sunrise?" She nodded. They climbed down from the hay and just held each other, not wanting to say goodbye. He had fallen hopelessly in love.

The next morning they met in the ring and walked back to the elephants. In the before-dawn grey light he noticed she was wearing one of the robes the acrobats all used before they climbed to the trapezes.

"Your pa had you practicing already, Rosa?" She shook her head no and smiled. They climbed up on the hay bales and sat looking toward the eastern sky. Rosa pointed to herself, counted to fifteen on her fingers, and pointed to where the sun would rise. "You want fifteen sunrises? . . . No! . . . The sun will rise in fifteen minutes? No! What?" She pointed to herself again, waiting. "You!" he said. She nodded, counted again to fifteen and waited. "You're fifteen." She pointed at the rim of the sun just coming up over the horizon, and grinned, happily. "You're fifteen, today? Today? Oh, happy birthday!" Rosa put her finger to his lips to be quiet. "Happy birthday, happy birthday," he whispered, leaning forward to kiss her. She put him off and smiled broadly. Pointing to herself again, she touched the little elephant on the cord around her neck, cupped both hands together, and made a gesture outward toward John.

"You're gonna give me back the elephant? No. You're gonna give me a present?" She nodded. "But I should be the one giving you a present. It's your birthday." She shook her head and told him to close his eyes and count to ten. When he opened them, she was kneeling, naked, in the sunrise.

"Oh, Jeeze. Oh, Jeeze," he breathed and watched transfixed as she rose and turned round and round until the sun was full over the horizon. Then she smiled at him and, extending both arms out to each side, as she did at the end of all her circus performances, bowed, put on her robe and tied it.

"What a beautiful present. Nobody ever gave me such a beautiful present. I wish I'd'a known it was your birthday. I don't have any present to give you." Rosa nodded her head and grinned. Touching his shoulder, she pointed to the sun, then shook his shirt and covered her eyes with her hands. He sat a minute, looking at her, not sure he understood.

"You mean you want me to show you my birthday suit?" She laughed, nodding, as he laughed, too. "Ok, if that's what you want for your birthday. But I ain't pretty like you." He stood up to pull off his shirt, laughing into the sun. A voice out of the dark below them made Rosa gasp in fear. It froze them both.

"Get down from there, you bum! What you do to my Rosa? I kill you, you son of a bitch," the angry voice bellowed. "I kill you, you ruin my Rosa! Get down here. Rosa, you come down!"

John's mind was flying. How can I get her down from here? How can I get her out of here? He jumped into action, climbing down from the haystacks, shielding Rosa as he helped her down, guiding her to one side. He stood in front of Carlo and answered his thundering adversary, as much control in his own voice as he could muster.

"I ain't done nothing, sir. We ain't done nothing. It's her birthday today and we were just watching the sunrise on her birthday. I ain't ruined Rosa, sir. I ain't ruined nobody." John hoped that Carlo hadn't been watching long enough to see his daughter standing naked in the sunrise, too. But if he had, John figured, he'd a' hollered a whole lot sooner and a whole lot louder. "I wouldn't hurt her, sir, I love Rosa and we ain't done nothin' wrong."

Carlo seized hold of John's shirt and pulled him up close, face to face, growling, low and menacing.

"You don't talk to Rosa no more, you hear? I kill you, you bum."

John had been calm and respectful up to this point, for Rosa's sake, but now his own anger rose up in his throat and he wrenched free of Carlo's grasp.

"Hey! Leggo! Keep your hands offa me. I told you, I ain't done nothin' to Rosa, so lay off. And I ain't no bum!"

Rosa touched John on the face, trembling at her father's fury, then turned and ran. Carlo shook a fist at John and snarled. "I fix you, you bum. I fix you." He turned abruptly and followed his daughter.

Shaken by the whole morning's experience, John stayed with the elephants. He found a certain calm again in the physical labors and the peaceable swaying of the huge beasts. One of the rigger's walked over to him.

"Hey, John, Mr. Sanford wants to see you in his office."

"What's he want with me?"

"Don't know, kid. He just told me to tell you, and not to dawdle."

"Okay, thanks, Joe."

On the way over to the side show tent where the boss had a space sectioned off for his office, John thought, *Maybe he's gonna give me a new job or something.*

"Hello, Mr. Sanford, you wanna see me?"

"Yep, sure do." He handed John his pay and said, "You're off the payroll, Son. Sorry."

John was stunned. "Why, Mr. Sanford? Ain't I done my job right?"

"Sure have, John. You're a real hard worker. This isn't about work, it's about business. I don't know what happened and I don't wanna know, but Carlo and his family are my number one act. They're a damn good draw and I can't afford to lose 'em just because his little dummy has a yen for the elephant boy."

"Don't you call her a dummy. She ain't no dummy. She's smart, and beautiful, and kind, and good. She ain't done nothin' wrong. Neither have I."

"It don't matter one way or the other to me, John. You got caught doing something Carlo didn't like or imagined he didn't like. It's all the same. He came in this morning blowin' smoke and fire, ready to tear my head off. Gave me an ultimatum. Either I kick you out on your behind, or he takes his family and leaves for Texas or Louisiana or Florida and some other circus."

"That ain't fair, sir. That just ain't fair."

"Fair don't count worth shit, John. He's just more important to my business than you are. Water boys are a dime a dozen. Good flying acts are hard to find, and they're the best I can get. It's simple as that, John. Business is business. So, you got your pay, now get your gear and get off the property, or I'll get the sheriff and have you hauled to jail. Nothing personal. I wish you good luck."

"Yeah, business is business," he mumbled. He walked away feeling betrayed again by the world. Angry, miserable, alone, he headed for the only place he could think of to solve his problems.

In the maze of tracks and cars in the Kansas City train yard, he wandered like a lost soul. *Geeze! This sure ain't like Marion or even Little Rock I don't know which way any of these trains are going. Ahh Nuts! It don't matter which way I go, anyhow. Just so's I get as far away from this place as possible.*

John stared out at the moonlit Kansas landscape flying by, but all he could see was Rosa shining in the morning's brilliant sunrise. The night turned colder and he huddled in the corner of the boxcar trying to get warm. It wasn't much of a place to bed down. He wished he had a blanket.

GOLIATH

(EXCERPT FROM THE NOVEL *A GOOD FIST*)

by Barbara E. Rowe

T HE SMELL OF FOOD cooking made him intensely aware of his complaining belly. The faded sign on the door said "Gus and Gert's Diner." He went in. Another sign, printed on grey cardboard and tacked on the wall behind a worn wood counter, informed him, "Good Food—$1.00."

No one was behind the counter but, when he closed the door, a balding man with a toothpick in his mouth pushed aside a curtain covering a doorway to the rear. His face was round and flat, like a pie pan, with ruddy, leathery skin. The man was thin and a little stooped. His pants were very loose around his middle and held up by suspenders. It reminded John of circus clowns who walked around inside painted cardboard barrels held up with wide red suspenders. The man took the toothpick out of his mouth and raised his eyebrows making his forehead wrinkle like a washboard.

John asked, "Can I get me something to eat?"

"Venison, turnips and potatoes, stewed tomatoes if you want 'em, and apple and raisin pie. You got enough to pay?" He pointed at the

313

"Good Food—$1.00" sign, waiting for proof. John nodded, dug in his pants pocket and counted out the change.

"You happen to have any makin's?" The man nodded. "You got some coffee, too?" He went through the curtained doorway. John heard a woman's voice low and muffled. *I guess they must be Gus and Gert.* John smiled to himself. Gus brought a mug of coffee. Seeing no sugar bowl, John asked, "You got any sugar, Mr?"

"Right there in that box." The man pointed to a blue box. John opened it and saw little cubes that reminded him of dice. He'd never seen sugar like this before. He took one out, looked at it quizzically and put it in his mouth. It was hard and crunchy, like a piece of peanut brittle. He smiled, put three more cubes in his mouth and three in his coffee and, stirring, felt the lumps collapse against his spoon. He poured cream into his cup from a spouted jug and watched it swirl and change the coffee from dark brown to a golden caramel. Gus brought out a plate of stew with turnips and boiled potatoes and gravy. The venison was as new to John as the sugar cubes. It was good. Gus went back behind the curtain again and John slyly put a handful of sugar lumps in his pocket.

Part way through his meal, three men came in together and sat at the counter.

"Hey, Toivo," one hollered, "leave them beauts of Lena's alone and git us some coffee." John grinned to himself. *Well, I guess Gus ain't Gus, he's Toivo and Gert ain't Gert, she's Lena. What's Lena's 'beauts?'*

Toivo returned, tossed John's tobacco and papers on the counter and raised his toothpick to his forehead in a casual salute to the new customers.

"Hello, Sheriff," he said, putting the toothpick back in his mouth. He set up three mugs and poured each full of coffee. Then he gestured to John, "Hey buddy, pass that sugar down this way, will ya?"

John nodded, but first helped himself to several more cubes before giving the box a push. Nonchalantly he deposited them with the collection already in his pocket. While he ate his pie, he listened to the men discussing a convict who had escaped from Leavenworth, Kansas a week before and had been seen headed north over the Nebraska border.

"He's a great big son of a bitch. And mean. Doing time for slitting some guy's throat." The sheriff took a long swallow from his cup, set it on the counter, looked up at Toivo again. "He killed a guard with his bare hands escaping. Broke the poor bastard's neck. He'll hang sure, now, when they catch him. Gossip along the line is he's one a' them that does it with boys, you know what I mean? Jesus!" The sheriff shook his head slowly, and looked in John's direction. "Just come in to tell you to be lookin' out for him. He's sure to be looking for food and he'll be easy enough to spot. Six feet seven is too big to sneak around corners."

"Six feet and seven, hey? Wheee-ew!" Toivo shook his head in awe and went back into the kitchen, apparently sharing the news with Lena. Soon, a large, dark-haired woman came through the curtain. She wore men's brown wool pants held up with suspenders over a man's flannel shirt, much like Toivo's. John noted, however, that there would be no mistaking her for a man. Her pants were not loose anywhere and her breasts were an enormous swelling that filled the front of the shirt. Grinning to himself, he realized what Lena's beauts were. Lena planted broad, red, chapped hands flat on the counter, and leaned forward earnestly.

"Just how close is this convict supposed to be, Sheriff? I'm not anxious to mix it up with some murdering Goliath. Maybe we oughta just close up for the night and go home?"

"Don't know how close he is, Lena. My guess is he might be heading for Canada. Maybe he's there already. Don't know. Just figured he'll likely be needing food wherever he is. If you're asking me, I guess you might be wise to close up."

"I'm askin', Sheriff. Thanks for comin' by." She turned then and looked at John. "Dinner okay?" she asked, and caught John staring at her breasts. "You thinking about dessert that ain't on the menu, Sonny?" She chuckled. "Seems to me you better be thinkin' about keepin' that cute young ass outa' some big trouble. Right, Sheriff?"

All the men at the counter laughed lightly at her remark, nodding agreement. John went back to his pie and coffee. Toivo gave the woman a withering look then turned to John.

"Anything else, Mister? We're about to close up." John shook his head no. "That'll be a dollar and a quarter; dinner, pie, coffee and tobacco."

John watched the sheriff and his men walk out, then asked, "Hey, Mister, you know when the next train comes by?"

"Just before dark, usually. Loads water and wood and don't stay long. The track's electrified just this side of Butte, so they won't stop again for fuel. It's only freight, though, no passengers."

"Okay, thanks, Toivo," John said, risking being a little familiar and enjoying the sound of the strange name on his tongue. He pushed the change across the counter, pointed at the cardboard sign and said, "Good food, too. 'Night." Toivo nodded, went through the curtain again as John closed the door. *Well, at least I know I'm in Montana now, because I know Butte is in Montana and I know a train'll be here before dark.*

A little beyond the last house, he sat on the tracks to wait. He watched the drama of the great western sky, its royal colors splashed across the clouds; purple, magenta, red and orange. The moon, freeing itself from the treetops, rose full and round, dyed red as blood in the sunset's reflection. He had not been sitting there more than five minutes when he felt the rails tremble and, shortly after that, heard the train whistle announce its coming.

He smiled, remembering one of his mother's favorite old hymns. He hummed "This train bound for Glory, this train. . ." then sang in a whisper, "Get on board little children, there's room for one and all." He rolled and lit a cigarette and watched his first exhalation of smoke bloom like a mushroom then melt away into the vast purple haze on the western horizon.

The business of loading wood and sluicing water from the tower into the holding tank behind the engine began, and the men talked of the weather, their women, the full moon and the convict at large.

"If he's headin' for Canada, this train wouldn't be getting him any closer to it, Joe," one of the voices speculated. "Except maybe in the mountains. But this sure as hell is no time a' year to be wanderin' around in the those mountains. Early snows can come out of nowhere, hard and deep." As the men worked, John walked around the train and peered inside an open car. It was pitch black. He pulled himself up and sat in the open door.

True to Toivo's information, the train didn't linger. The clickity clack of the wheels on the rails picked up speed and seemed to rattle a staccato code, faster and faster, like a telegraph key sending his name: J.P.D., J.P.D., J.P.D. . .

Full of a hearty meal, heading west where he wanted to go, out of the weather, free of snoring hobos, wandering animals, snakes, bedbugs and other assorted irritants, he could sleep undisturbed. He sat for a long time, just watching the miles fly by, thinking about where he'd been, where he was going. He felt good. He stood at last and stretched, looked around the car again, deciding where he'd sleep. In the shadows of one comer was a mound he had not noticed in the darkness before. He was not alone after all.

Adrenaline surged. His heart raced. JUMP! JUMP! His brain urged his body. *You can't jump now, you idiot. This train's goin' too fast. You'd kill yourself sure. Maybe he's just a hobo. Maybe I'm just jumpy from the talk in the cafe. Maybe we'll sleep till morning and go our separate ways and that'll be that.* Even as he thought the thoughts, he knew they were wishful thinking. He moved to the opposite corner of the car, to give himself distance and time to respond with any action that might be necessary. *Why the devil didn't I take the other car? There were two of 'em open. Never mind. Just make the best of it. Maybe he'll sleep until daylight. Just don't go to sleep and don't make a sound!*

John leaned against the wall of the car, slowly sliding down to the floor. His mind raced. *What if he wakes up and sees me and starts talkin'? What'll I say to him? If he stands, I'll stand, that's for sure. If he comes at me, I'll keep a heap of space between us.* Two hours passed. His eyes were heavy and he wanted to close them and rest.

He reached into his shirt pocket and pulled out his cigarette makings to ward off sleep. The moon had risen higher in the sky and slowly an edge of light crept into the open box car. John struck a match. It flared for an instant, igniting the cigarette paper. He took a long draw. From across the car a deep voice broke the silence.

"Hey, you got a butt to spare?"

John's thoughts raced again. *Shit! Why did I go and light up? Should I answer him? Should I give him a smoke? Should I get up or make him come over to me?*

"Just the makin's. Catch!" John threw the tobacco pouch, with the papers and matches pushed inside. The air, the sound of the wheels on the tracks, the crick in his neck—everything seemed older, louder, more painful. Larger than life. But he was wide awake! No chance of going to sleep now. Mounting fear blunted his pleasure of the smoke. In the opposite corner a match flared and he heard a deep exhalation of breath.

Finished with his own smoke, he stubbed out the embers on the floor of the car. The hypnotic cadence of the wheels clicking across the joints of the rails made him edgier. They seemed to be warning him of doom. "Clickity-clack, watch out or you're dead! Watch out or you're dead!" Every minute seemed like an hour.

A tiny spark arched through the open door and he knew the

stranger had flipped his cigarette butt out. The man groaned, or cleared his throat, John couldn't decide which, curled up on the floor and was quiet.

I wonder if he's sleepin' or pretendin' or just waiting for me to fall asleep. Would it help if I share my blanket with him—or my sugar cubes? Help what? Are you crazy? Just keep your eyes open. Be ready. Be ready. Ready for what? Boy, he sure can snore! At least I'll be safe as long as he's snoring.

Several times during the dragging hours the man groaned and turned. John went rigid with dread each time. Once his neighbor raised his head, looked around, but didn't seem to be bothered by John's presence. But when the man rolled over and stood up, John's whole body contracted in tense anticipation. The man yawned and stretched his arms. They reached almost to the top of the car. His chest and shoulders were massive.

No doubt at all, now. This was the convict they'd been talking about. Moving with easy nonchalance, one hand holding the open door for support, he turned and relieved himself on the unsuspecting landscape.

John took in every aspect of the great frame silhouetted in the doorway, the big ears that stood out like wings from his head, his long arms and the great girth of his torso. The convict turned, moved away from the door and spoke.

"Mind if I make myself another smoke?" The hair on the back of John's neck stood on end. "Or maybe I'll keep the whole bag. What else you got, Runt?" His voice filled the boxcar. "I can use a lot a' things. Money . . . Food . . . That blanket roll. You ain't gonna need any of 'em much longer, anyway.

The waiting was over. Cautious, expectant, fear jangling every nerve, John slid up the wall and stood, ready.

"You plannin' on goin' somewhere, Runt?" A sound like thunder rumbled out of the cavern of his chest into laughter. Terror tightened John's belly, saliva collected in a pool under his tongue but his throat was so dry he couldn't swallow.

"You gimme any trouble, I'll break you in two and feed you to the coyotes. Let's see what else you got in that bed roll." Arms wide, swaying with the motion of the car, the new world Goliath came forward, ready to surround his quarry in the corner. John scrambled to the back side of the car.

He looks like one of my old circus elephants. Them ears are damn near big enough to flap, and them arms swingin' like two trunks lookin' for hay. The mental picture might have made him laugh, if he wasn't so scared.

All his attention riveted on his adversary, his mind flying through every conceivable possibility. He reached in his pocket and his hand closed around his trusty iron railroad nut enclosed in its sock. He let the weighted sock hang down beside his leg, twirling it in small circles in the dark, getting the feel, getting the rhythm, measuring the distance. The convict was now between him and the open door, a massive silhouette against the moonlight.

"What you got there?" The big voice boomed. "Hand it over!"

"Leave me be," John said. "I'm telling ya', leave me be, or I'll drop ya'."

As the giant lunged, John whirled the iron laden sock in a wide arc with all the speed and force he could muster. It came down on the side of the convict's head with a thud. Goliath stood, wobbling a minute before he crumpled and fell, teetering half in and half out of the door. For an eternity of seconds he hung, balanced in space. Then the sway of the train toppled him into the night.

It was over almost before it had started. John stared, in shock, with the sock still in his hand. On the floor in front of him something glistened in the moonlight. He took a step toward it. It was an ear ripped from the big man's head by the force of the blow. John gagged with the realization of what it was and quickly kicked it out the door to join its owner in the wilderness.

Suddenly his whole body began to tremble, his knees buckled

and he had to sit down. He thought he might be sick, and wished he hadn't eaten so much. Then a deeper shock took hold of his mind and he couldn't think of anything else. *What if the convict is dead. What if he, John Debbs had killed a man? Geeze! I didn't wanna do that. I didn't even think about doin' that. All's I wanted to do was stop him from comin' any closer.*

It had all happened in one clickity-clack of the train wheels. He couldn't free his mind. Then he thought of another possible consequence.

Geeze! What if he isn't dead? What if he was just knocked out and when he wakes up without his ear, he starts huntin' me down? He killed other people before. Boy, wouldn't he just love to get even with me! The dark stain of blood from the convict's ear gleamed in the moonlight. Suddenly, he heaved the weighted sock as far as he could throw it. He was tired but his mind kept at it like a dog with a bone. When sleep did come, it was filled with fearful shapes and dreams. The train's slowing motion roused him.

Gotta' get out of here quick, he thought and stood, watching ahead for a smooth place to land. For one brief moment he was a bird flying in the grey dawn, then he was bumping and tumbling over rocky terrain as the train rolled on by, carrying the blood stain with it.

After walking an hour or so through rocky terrain he saw the glow of a drifter's campfire and headed toward it. Just as he had decided to head into the open and join the hobos, three horsemen rode into the camp. One of the rider's jackets glinted in the firelight, and John caught the flash of silver. *That's a sheriffs badge. Damn! That's a sheriff and his posse. How the heck did they find the convict so soon?* He crouched quickly into the shadows of brush and rocks and waited.

AND A FEW BOTTLES
OF "BLUE"

by John Rowe

T HROUGH FIVE YEARS OF fishing trips Randy, Bill and I had talked about landing one of those monsters of the deep, a muskie. This year, the camp owner, Marv, told us about this great muskie lake he could fly us to, and kept bragging about his new float plane, a 180 Cessna, that would hold four people plus equipment. Randy, however, had always been afraid of flying and had never set foot in a small plane. He flatly refused to go. Bill and I flatly refused to take no for an answer. So, after many hours of nagging and belittling, and a few bottles of Blue, Randy finally said, "OK! OK!"

By 8:00 AM the next morning, in a pouring rain, we had loaded our outboard, six gallons of gas, three seat cushions, oars, all our fishing equipment, sandwiches, candy bars and a playmate full of bottles of Blue. Besides all that gear, Marv and I weighed around 200 lbs apiece, Big Bill tipped the scale at 260 and Randy was at least 240 lbs. Because of the early morning rain, we all climbed aboard with the added poundage of full rain suits and boots. The plane was really loaded.

Marv taxied to the far end of the inlet, turned into the wind and away we went. After several minutes of full power, it was apparent we didn't have enough space to take off. Marv cut back on the throttle, turned to us and said,

"I'm going to make one more attempt, but you guys will all have to lean as far forward as you can." Randy's eyes were big as pie plates.

"I knew it! Oh, God, I just knew it. I want outa here," he moaned. Everyone leaned forward. Marv revved the engine and the plane bounded along the water for what seemed like miles. Suddenly we were airborne! We cleared the trees just in time and three grown men cheered like a bunch of school kids at a football game. . . The fourth one looked like he was going to be sick. We were flying over small islands at the north end of Eagle Lake. The rain had slacked off but a heavy mist was moving in.

"Boys," Marv said, "the ceiling is so low; I can't see a thing. I'm going to put the plane down right here."

Randy gripped the seat so tight his knuckles went white. Marv landed the plane nicely.

He picked up the radio weather station at Kenora. They were reporting a front that would pass our area in about half an hour.

"Well," Marv said, "that means we sit here for awhile." He opened the door and said, "I gotta take a whiz."

"How do you do it on a sea plane?" Bill asked.

"Hold on to the door, stand on the float, grab the wing strut, close the door and do what you gotta do."

Bill followed directions but called back to me.

"Hey, Jack, is the float supposed to be this low in the water?"

We looked out and saw that the rear part of the pontoon was halfway below water and the plane was sinking tail first. Marv saw what was happening, too.

"Bill, move to the front of that pontoon." Marv yelled. "Stand

between the wing strut and the propeller—AND DON'T MOVE."
Then Marv jumped into his seat and started the plane engine. Randy
was white as a corpse and kept mumbling, "I gotta get outta here."
The power of the motor pulled the pontoon up slowly. As the mist
cleared, we could see a small island about 100 yards ahead. Marv
cut the engine.

"I'm going to coast to that island. Randy, get out on the other
pontoon and help Bill fend off any rocks along the way." Randy
looked stunned.

"Me? Why me?"

Marv gave him a scathing look. "Because I said so."

Randy got out on the pontoon and held the strut for dear life. Just
as we were about to touch the island, he pushed away from a rock
but his foot slid on the bird droppings that covered it. He kept the
plane from hitting the rock but fell into the lake, his rain suit bal-
looning with water.

Once the plane was tied down, Marv checked the pontoons, then
got two hand pumps from the back of the plane and gave one to me.

"Water must have gotten in from the control cable openings at
the rear of the pontoons," he said. "Pull the plug at the rear end of
that pontoon, insert that pump and start pumping. I'll get this side."

It took about 15 minutes to pump all the compartments dry. Talk
about extra weight! There must have been 10 gallons of water in
each pontoon. No wonder we had such a time taking off.

As the weather cleared, Marv looked Randy in the eye.

"Randy, you been bellyaching about wanting to get out. You stay
here on the island while I take Jack and Bill to the lake. I'll be back
later for you."

Now this island was about the size of the *Tribune* sport page.
Except for a few pines and birds, Randy would be all alone. He
looked like someone had taken his last beer. Then he just threw up
his arms and sighed.

"Oh, what the hell! At least I'm on land." He took off a boot and emptied it of water. "I might as well die happy. Gimme a rod, some lures, some candy bars and a bottle of Blue."

Without Randy's weight and the excess water, we took off with ease. As we circled the island and flew off, we could just see Randy struggling out of his soggy rain suit. We had no trouble finding Marv's lake and the boat he had stashed earlier in the year. After unloading the plane and getting the boat set up, Marv told us some of the best places to try our luck. As he took off again to look for the tiny island and the marooned Randy, we set out for the fishing spots with fervent hopes of catching the really big one. Before the sound of the motor faded, Bill had his first strike.

Meanwhile, back on that small atoll, stranded Randy, slipping and sliding on the bird-fouled rocks, had some visitors. Out of the mist a boat with two fishermen pulled within earshot and called out to Randy.

"You O.K.?"

"Yup," Randy answered casting his line.

"What are you doing way out here?" they asked.

"Fishin'."

"Where's your boat?"

"Don't have one."'

"Are you lost?"

"Nope."

"Do you want a ride?"

"Nope."

"How are you gonna get off that island?"

"Plane." He reeled in a northern.

The two fishermen shook their heads indicating Randy must not have both oars in the water. As they pulled away laughing at this weirdo stuck in the middle of nowhere, the drone of a plane caught their attention. It flew in, circled and landed. As the two fishermen watched, dumbfounded, Randy, slipping and sliding, eagerly climbed on board "his plane." We all roared with laughter later as he described his encounter.

We boated thirteen muskies that day, put them all back to grow for another year, ate peanut butter and jelly sandwiches, finished the beer and counted the day one of our best. We hauled the boat up onto the big flat rock where we had found it, turned it upside down, stored the motor and gas beneath it, ready for the next fishermen. Toward evening Marv flew in to pick us up. Flying back to camp, Randy didn't make a peep. He told us later he was afraid Marv might drop him on another God-forsaken island just to teach him a lesson.

All in all it was a trip we would never forget; the kind of trip that makes for a good story. By the way, did I ever tell you about the time the muskie towed our boat over the waterfall?

Retired architect, ex-flyer, fisherman, father and grandfather of a bunch of fishermen (where all my stories come from).

JOHN ROWE

MISHKA'S TEDDY BEAR

(A STORY OF WAR)

by Larry E. Scott

"The earth is given into the hand of the wicked:
he covereth the faces of the judges thereof;
if not, where, and who is he?"

—Job 9:24

I

KOSOVO, YUGOSLAVIA–MARCH 24, 1999

"Thump. Thump. Thump." The mittened fist beat against the door. "Chevki! Chevki! Come! Come! Come to the door!"

Chevki Mlitnikov bolted from his sleep, pulling the bedcovers with him. Eleska, his wife, naked beside him, shivered in the cold night air.

"Chevki, what's wrong?" Eleska asked. "Give me the covers. I'm cold."

"Sorry, dear," Chevki replied, placing the covers over her. "Someone's at the door." Eleska didn't hear his words. She'd already curled back to sleep.

"*Thump! Thump! Thump!*" The knocking came, more insistent.

Chevki quickly put on his robe and slid into his slippers. They felt warm. But not warm enough to melt the terror—the icy terror—stuck frozen in his gut. Chevki crept through the dark, feeling his way to the door, afraid to strike a light. He reached in the corner and grabbed his gun—an old shotgun passed down from his grandfather to his father to him. Then he reached for the bolt on the door.

"Who's there?" he whispered. . . . No response. . . . Then, louder, "Who's there! Who's there!"

"It's me! It's Malachi! Hurry, Chevki! Open the door!"

Chevki unbolted and opened the door. "Come! Come in! Get out of the cold."

Malachi entered, pulling off his mittens with his teeth. Frost glistened on his stocking cap and across the shoulders of his heavy wool coat. Steam huffed from his mouth and nose.

"What are you doing, Malachi, out so late as this? What's wrong? What's happening?"

Malachi heaved, catching his breath. "The Serbs! The Serbs! They've come! They've come! Their tanks! Their guns!"

Chevki looked into Malachi's eyes—bright and wild, they bulged. Eyes of a beast. Eyes of a mad man. Distant eyes. Vacant eyes. Eyes of a man who'd seen death.

Chevki reached and shook Malachi's shoulders. "Where are they, Malachi? How far away?"

"Th..th..they're in Pristina. They're coming now," Malachi shivered. "Twenty, thirty kilometers away. You've got to leave. Take your family. Go! Go now! You must! You must!"

"Go where, Malachi? We've no place to go."

"Go to the mountains. Find a place, any place. Just find a place to hide. You can't stay here. Here, you'll die!"

"Die? Malachi, you're so upset. Surely its not so bad as that. If they come, we'll just do as they say. . .

"No! No! No!" Malachi screamed., wildly shaking his head. "I've been there! I've seen! With my own eyes! Yes! I've seen! I've seen the families thrown in the streets. The old, the men, the women, the children—all of them—they shoot them dead! Dead! Dead! My eyes—my eyes—they see these things! They burn the houses! Everything! Dead! All dead!"

Chevki watched as Malachi ran, mad, into the cold, black night. Chevki stood, numb in the doorway, oblivious to the cold. Then, in the distance, he heard strange sounds. Ominous, brutal, frightening sounds. He saw what looked like sheets of lightning come across his fertile fields—the fields he tilled—the fields he loved—the fields where lay his ancestors' graves. *Pfoomf. . . pfoomf. . . pfoomf* came the sounds of cannons. *Pfoomf. . . pfoomf. . . pfoomf* came war.

II

Chevki turned quickly, closing the door. With trembling fingers he struck a match and lit the kerosene lamp. His eyes, like a camera, snapshot the room: *Click*—the hand-carved walnut grandfather clock. *Click*—the rack of antlers above the mantel from the buck he'd shot when he was ten. *Click*—his fragrant tobacco; his humidor; his favorite meerschaum pipe. *Click*—the rocking chair by the fireplace where, at day's end, he'd sing lullabies and rock tiny Mishka to sleep. Mishka, their joy—their four year old daughter. Mishka, the light of their lives.

Chevki fell to his knees. *"God! Oh, God! What shall I do? Tell me, God! Tell me, please! Stay? Go? "Where to? Where to?"*

"We must go," whispered the voice behind him. Startled, Chevki turned. It wasn't God. It was Eleska. Naked, except for a shawl on her shoulders, she stood, statuesque in the flickering shadows. Chevki's eyes pored over her beauty. Never had he tired of her. Each season she ripened more and more. Olive skin. Waist-length hair, black and shiny as a raven's wing. Tiny breasts. Rounded hips. He knew her scent. He knew her taste. He knew her touch in the dark of night. Oh! How much he loved her!

"But, what shall we . . . ."

"*Shoosh,* my love," Eleska whispered, moving toward him. "We must go, no matter where. We must leave. We must go now."

Eleska stood before her husband, looking down at him on his knees. Gently she drew his head to her belly. She held him close. She felt his tears, his silent tears, trickle down her satin skin into her thicket of pubic hair. She felt his breath—hot, moist. She heard the *tick. . . tick. . . tick* of the clock. She saw from the light of the lamp as it flickered, the shadows of all that filled their home—the shadows of their life together—the memories, the dreams, the hopes.

"Come now, Chevki. We must dress. We must dress and pack our things. Then, we must awaken Mishka. But first, I'll fix us breakfast. We must eat well. Eat all that we can. Our journey will be cold and hard. So, come. Come here. Give me a kiss. Kiss me, my love. Kiss me now."

Chevki rose—a strong, hard man—and wrapped his arms around his wife. Fiercely they kissed. He tasted the blood from her split lip. He tasted the salt of her tears. They kissed with passion—a deep, stirring passion—the passion of those who face death.

Surrounded by the power of him, Eleska felt wonderfully safe. Her tears streamed down. She sobbed and sobbed. With every sob she tried to touch and taste and smell and hear each thing that lived inside their home. She tried to paste them in her heart, for it would be her scrapbook. It would hold the world they'd known— all of it—all of it. Anything that she forgot—that she couldn't carry inside her heart—forever would be lost.

Chevki wiped her tears with the sleeve of his robe. She cried until she could cry no more. Then they dressed and got to work. The time for prayers and tears was over. Chevki packed what they could carry while Eleska fixed their breakfast.

"Breakfast's almost ready, Chevki. Please, awaken Mishka."

Chevki walked to the corner of their bedroom and drew back the hanging sheet that marked the privacy between their bed and hers. Long he gazed at the sleeping child—her curly, black locks; her mother's high-boned cheeks; her eyelids and lips aquiver, perhaps in the midst of a dream. How he hated waking her. How he hated taking her from where she was, so safe and warm, to the fear that was to be.

Dear God! I pray with all I am—with all my soul—please keep her safe. Please let her live. Please take her through this dark, dark night.

"Mishka. . . . Mishka. . . . You must get up," Chevki whispered, stroking her hair.

Mishka's eyes fluttered open. She yawned. She stretched. "But, Daddy . . . Daddy . . . I was having a dream—a real good dream. Don't wake me up. I'm not ready yet. Let me go back to sleep."

"No, Mishka, you must wake up. Mommy's fixing breakfast. It's almost ready."

"But me an' *Teddy* were playin' in the fields an' they were all filled with candy," she said, pulling her teddy bear close to her. "Please, Daddy, please. Let me go back—let me sleep—just a little more."

"No, my wee one. You must get up. Come now. Let me help you get dressed."

In the dim-lit room Mishka stood in her slumber. Chevki dressed her, layer on layer, with the sturdiest of her clothes. Nodding between being asleep and awake, she clutched her friend, *Teddy,* close to her chest.

"Here, Mishka. Give me *Teddy,*" Chevki said, gently pulling her bear from her arms. "Let go of *Teddy* so I can put on your sweater."

"Breakfast's ready," Eleska called. "Time to eat."

"Come, now, Mishka. Time for breakfast. Grab *Teddy*. He needs to eat, too."

"O.K., Daddy," Mishka replied, rubbing her eyes, grabbing *Teddy* by the scruff of his neck. "Come on, *Teddy*. Let's go. Let's eat."

They sat together at the dining table. Chevki and Eleska caught each other's eyes. Eleska's eyes asked, *Does she know anything? Have you told her yet?*

Chevki's eyes answered, *No, I haven't.*

For a moment their eyes locked in silence, knowing not what to say.

"Let us pray," Chevki said, bowing his head. "Our Father, bless this food and our souls. Today we shall go on a very long journey. We will walk through the fields to the forests and mountains. There we will camp for awhile. On our journey we'll see wondrous things—things we've never seen. But, at times, we might be cold. Sometimes a little hungry. Some things might even scare us a bit. But, that's O.K. For You are with us. And we are with each other. Protect us, we pray, on our camping trip. Thank you, Lord. Amen."

Chevki looked up from his prayer at Eleska. She smiled. Her wet eyes glistened. She nodded her approval. "Now! Let's eat!" she said, passing slices of hard-crust bread; a platter of hot fried eggs and sausage; then, pouring glasses of icy cold milk.

"What's camping, Daddy?" Mishka asked.

"It's an adventure, Mishka. It's—well—it's like your dream. It's going to another place where you've never been before. You go to the mountains and find a place in the woods to stay. You try to be quiet so you can see the birds and deer and other creatures. You watch all the wonderful things of nature. The trees. The rocks. The sky. The streams. Then, after awhile, you come home."

"Oh, that sounds like fun. I know *Teddy* will like it." She paused a moment, deep in thought. Then she continued, "Maybe he'll see some of *Teddy's* friends. Maybe that's where teddy bears live. Do you think so, Daddy?" she asked, excited, with wondering eyes. "Yes, my wee one. That's where they live. But they're awfully hard to find. That's what makes *Teddy* so very special. When we go to the woods, keep looking and looking. Maybe you'll find some of *Teddy's* friends. Maybe, just maybe, you will."

III

Then it came. A shrieking, shrill whistle—the whistle of mortar shells. For but a moment all was silent. . . 'pin-drop' silent. Then . . . *Kaboom! Kaboom! Kaboom!* Stones from their fields hailed on the roof, rattling down the slate shingles. The wooden floor beneath them shuddered. Then, the world grew still.

Like a feather dropped from an eagle's wing, they watched the world they'd always known flutter away on the wind.

"Come," Eleska said with resolve, rising abruptly from the table. "Now is the time. It's time to go."

"Mommy! Mommy! What went *boom?*" Mishka asked, fear in her eyes.

"A storm, my wee one. A bad, bad storm. We must go now and get away from it."

"O.K. Let's go!" Mishka replied, climbing down from her chair. In her tiny mind of candy-filled fields, a storm, a bad storm, made sense. "Come on, *Teddy*. We've got to go. We're going to visit your friends."

Quickly they gathered their few things together. Into the night they fled. As they walked in the dark from their farm to the road, Chevki suddenly stopped and said, "Eleska. Wait. I must go back. I forgot to lock the door."

"What for, Chevki?" Eleska replied, not breaking stride, not looking back. "What does it matter? What good would it do?"

With those few words the war hit Chevki on yet a deeper level. "Yes. Of course." he muttered, numbly. "Of course. . . Of course. . . No difference. . ."

Chevki trudged, step by step, on in the night to the road. War is a song—a terrible song—a song of many verses. Chevki had just heard one such verse. How many were yet to come? They neared the road. "Mommy! Mommy! Hear the voices? Hear the people?" Mishka asked, tugging hard at Eleska's hand. "Are they going with us? Are they going camping, too?" "Yes, Mishka. They're going, too."

They weren't prepared for what they saw—what little they could see through the night. The road was packed with human shadows, shuffling, weary, in cold, dark silence.

Hand-in-hand, they waited for a break in the human chain that passed before them. Then, when it came, they stepped in line. The march had, now, begun.

"*Wheeee! Wheeee!*" the mortar shells screamed. "*KABOOM! KABOOM!*" they exploded. The crowd ran, scrambling, to the ditches, pressing themselves flat against the earth. The shells had landed almost upon them! Stunned, they stood, ears ringing, the stench of gunpowder scorching the air. Then came the chaos: The screams! The shrieks! The wailing! The cries! The moans of the dying! The silence of death!

"Daddy! Daddy!" Mishka cried. "I'm scared! I'm scared! I wanna go home! I don't wanna go camping! Don't make me go! I wanna go home. Don't make me go camping, Daddy!"

Chevki dropped one of the bags—a bag full of all they had left in life. Down he reached and picked up Mishka, wrapping her tightly in his arm. "Hush, now, wee one. It's O.K. It's O.K. Now, I'll tell you what we'll do. We'll say your favorite prayer together—your night-time prayer, O.K.? Chevki started saying the prayer, hoping for Mishka to join him. "Now, I lay me down to sleep. I pray the Lord, my soul to keep. . . .

"But, Daddy! Daddy! I've lost *Teddy! Teddy's* back there. Back there," Mishka pointed—back in the dark—back in the road full of thousands of people. "Go get *Teddy!* Please, Daddy! Please!"

Chevki looked in her pleading eyes. Never before had he failed her. He was her Daddy. He could do all. Nothing was bigger or braver than he. Not, that is, until now.

Yes, war is a terrible, terrible song—a song of many verses. Chevki had heard, now, another verse. And, this verse broke his heart.

"No, wee one. No. I cannot go back for *Teddy.* It's too dark. Too many people. We must go now. I can't go back."

"*Teddy! Teddy! Teddy!*" she shrieked. Step by step by step she shrieked. Then she cried. Then she sobbed herself to sleep, curled in her heartbroken daddy's arm.

IV

Came, then, the dawn. The sun crept up, warming the earth. Here and there, a song bird chirped. Hoarfrost sparkled on tips of grass. Steam rose from the fields.

Teddy stretched, not yet awake. Slowly he opened his eyes. "*Brrrr* . . . I'm cold! Oh! So cold!" he shivered all the way down to his bones. "Where am I?" he asked, looking left, looking right, seeing nothing at all familiar. "Mishka! Mishka! Where are you? Mishka! Mishka! I'm scared—so scared!"

But Mishka didn't answer.

Flat on his back in the road he lay—cold, so cold—and all alone. Shoes and boots clomped all around him. Thousands and thousands and thousands they came. Thousands and thousands and thousands they went. First they shuffled. Then they walked. Quickly they walked. Then, at the last, they ran.

Then came the old ones, the sick ones, the young ones. The mothers with babies clutched in their arms. The ones who'd gone as far as they could. They sat and knelt, exhausted, around him. They couldn't go on. They'd reached the end.

So silent that he didn't notice, a woman came and sat. She drew her daughter to her lap. She pulled their few little bundled things close beside her. Placing her cheek against her daughter's, she rocked to and fro, humming a tune—a gentle lullaby.

Then, from the quiet, the little girl said, pointing at the sodden, muddy road, "Mommy! Mommy! Look! Look there!"

"Why, yes. Oh, my! It's a teddy bear!" the mother replied, reaching for *Teddy,* ragged and trampled, covered in mud. She tugged and tugged to pull *Teddy* free. Finally he came—all but one arm. It remained, stuck in the mud.

"Can I have him?" the little girl asked. "Can I, Mommy, please?"

"Of course you can. Of course you can. Oh, look! It looks like he's been hurt! Something's happened to his arm. You must take special care of him. You must make him well, O.K.?"

"O.K., Mommy! I will! I will!" the little child chirped with gleeful eyes. But a cloud of worry then crossed her face. "Mommy? Mommy? What do I do? How do I make him well?"

The woman reached down to the hem of her dress—her very best dress—the dress her husband had given her but a few days ago. Wrapped so nice in lovely paper. Wrapped in a red satin bow. Her anniversary gift. Ten years . . . ten years . . . they'd been very good years . . . the best years of her life. . . . She reached to its hem and, with tears in her eyes, she ripped a long, narrow strip.

"Here, my child. Here you are." She handed her daughter the strip of her dress. "Give him a kiss and wrap him in this. It's all he needs to make him well—just this and a whole lot of love."

The woman sat at the edge of the road, holding her daughter in her lap. To and fro the woman rocked, the rhythm bringing comfort.

She'd given all she had to give—a strip of her dress and a song.

Yes, war is a terrible, terrible song—a song of many verses. The mother hummed the verse she heard. The little girl tended to *Teddy.*

Then came the belching diesel engines and the *clank. . clank. . clank* of the tanks.

Then came the stomping, marching soldiers. . . .

Then came the *rat-a-tat-tat-tat-tat . . . The rat-a-tat-tat* of machine guns. . . .

Then came the muffled *thud* of the dead, falling in the road around him. . . .

Then came the whimper, the trembling whimper, of the dying mother clutching her child—clutching her child and *Teddy.* . . .

Then came the eyes of the soulless soldier. . . .

Then came the smirk of his curling lip and his rotten, tar-stained teeth. . . .

Then came the foulness of his odor. . . .

Then came the muzzle of his rifle. . . .

Kapop! Kapop! Kapop!

THE PRIZE OF ICE-OUT

by Willa J. Shulman

BORN FIVE WEEKS EARLIER than the predicted delivery date, the infant Aaron arrived pink and warm and wailing. The nurse admired his healthy body and full cheeks, scrubbed and wiped dry all the little crevices and wrinkles. "Sure was anxious, this little one. Couldn't wait to get started." She smiled at the wee newborn and then turned her attention to Brenda lying in the hospital bed. "Got all his finger and toes . . . got everything he's supposed to."

The nurse wrapped the newborn firmly in a soft blue receiving blanket, placed the infant in Brenda's waiting arms and said, "Here you go, Mrs. Fischer, finally got yourself a boy . . . and a fine looking baby boy he is . . . all the parts in all the right places . . . a real little prize package." She stood back away from the bed, her head tilted to one side, and observed the scene before her of mother and son content with each other.

"I'll be leavin' you two to get to know each other. Ring the buzzer if you need anything."

Brenda lay open the blanket and checked the tiny infant. She noted little strands of red hair slicked back against his damp head. She inspected his toenails and studied his long eyelashes, his tiny

338

button nose and small mouth. "Too bad your sisters didn't get your Daddy's red hair," she murmured lovingly to the newborn.

She nuzzled the newborn against her cheek and continued her critical inspection. Opening his palm she read a long lifeline and noted his slim, elongated fingers . . . ten of them. The infant clasped his hands shut making tiny fists, whimpering softly. "Aaron," she said, listening to the sound of her voice, "we'll call you Aaron. It's such a good name." She cradled the infant's head in the crook of her arm. "Three girls and finally, my son. God has been good to us."

As Aaron grew, his body never caught up to his hands. They were large, oversized. They dangled. They hung down and swung at the end of his wrists as though not belonging to him. He tried to hide them.

Each day began with Anna's teasing, always Anna, the eldest of his three sisters. "Hey, Red Aaron," Anna would laugh, "what's hidden in your mitts today? You hidin' a basketball?" His hands tightened into fists under the table each time Anna started in on him. "Wanna play patty cake?" she'd continue.

He was relieved when Brenda bought him overalls and said he could wear them to school. He shoved his hands into the loose pockets. He hid them under the bib and, looking up at the blue sky, pretended to be busy. And in the schoolroom he kept them tucked away under the desk. Not once did he raise his hand in class to volunteer an answer. The teacher thought he was good natured, just not very bright. But outside of the school room he couldn't escape the mocking of his classmates. "Put up your dukes," they'd yell after him as he raced down the road toward home, his hands flapping against his knees.

He'd run up the front porch steps and find Mama waiting for him, her arms stretched wide, warm and safe. He'd wrap his enormous hands around her waist and press his face into her soft belly, sobbing and crying. And Brenda? She'd pull back and look him straight in the eye and say, "Red Aaron, you are my special prize package. Your day will come. Now, dry your eyes and stop this foolishness."

It was the best time of day, having Mama all to himself. They'd rush down off the old wooden porch, past the vegetable garden, run around the yard out back, bending down under the sheets hanging from the clothesline, and head straight for the lake. Giggling like a child, Brenda would kick off her shoes and edge her tired feet into the cool, clear water. She'd carefully step from stone to stone, Aaron following, his fingertips skimming the tops of the smooth rocks.

As Aaron grew in height, his hands continued to grow in length, hanging awkwardly past his knees to well below his calves. He stopped attending school at age fifteen and stayed close to home. He worked the farm alongside his father from early morn to sundown. Often times, Brenda would peer out of the farmhouse and spot the two red heads, Aaron and Jason, bobbing up and down between the planting rows and she'd sigh contentedly, ". . . like father. . . like son . . . a fine team."

With Aaron's help the farm produced abundant, profitable crops. The livestock were well-cared for, the machinery finely tuned, tools were at the ready, and wood was split and piled for long winter nights. Brenda and Jason were proud to have raised a "real farmer." Life eased for them all.

And the girls had stopped their teasing. They watched Aaron slaughter a chicken with a mere twist of his wrist, pluck a fish quickly from the nearby lake, husk an even dozen ears of corn without effort. Anna observed quietly with her sisters how Aaron's calloused hands never stopped moving, how his lengthy fingers drummed incessantly on his ankles, how the blood pulsated through the veins, moving rapidly through the vessels. They watched as he pulled bales of hay from the loft without need of a ladder. They stood wide-eyed as complex engines were carefully taken apart by his huge hands and deftly put back together to perform like new.

The girls stood beside the open barn door as Aaron's hands pulled at the cows' teats, watched as his long fingers combed through his thick, red hair, drawing the long strands off his forehead. They said not a word as he reached an enormous hand down the length of the dinner table for the tub of butter, knowing nothing would be turned topsy turvy in the path of his hand. They listened to the endless cracking of his knuckles and watched his teeth nibbling and chewing his cracked upper lip as he washed at the kitchen sink, turning his palms this way and that, and all the time shaking his head ever so slightly as if to be saying "no . . . no. . . . "

Brenda insisted Aaron attend church with 'no excuses.' "We're a God fearin' family. You have been touched for something special. You will respect the Sabbath and learn to be thankful." Sunday's Aaron tucked his hands under the pew and prayed for the Lord to send a message. "Send me a sign . . . Tell me why."

Though his hands were truly unsightly, they proved to be strong and sure. More than once Jason, bewildered by the power and strength of his son's hands, had said in awe, "Aaron, you are somethin' else . . . a one of a kind, is what you are."

On those occasions, Aaron would rush from the field and head for the lake, his hands trailing in the earth behind him. He'd sit by the edge of the lake till the sunset turned the sky to a rainbow of color. Then he'd swim out swiftly to the middle of the lake and wait patiently for the moon to rise high, lay his head back and count the many stars. He'd listen for the loons crooning across the lake on a warm summer's night.

He loved the lake just as well in mid-winter when it froze over. He'd hum softly to himself while he etched designs in the thick ice with his forefinger. He wondered if the stories Jason told about the winters in the 'good ole days' had any truth. "Dad", he'd ask, "were you really able to drive your truck across the lake? Did the lake really freeze two feet deep all the way across the nine miles to town?"

That was all the prompting Jason needed. He'd launch into stories of his youth. He'd sit by the fire after dinner dishes were washed and wiped, telling of ice fishing. "Right here on Long Lake we'd go out about a mile from shore, drill holes in the ice, drop our lines and talk. We'd talk all day and try to keep warm. We'd pray a big fish would be caught on our hooks, and we'd try to figure what day the ice would break up. Lotta money to win if you bet the day and time of 'ice-out' exactly right."

"Guess that part's true enough," Aaron would nod. Then he'd shake his long finger across the room to Jason and ask, "What's our bet this year, Dad? We shootin' for late March or early April?"

The Fischer family would sit by the fire on long winter nights trying their darndest to figure out how to win the town's contest. They talked about coming close to winning that prize money a few years back, missing 'ice-out' by only a couple of hours.

The family unit grew larger as each sister married and settled into their own farms close by. Nieces and nephews sprang like weeds. Aaron was their favorite baby-sitter. He'd throw the children high into the air and deftly catch them in an arc overhead. He'd place them on high branches of the oak tree, and they'd giggle and laugh and shriek with glee. "Get me down, Uncle Aaron. I promise to be good."

After his daily chores, when the sun seemed to scorch the earth, Aaron would take the youngsters down to the lake and hoist them high up on a strong limb. They'd grab hold of the rope swing he tethered each year, and out they'd swing, out over the clear water, laughing and squealing, their arms and legs pumping in glee till they dropped into the lake. One after another they'd beg for yet another turn.

He'd put them atop the haystack playing king of the mountain.

He'd laugh when they called out to him, "Hey, Uncle Aaron, you are so H A N D some." He thought them clever saying, "Uncle Aaron, did you ever take a H A N D out?" He'd take them ice skating out on the lake, whirling and twirling them till they spun off in all directions.

One day he brought the youngest one home early, leaving the other youngsters on their own. He carried Molly up on his shoulders singing "Home again, home again, jiggidy, jig." He stomped the snow off his heavy boots out on the porch and charged into the house.

"Anna. Anna. Come take care of this child. She's near froze to death." He called out to his sister a few times to be heard over the laughter and loud voices coming from the parlor.

"Anna, would ya listen to that wind howl. It's fierce today down by the lake. Good thing the sun is strong. Makes me want to press my face right up to the sky."

"You surely are the romantic one." Anna had a soft spot for her brother. She admired how strong and sure of himself he'd become, no longer testy, though not yet at ease. "Come sit with me a bit."

They sat across the wooden table sipping hot chocolate, Anna cooling Molly's with a spoon, stirring the marshmallow so it would get soft and gooey.

"Wish we could win all that money this year. Then things would be different."

Anna shook her head slowly. "It's time you got on with accepting things as they are. Ain't so bad . . . be thankful for what you got."

"Now you sound just like Mama."

A thunderous sound threw Aaron from his seat. He sprang forward, mouth open, lips pulled back taut against his teeth. "Run!" he yelled. "The children! Run!" The earth shattering noise was deafening. He smashed open the kitchen door and flung himself over the porch railing. "Ice-out" he shrieked, the word tearing out his insides.

The deafening sound of ice breaking against the rocks along the shore blanketed his cries.

The wind threw huge chunks of ice against the rocks, then shifting course, moved the glacier-like mountains away from the shoreline. The crashing ice breaking up left pools of water and created jagged peaks, the earth vibrating with the force of the weighty attack. Aaron raced to the lake, his shouts of "Help . . . the children. . ." echoing and cracking in the brittle air, his mind paralyzed with thoughts of the solid lake breaking up under the skates of the children . . . of the lake swallowing the children.

Aaron raced forward into the icy waters. Tasting the madness of fear, he climbed up onto the moving chunks of razor sharp ice, his eyes searching, his hands frantically plunging deep into the black waters below. Gladly, he would give up his life in exchange for the children. Using his monstrous hands as powerful tools, he wildly raked huge circles seeking the familiar forms, sweat and fear mingling on his sodden clothes. He struggled and probed the walls of ice, terror seizing his throat, the air burning deep into his lungs. "Take me," he screamed toward the darkening skies. "Take me," he pleaded, exhaustion weakening his cries.

The children huddled one against the other, the ice under their skates moving them rapidly away from land. They screamed in panic, "Uncle Aaron! Uncle Aaron! Save us! Come get us!"

Over the crashing sound of 'ice-out,' Aaron heard their shrieks.

As the mountains of ice shifted in the raging wind, Aaron spotted the tiny figures of the children hidden behind a sheer pinnacle of ice far from shore. Using his frostbitten hands, he pulled his rigid body over mounds of ice back to the waiting oak tree.

With his massive hands he grabbed hold of the rope swing and propelled himself, swinging out over the icy waters. He hurled himself back and forth as a pendulum, picking up momentum, increasing the distance of the swing, closing in, closer and closer to the children. Holding firmly with one hand, he stretched out extending to his maximum reach. With enormous energy, the apex of the swing launched him just beyond the frightened children. He opened his huge hand, and at the down sweep, grasped the winter jackets of the children with his long fingers. He struggled with the force of the wind and wrestled the children off the ice floe and clasped them close to his chest as the rope catapulted them up away from the icy waters below. Clutching the whimpering youngsters, he thrust his legs towards the shore and swung them unharmed from the grip of 'ice-out.'

Safely back at shore the trembling children, shivering with fear, hugged Aaron and yelled, "It's 'ice-out.'" Their eyes wide with innocence they shouted, "Uncle Aaron, Uncle Aaron, did we win? Did we win the prize this year?"

Panting and weeping, Aaron hugged each of the children, tears gushing down his cheeks. "Yes . . . ." Aaron sobbed, his face beaming with love and relief. He lifted the children high in the air. "Yes . . . " he said. "We've won . . . we've won a great prize . . . we've won the greatest prize of all."

After graduating Bennington College, taught modern dance to both children and adults. Along with raising two daughters, choreographed and performed with several professional dance companies in the New York area. Currently, focuses on translating themes used in her choreography to the written word. Several short stories published in The Writer's Journal, The Critic, A Journal of American Catholic Culture, *and* Being, a Celebration of Life. *Now resides in Florida.*

WILLA J. SHULMAN

"O.K. ANNA, DEAR"

by Arlene Silberman

I CAN SEE ANNA MCGOVERN sitting on a Central Park bench alongside of her friends, Margaret Duffy and Monica Kelly, as if I had a Kodak Brownie camera embedded inside of me from the time I was born until I was six years old. Anna's freshly starched, white uniform was crisp and spotless, forbidding a childish hand from touching the pristine garb, at the risk of leaving so much as a fingerprint. Certainly, I would never have been so bold. Nor would I have dared to climb into her lap, assuming one was there. One couldn't be sure. Even Anna's white oxford shoes were unsmudged, despite New York City's dusty pavements, and the straight seams of her white stockings never wavered from their point of departure behind the heels of those shoes to some dark, mysterious place unknown to me.

The only time I summoned up the courage to whisper and ask permission to play on a little hill directly behind Anna's bench (not the Big Hill where the other kids played on the rocks), her refusal was far louder than my timid request. "You will do no such thing," her brogue rang out. "I'll not have you getting your good clothes filthy dirty." Anna always said "filthy-dirty" as if they were part of the same word. Since I had no play clothes, it was hard to be sure what "good clothes" really meant. Everything came from Saks Fifth Avenue, Best & Co., or Bonwit Teller. In fact, before the buyers went on their semi-annual buying trips to Europe, they typically made a personal visit to our Park Avenue apartment to discuss colors and fabrics with Anna and my mother, each seeming to have an equal voice. But I was less afraid of my mother.

I only felt embarrassed during those personalized sessions. But embarrassed wasn't as bad as feeling powerless in Central Park every time that Anna's friends, Margaret and Monica, mocked me with the bemused nickname with which they taunted me: "O. K., Anna dear." Didn't they know that I always chose those words to placate my governess? And govern she did. What neither they nor I knew was that ever since my mother's brother, Belmont Elwood, died in the flu epidemic of 1918, my mother lived in a state of paralyzing fear about head colds, sore throats, coughs and—heaven forbid—measles, mumps, and chicken pox. From 1929 to 1937 Anna's primary responsibility was to rule as Health Czar, keeping me—and later my brother Richard—free from dirt, germs, and contagion from other children. Also free from any sense of adventure and independence, fun and friendship. My sister, Bunny, escaped such tyranny because her real name is Bernice Ellen, and she was Belmont Elwood's namesake. Consequently, Grandma became her mother and her grandmother, and the thought of a governess for "her" little child was out of the question. But I wasn't named for anyone, nor was Richard, so Anna McGovern wielded total authority.

In those days, unless I am mistaken, there were no nursery schools or kindergartens, where children freely swapped infections with each other, the way my children did a generation later. I don't even know if there was such a condition as a "virus" much less "something that's making the rounds." As a mother, I took it for granted that the first year that pre-schoolers stretched out on mats, one next to the other, for a nap, or gathered together in a circle for "story time," they would be sick at home as many days as they would appear to be well at school. Ultimately, they built up an immunity to each others' bugs, I guess, and until they did, I tried to be loving and patient. Sometimes I succeeded.

Even now, when I am a *grandmother* six times over, I find myself recoiling at the tyranny of Anna McGovern as I remember the harshness of her words. "Almost doesn't count," she used to snap when I tried to tie my shoelaces and was only half-way successful. So ingrained is the response that forty-six years ago, when my not very agile son, David, was daring to go a little higher on his climbing bars in our backyard, and called out, "Look, Mommy, I almost reached the top." I had to force the words "almost doesn't count" from escaping my mouth. Of course, almost *does* count! It counts very much. But I didn't know that when I was a little girl.

Another of Anna's favorite aphorisms was equally demeaning: *"Not bad is not good."* To silence me if I dared to show even a trace of childish impatience, Anna would shout, *"I'll come when I'm good and ready and not a second before."* How I cowered! Also *"I'll do it in my own sweet time."* Even a scraped knee or elbow got no more consolation than, *"It'll get better before you get married."* "Anna-isms" could fill a book or break a child's spirit.

Now that my childhood years are long behind me, I watch parents and grandparents feeling totally powerless when their young charges fling themselves down on the floor, refusing to budge an inch. Or clearly embarrassed when a little one screams without pausing to take a breath, while someone sitting in a coffee shop's next booth is obviously irritated. These kids are full of power! And they know it! The likes of Anna McGovern and her park bench friends, Monica and Margaret, have long disappeared from the scene. They wouldn't have put up with spirited children for a minute. "I'll teach *them* who's boss," the governesses of yesteryear would have said. This much I know without a doubt: Anna taught me—and I have paid the price ever since.

※

The author of Growing Up Writing (Times Books, 1989), *which* The New York Times Book Review *called "required reading for new parents, along with* Benjamin Spock *and* T. Berry Brazelton." *Her articles have appeared in* Ladies' Home Journal, Family Circle, Redbook, The New York Times, Family Weekly, Pageant, American Education, Cosmopolitan, Instructor, *and* IBM Magazine.

ARLENE SILBERMAN

MOZART PIANO CONCERTO NO 21: AS DESCRIBED TO A DEAF WOMAN

by Sean Toner

First movement:
By the dim candlelight of dawn,
Beneath strips of wispy cirrus clouds,
Hourglass shaped butterflies flitter through
The red and orange and yellow fireworks display
Of autumn leaves
Kicked up by children at play,
The Monarchs glide, and lift, and alight
On rest-stop trees as if to check their maps,
Then pass preteens skipping and running and jumping,
men combing lawns with mowers,
And housewives pruning rose vines climbing as high
As the traffic lights of day and night will allow.

Second movement:
The indigo crushed velvet of dusk settles
like cool sheets over the day,
Street lamps and household lights flicker on
As if they were fireflies caught in slow motion;
Unfettered felines slink,
Catching every once or twice a wink from the Moon
As they clamber into position to spy the preparation
Of the sprites and pixies and fairies
To dole out peaceful dreams and glad tidings
To slumbering humans
Whose clockworks and measuring sticks
Had counted magic out of the world.
Third movement:
The morning becomes electrified with flight;
With rising redbirds and blue jays and hummingbirds
Riding thermals south like invisible elevators of elation
To the top floors of Creation and then down again
To the ground where the young and the youthful
Imitate, with frisbees and balls and gliders,
And the wings of their lips in smiles,
The flight of day into dark
And then back again into light.

❧

This blind novelist's credits include stories in Romance Recipes for the Soul *and the forthcoming* Haworth Society Anthology 2000. *The poem featured here is taken from his current project,* Echoes of Light, *a novel about a blind man and deaf woman's difficult love affair. His E-mail is: echo@snip.net.*

SEAN TONER

ELLIE'S CLOSET

by Patrika Vaughn

THE DINING ROOM FLOWERS, now three days old, were beginning to fade. Rusting edges encroached on the bright centers of the peonies and forget-me-nots, reminding Ellie more of autumn than of the winter wedding anniversary they commemorated.

She looked at the flowers and tried to comprehend the forty years—two thirds of her life—and the familiarity with George they represented. Absently, she set plates of poached eggs on chintz placemats at both ends of the oval oak table. A scent of decay washed over her as she bent over the flowers' sepia edges.

"Do you know the difference between a circus and The Rockettes?" George grinned, sitting down to breakfast.

A flake of dandruff floated from his shoulder into his poached eggs, sending a pulse of rage through her. She looked away, avoiding his ruddy unshaven face as she passed the toast and managed a neutral, "No, George."

George salted his eggs and chirped, "Ah, then let me explain, my dear. A circus is a cunning array of stunts while The Rockets are a stunning arr. . ."

"I'll get the coffee," Ellie announced, jumping up to escape. But in the kitchen, trying to work around the sawdust and tools covering the unfinished counters, her disgust threatened to smother her. She held herself very still, taking several, deep, even breaths.

A soft steady light poured through the window, erasing thoughts of George. It would be a perfect morning to paint.

Ellie poured two coffees and hurried to the dining room where George was crumpling his napkin. "Think I've figured out a shortcut on the cabinet doors, El. I'll have them done in an hour or two. If you paint your damned designs on them this morning, I can hang the upper cabinets this afternoon."

"This morning, George? I . . . I won't have time."

"Well that beats all. After hounding and nagging for three weeks about getting the kitchen done, now you don't have time to slap a little paint on the doors! Remodeling the house wasn't all my idea, you know. Lost interest?"

"No. Not at all. It's just that I have something else planned for this morning, and it won't wait."

"Okay. Suit yourself." He scraped his chair on the hardwood floor and, as he stomped toward the kitchen, Ellie called pleasantly, "Since you won't be working in there today, would you mind gathering up those tools on the counter?"

George grumbled, swept hammers and saws into a metal tool chest and carried it to the basement. Ellie sat drinking coffee.

The soft morning light held as Ellie washed the breakfast dishes. She moved slowly, studying the dining room flowers bathed in late winter sun. The morning sun gave them a new quality, something she hadn't seen when she had begun painting them a few days ago. The flowers had stood straight and fresh then, and she had been captured by their brilliance. Now she was riveted by the tall forsythia branches that framed the fading flowers, casting bold shadows across the table. There was something timeless and peaceful in the stark design of those shadows against the bare oak, something that would be gone the moment the sun rose above the roofline. She felt an urgency to capture this on canvas.

Reaching absently for the coffee cups on the counter, Ellie felt a sharp, clean pain slice across her index finger. She looked down at blood, dripping onto an overlooked tool. George's carpet knife. The cut was deep and would have to be bandaged. Her left hand. She would do no painting today. A single whimper escaped as Ellie stuck her finger in her mouth.

At dinner that night, when she explained her bandaged finger, George said, "Damn, El. Guess you can't do the cabinet doors tomorrow either. Better leave the dishes 'til morning, give it a rest."

They finished breakfast late the next morning. Ellie hurried with the dishes, annoyed by the rubber glove that kept her bandage dry. Her finger throbbed but would not prevent her from sketching. She was thankful that George was working downstairs.

"Ellie, is my hammer up there?" George called from the basement. "Bring it here, would you?"

She found the hammer, took it to him and hurried back to the sink.

The light still held. She studied the forsythia, forgetting to breathe as she noted the way the coppery branches blended into a thick purple haze at their base. Fallen petals turned the haze into a rich mosaic of somber colors, reminding Ellie that in a day or two only bare stems would remain.

"Hey, El, would you toss down the steel wool, next to the sink?" She threw it down the stairs and ran to her studio for a sketch pad, dishes forgotten. Her hand raced to capture the pattern of light and dark before the sun cleared the rooftop.

"Oh, damn! Ellie, can you come down here a minute? I need an extra hand."

"Can it wait five minutes?" she called, sketching rapidly.

"Not a second to spare. Hurry, before this glue dries!"

"What IS it?" she demanded, stomping down the stairs.

"This joint is . . . something wrong, El?"

"Nothing. Just tell me what you want me to do, quickly."

"Here. Push these pieces together as hard as you can. Use your right hand, El, so you can get a better purchase. Now, with your left . . . oh for God's sake, take off that damned glove!"

By the time she returned, the dining room was washed in bland sunshine, the wonderful shadows erased. She returned the sketch pad to her studio and went back to the dishes, promising herself she would capture them tomorrow.

She decided to cook ahead, to allow more painting time tomorrow. A casserole, using leftover turkey from their anniversary party. She hummed a tuneless ditty, one she and the children had made up when they'd first begged to help in the kitchen. "This is the way we gather food, gather food, gather food," she hummed, placing the turkey, onions, lasagna, cream and spices on the counter.

She had been astonished, once the children were grown, to find herself again consumed by painting. She was even more astonished when her paintings began to win prizes, and amazed to find herself excused from charitable obligations because of "her work." Ellie felt deep pride in having taken first prize at the Rabun County Fair for the last five years. This was no small accomplishment in a county which boasted a Thomas Higgins, famed throughout Georgia for his landscapes, not to mention Mable Smith who excelled at the human figure. Ellie herself tended toward still lifes, and her Winter Apples hung in Stillwell's Chamber of Commerce office.

She had painted only during the week when George was at work, accepting his opinion of her art. "Well, it keeps her off the streets, this little hobby," he would say, smiling fondly at her when congratulated on his talented wife. She always smiled back, never challenging his view.

She had gone through evenings and weekends by rote, waiting on

George, accompanying him to pie suppers and other social functions, and cooking three meals instead of two each day. Weekends were her purgatory. She had done all that was expected of her in order to earn her way into heaven every Monday morning. She hadn't resented the years of useless virtue when weekdays were her own.

Ellie turned to the single intact cabinet, where her cookware was kept. "And this is the way we—oh, damn. GEORGE! OH GEORGE! DO YOU KNOW WHERE MY RED ENAMEL BAKE POT IS?"

She heard the skillsaw and waited. When the ripping stopped, she called down the basement steps, "George, have you seen my red pot?"

"Wha . . .? Oh, yeah. Garage."

"Thank you," she called, moving toward the garage. When a five-minute search failed to unearth her pot, she called down again. "WHERE in the garage, George?"

"Oh, for—right front corner, under the tarp with your other pots and pans—and please don't interrupt me again. I'm taking some exacting measurements."

By the time Ellie put the casserole into the oven, she felt disoriented and out of sync. Few things remained in their accustomed places, and her kitchen rhythms had been obliterated. She felt foreign in her own kitchen.

She dried the dishes and wiped the counter, comforting herself with these familiar motions.

She couldn't blame her parents. Nobody, in those days, sent maiden daughters off to art school. And she had been fond of George all through their school years. Part of her had felt relief at the familiarity of their partnership, at the comfort of staying in this dear little town. George had worked hard to provide, and she was grateful to him for her carefree years of raising the children. She had been content doing needlepoint as she watched the children play, but now she was tired of needlepoint, of cut fingers, of crumbs.

As she put away the last clean cup, George called up the stairs, "Hey, El, how about a coffee break?"

Ellie sighed and put on a fresh pot, her confusion returning.

Her scatteredness became panic as George distracted her with prattle. She had not realized, before his retirement, that George babbled. Constantly. Tired old jokes if he could think of nothing else to say. Being friendly, he called it. In self defense she had revived her motherly nods and murmurs, surprised at how easily she ignored his meaningless chatter and focused on shapes and shadows instead.

George was set in his ways, it was true, and a little thick sometimes in his common-sense way, but he was also cheerful, devoted, and hard working. He had been a good father and husband, if not a stimulating companion. She was fond of him, like an old shaggy dog she'd had since its puppyhood and was in the habit of protecting. George did not like to have his cheerfulness interrupted by change.

"Dammit, El, you're not listening!"

"I'm sorry, George. What did you say?"

"I said, will you need the car tomorrow? If not, I'll drive down to Atlanta and pick up the faucets so we can get on with it."

"Really? You can do that?"

"Sure. Otherwise we have to wait till next week's delivery to Elmer's Hardware."

"That sounds fine. I can do without the car."

"Okay. I'll get the faucets and you do the cabinet doors, right?"

"I'll do them today."

By four o'clock the cabinet doors were painted and Ellie was relieved to have them out of the way. They would be the final decorative touch in the new kitchen, and she was pleased at how well they had turned out. Planning to relax a while before starting dinner, she poured a cup of coffee and carried it to the dining room. Her jaw tightened as she watched a faded petal float onto the table.

Well, tomorrow would be different, with George gone all day. The quiet house would nourish and restore her. She would be able to complete the sketching, even with a bandage.

They breakfasted early the next morning and George left before daybreak. Ellie waved goodbye, calling to him to drive carefully, although she knew he wouldn't.

"Hey, what are you doing in the dark?" George called from the front hall.

Ellie put down her brush and rubbed her eyes. Her temples pulsed as she glanced up at the clock. Five o'clock! Where had the day gone? Late afternoon gloom shrouded the dining room. She must have been straining her eyes for hours.

Ellie pulled her smock over her head and took a step back, looking at the canvas before her. She caught her breath. It was perfect! Somehow, in spite of the shifting light, she had captured her morning vision. Only one more day was needed to complete it. Smiling, she ran to greet George.

In no time at all she removed her paints and easel, popped the casserole into the oven and set the table. By the time George turned off the evening news, she had placed a salad and hot rolls next to the silver candles which flanked the flowers.

"Smells great," George purred as she carried in the warm and fragrant casserole.

Ellie smiled as he attacked his meal with gusto. As she brought out coffee and dessert, he pushed back his chair and said, "Forecast calls for high thirties tomorrow. Want to take a ride out to the cabin? We haven't been out since the big freeze. Be a good idea to check it out, make sure no pipes have busted."

Ellie held her coffee to her nose, blotting out the sickly smell of the flowers. More petals had fallen and they would surely have to be thrown out tomorrow. Would they last through the morning? Could she finish the painting without them?

"Ellie?" His tone was flat, insistent.

"Tomorrow, George?" she said at last, ashamed of the exasperation in her voice.

"Sure, why not? It'll be a beautiful day. Perfect for a drive in the country."

"But we wouldn't get there 'til noon. The cabin will be freezing and the kitchen's not stocked."

"We can pack a lunch and there's plenty of firewood," he answered, slurping coffee.

"I thought you were going to finish the kitchen this week," Ellie said, her voice now calm, but thick as mud.

George didn't seem to notice. "Can't, Hon. Next step is installing the sink and we still don't have the faucet hardware."

"But I thought . . ."

"So did I, but there's some kind of materials shortage and the damned hardware production's behind schedule. Next week, they said."

Ellie pushed away her pie and smoothed her rumpled placemat. "You could put the doors on the cabinets while you're waiting, couldn't you?"

"I could, but then they'd be in the way when I connect the sink pipes. Look, El, I know it's tough having your kitchen torn up, but there isn't anything I can do about it now. So why not take a break? We can make a holiday out of it . . . picnic in front of the fireplace, like we did when the kids were little. You used to love that. And we can have dinner at Ma's Kitchen on the way home. Come on, isn't that what early retirement's all about?"

"For you, maybe," she snapped. "Just one big kindergarten outing, but that's not *my* idea of a good time."

George's sunny blue eyes turned a cold grey. "Kindergarten? Just what the hell do you mean by that?"

Ellie shrank back in her chair, her words echoing in her head as she glared back, angry and afraid. She welcomed the fear, so much cleaner than disgust, but regretted her loss of control. Her hands brushed away crumbs as if by removing this brittle debris she could erase the growing tension between them. She wasn't ready to face him. Not yet.

"I don't know what I mean, George. I just don't want to go."

George shifted in his chair, indecision and disappointment registering on his face as he watched Ellie rub her greying temples. "It's your painting, isn't it?" he demanded. "Your goddam studio!" he accused.

"What about my studio, George?" The constriction in her throat made it hard to talk.

"I never should have gone along with it. It's ruined everything. You're getting moodier, more and more self-absorbed, dropping out of your civic work—and for what? To hole up in that damned cubbyhole, day after day, like the rest of the world didn't exist. It's not right, El."

Ellie thought back to the guilt she had felt ten years ago when, suddenly, and without consulting him, she had remodeled the pantry. It was a tiny room, a mere closet off the kitchen on the north side of their large, old house. Ellie had ordered windows and a skylight installed, had painted the walls white and set up her easel and paints there. George had been angry, asking why she had not simply used the guest room or one of the children's empty rooms upstairs. But she had insisted on the pantry's northern light. They could easily afford the expense and, when she had begged his indulgence, George had relented.

"That pantry remodeling was a big mistake. I can see that now. Maybe the kitchen remodeling is, too. God knows you've had little to do with it. You were so excited about fixing up the house, especially the kitchen. You've complained for years about that old kitchen. I thought we were going to do this together, that it would bring us closer. Instead, all you do is gripe about grease on your dish towels or bitch about grease I left when there wasn't anything around to wipe it on. I don't understand, El. I haven't understood you for ten years!"

Ellie hung her head, but made no reply.

"And that's another thing," George went on. "It's like pulling teeth to get you to help. When you're not hidden away in your damned closet, you're following me around with a damned dust mop or vacuum cleaner. I'm not as young as I used to be, and some of those pieces are damned heavy. It would go a lot faster with help."

Ellie made no reply.

"I know it's going slowly," George continued, "but what do you expect from a beginner? Hell, when we planned this, I let you go on and on about 'nuances' of style and design that meant nothing to me. You insisted on Victorian faucets, stuff I sure as hell didn't care about, that complicated the whole project. But I agreed to do it your way. You know, six months ago I was looking forward to retirement, excited about learning carpentry and about us working together, like we used to when the kids were young. But now . . . hell, now I wish I'd stuck to fishing."

"I'm going to need the house to myself tomorrow. Why don't you go fishing?" Ellie said.

George's unbelieving stare unnerved her. "Look, George, I'm sorry. But the house will be here next week and those flowers won't. Maintenance and repair go on forever. If I wait for everything to be done, I'll never paint!"

"It means that much to you?" He sounded hurt.

"Yes. This is the best thing I've ever done, George, and it's almost finished. I've got to finish it. I'll need total concentration to get it right." There was no hesitation or self-consciousness in her voice.

George smiled, relieved at her openness. "Okay. I'll fish in the stream behind the cabin—but only if you come, too. Bring your paints, finish it there. You always said the light there was perfect. What do you say, El?"

Her grip tightened on the pepper mill, then eased. He was being reasonable. She couldn't say no. "Well, I guess that would work— if you promise not to talk!"

"Have you ever known me to talk when I'm fishing?" he chuckled.

George whipped the Blazer over patches of ice that gleamed in the headlights as they drove out of town the next morning.

"Now we've got plenty of time, George. No need to hurry," Ellie said, picking at her bandaid. She would remove it later, when her easel was up. It would be wonderful to paint without that obstruction. The night's ice would melt as soon as the sun was up. She wouldn't need gloves.

Streetlamps gave way to mercury vapor yardlights as they moved past town. It was still dark when they reached the bridge at the foot of Black Mountain, but Ellie was content in the warm car, planning her day's work—touches of black and umber here and there to give depth to the shadows, perhaps some white highlighting for contrast. It would be easy in the clear light at the bluff, and she would once and for all have captured on canvas a truth too amazing for words. George was mercifully quiet, reassuring her that he was concentrating on his driving. Ellie sank into the satisfaction of her accomplishment.

As they entered the curve on the far side of the bridge, George reached for her hand—a clumsy grab made with his eyes still on the road. Ellie's gasp was involuntary, as much from the unexpected intrusion on her thoughts as from the pain as her bandaged finger caught on the hand brake between them.

"Dammit, George," she screamed. "Damn you!"

Turning to face her, George twisted the wheel. The car lurched and skidded onto the ice along the bridge's edge.

The brilliant morning sun sparkled on ice and broken glass, and cast stark shadows into the twisted metal wreck, an unfinished canvas of peonies lay tilted toward the sun, in perfect light.

AT LOVE'S GRAVE

by Enrico B. Wallenda

She slithers with control,
hissing poison into my soul.
No escape once in the grasp
of this venomous asp.
Freedom, your sweetness sours
as constricting control devours
the love I once gave.
Love now a memory in the grave.

A PARTY

by Lilo Weidinger

A party for having fun.
A few friends coming to nibble and play.
A cake to be the crowning glory.
All ingredients carefully measured
An oven in perfect condition
At 350 degrees, to be trusted.
Alas, a burned cake. . .
And I had to go shopping for cookies instead.

THE SARASOTA LITERARY SOCIETY'S YEAR 2001 WRITERS' CONTEST

Essays and Short Stories: up to 5000 words.
Short-short Stories: up to 200 words
Poetry: no more than 2 pages.

FIRST PRIZE . . . $500
2ND PRIZE . . . $200
3RD PRIZE . . . $100
4TH PRIZE . . . $50
5th to 10th Prizes . . . $25

Entries meriting publication will appear in the 2001 issue of *New Century Voices.*

To Enter:
1. Entries must be typed, double-spaced, 81/2 x 11 white paper. (MS corrections for publication will be based on *The Chicago Manual of Style.*)
2. Include cover page containing name, address, phone no., word count, and title. Head each page of MS with page # and title—no other identification. Entries must be your own original work, previously unpublished. MS are not returnable.
3. Submit as many entries as you wish. Each entry must be accompanied by a $10.00 reading fee and the coupon (or fascimile) on the following page.
4. A request for a list of winners must be accompanied by a SASE.
5. Contest dates are September 1 through December 31, 2000.
6. Any non-conforming entries will be rendered ineligible.
7. Mail all entries to:
   Contest Editorial Panel–Sarasota Literary Society
   PO Box 4008
   Sarasota, FL 34230-4008

Questions? Contact Barbara E. Rowe (941) 366-5701

✂ -

ENTRY FORM AND PERMISSION
FOR ONE-TIME PUBLICATION

Enclosed is my entry for your year—2001 writing contest.

I, _____, hereby grant the Sarasota Literary Society

permission to publish (title)_____

_____

in their next anthology, *New Century Voices–2001*. I certify that this entry is my own original work, has not been published prior to date of submission, and publication rights are mine to assign. I retain all other rights. I agree to hold SLS and its officers and members harmless against all claims to the contrary.

Dated _____ Signature_____

$10.00 reading fee per entry is enclosed.

SASE enclosed if list of winners is desired.

To order additional copies of this volume, please use the attached order form:

ORDER FORM

for *New Century Voices—2000*

Please rush to me _____ copies of *New Century Voices—2000*

@ $9.95 each plus $4.00 shipping/handling *

Total $13.95 per volume.

TOTAL ENCLOSED: $_____

* Note: No shipping charges on orders for ten or more. Florida residents add 70 cents/book sales tax, total $14.65 per single volume.

SHIPPING LABEL

Please print legibly

FROM: Sarasota Literary Society
PO Box 4008
Sarasota, FL 34230-4008

TO: Name_____

Address_____

City_____

State _____ ZIP_____

MEMBERSHIP APPLICATION

Please enroll me as a member of the Sarasota Literary Society.
Enclosed is my check for the annual dues of $35.00.
(Membership year runs from April 1st)

Name _____

Address _____

City, State _____ Zip_____